Counseling Survivors of Sexual Abuse

Diane Mandt Langberg, Ph. D.

Xulon Press
www.xulonpress.com

To order additional copies, call 1-866-909-BOOK (2665).

What the Professionals Have Been Saying about Counseling Survivors of Sexual Abuse

"I have not seen a more satisfying book on treating sexual abuse. Finally someone is focused not just on technique or the horror of it all. Diane Langberg enters into the lives of sexually abused persons with great humility and respect, addressing their issues with the finest balance of insight and resources I have seen from a Christian perspective.

"With her focus on the framework of trauma as the best way to treat sexual abuse, this book gives a most refreshing approach to the subject. Her emphasis on special ways to help is useful for any Christian professional. It made me want to study at the feet of Dr. Langberg and learn more.

"Diane's insights about how God created us as persons and how personhood is destroyed by sexual abuse set a framework that is very thoughtful and biblically astute. The chapter about 'The Person of the Therapist' is something I believe every Christian therapist should read!

"Finally, Diane is a philosopher of the human experience of suffer- ing. What this book says about the nature of evil, suffering, and God has changed my way of thinking—it has changed me! I now want to be what Diane calls a 'witness' of the trauma of human suffering. We would all benefit from what Dr. Langberg writes in her outstanding book."

**David Gatewood,
Executive Director of California and Colorado Christian
Counseling Centers; Supervisor of Counseling Services for
Focus on the Family; Member of the Law and Ethics
Committee of the AACC**

"Every Christian therapist and pastor should read this book. Dr. Langberg has incorporated a sound theological framework into a caring and comprehensive treatment approach for survivors of chronic, violent sexual abuse. She presents a balanced perspective on current controversial issues and sounds a needed call to all Christian therapists to hold ourselves to a higher standard of modeling Christlikeness for our clients."

Dr. Miriam Stark,
Chairperson of the Department of Pastoral Counseling and
Associate Professor of Pastoral Counseling and Psychology at
Trinity Evangelical Divinity School

"A worthy, necessary addition to the library of anyone who works with survivors of sexual abuse. The chapter about false memory syndrome is exceptionally well done—fair, honest, and informative."

Dr. Rosemarie Hughes,
Dean of the Regent University School of Counseling and
Human Service

"This is an excellent book, demonstrating a genuine understanding of the survivors of sexual abuse and their healing process, as well as the impact on the counselors who hear the trauma. It is well-balanced, presenting a brief synopsis of the controversial issues in this field."

Dr. Arlys Norcross McDonald,
Author of *Repressed Memories: Can you Trust Them?;*
Director of McDonald Therapy Center

"One of the most powerful Christian counseling books I have ever read. From the onset you feel the horrible pain of those who have been abused, and yet you also sense how the Lord's love and power in and through the life of a caring counselor can bring healing and restoration. Diane Langberg's informative, professional, and compassionate treatment of these topics is must reading for all Christian lay and professional leaders."

Dr. Joseph A. Kloba,
Director of the Graduate Counseling Psychology Program;
Professor of Psychology at Palm Beach Atlantic College

Books in the AACC Counseling Library

Psychology, Theology, and Spirituality in Christian Counseling
by Mark R. McMinn, Ph.D.

Counseling Children through the World of Play
by Daniel S. Sweeney, Ph.D.

Promoting Change through Brief Therapy in Christian Counseling
by Gary J. Oliver, Ph.D.; Monte Hasz, Psy.D.;
and Matthew Richburg, M.A.

Soon to Be Released
Counseling in the Wake of Trauma
by H. Norman Wright, M.A., and
Timothy Thompson, Ph.D.

Other AACC-Tyndale Books

*Family Shock: Keeping Families Strong in the Midst
of Earthshaking Change*
by Gary R. Collins, Ph.D.

*Intimate Allies: Rediscovering God's Design for Marriage and
Becoming Soul Mates for Life*
by Dan B. Allender, Ph.D., and Tremper Longman III, Ph.D.

*"Why Did You Do That?" Understand Why Your Family Members
Act as They Do*
by Wm. Lee Carter, Ed.D.

*High-Maintenance Relationships: How to Handle Impossible
People*
by Les Parrott III, Ph.D.

*Longing for Belonging: Finding the Acceptance You've
Always Wanted*
by Sandra D. Wilson, Ph.D.

*On the Threshold of Hope: Opening the Door to Healing for
Survivors of Sexual Abuse*
by Diane Mandt Langberg, Ph.D.
(a companion book to this book)

The American Association of Christian Counselors is an organization of professional, pastoral, and lay counselors committed to the promotion of excellence and unity in Christian counseling. The AACC provides conferences, software, video and audio resources, two professional journals, a resource review, as well as other publications and resources. Membership is open to anyone who writes for information: AACC, P.O. Box 739, Forest, VA 24551.

To Linny
whose steadfast courage in facing hard truths
and bowing to the work of redemption
has shown me the face of Jesus.
With eternal gratitude

Contents

꧁❖꧂

Preface

༄༅

This book is meant to be both a challenge and a support to those in the Christian community who work with adult survivors of sexual abuse. Though sexual abuse is now discussed and written about with some frequency, there has not been a book focusing specifically on a treatment plan available to Christian counselors. It is my hope that this book will, in some measure, fill that gap.

Any work we do in the counseling field needs to be measured against the truth of the Word of God. We are also, as believers, bound to follow the highest ethical principles, serving our counselees in a way that is above reproach. Because the subject of sexual abuse and its treatment is emotion laden and because training in this area is a new phenomenon, many have fallen prey to unwise, unethical, and unbiblical practices. I hope that these pages will serve to call all of us to careful thinking and to compassionate, practical, and godly lives. It is my prayer that this book will challenge us to "hold fast the confession of our hope without wavering," while stimulating us "to love and good deeds" (Heb. 10:23-24, NASB).

I also long for this book to serve as a support to the many who work long and hard to minister to survivors. As I speak at conferences and seminars on the subject of sexual abuse, I am often overwhelmed at the many faithful, compassionate people who work in this area. They care deeply for those they feel God has called them to serve. They long for training and support in the work that they do. Again, I hope this book will begin to fill that gap.

As you read, keep in mind two things. The first is that when I speak of survivors of sexual abuse, I am by and large referring to chronic abuse that occurred in childhood. There are many kinds of sexual abuse, so obviously not everything suggested in these pages will be applicable to all survivors. Situations that were not chronic or that occurred in the later developmental stages will require modifications of the approach presented here. The book asks you to keep in mind that each survivor is a unique individual and therefore to apply carefully what you learn.

The second thing to note is that I have chosen to use feminine pronouns when referring to survivors. Current statistics suggest that a much greater percentage of survivors is female, and my years in practice have borne that out. The stories and examples used in the book (all of which are true) are based on the experiences of various women. I have dealt with men in my practice, and the book includes a section specifically related to their unique struggles, though I believe treatment is very similar for both populations. I also think the statistics will change as more men feel free to admit a history of sexual abuse.

This book is the result of twenty-five years in the therapist's chair. They have been rich and invaluable years. It is my desire that what I have gleaned over time will, for each of my readers, result in "the eyes of your heart [being] enlightened in order that you may know the hope to which he has called you, the riches of his glorious inheritance in the saints, and his incomparably great power for us who believe" (Eph. 1:18-19). I send this work out with the same prayer with which Amy Carmichael sent out one of her books:

> Take this book in Thy wounded Hand,
> Jesus, Lord of Calvary,
> Let it go forth at Thy command,
> Use it as it pleaseth Thee.
> Dust of earth, but Thy dust, Lord,

Blade of grass in Thy Hand a sword,
Nothing, nothing unless it be
Purged and quickened, O Lord, by Thee.

Amy Carmichael, *Gold Cord*

Acknowledgments

The longer I live, the more aware I am that anything significant we do consists of the strands of many lives woven together. This book is no exception. The influence and support of many people lie behind the words I have penned. It is a privilege to thank them publicly.

I have worked with survivors of sexual abuse for over twenty years. I have talked, wept, and struggled with many men and women whose lives have been devastated by the sins of others against them. They have trusted me with their stories, their fears, and their dreams. Many of them have prayed for me daily while I have written this book. Their courage in letting me into the truth of their lives, as well as their pursuit of redemption for "the desolations of many generations" (Isa. 61:4, NASB), has gifted me immeasurably. Each of them, in their own way, is part of this book. Each of them also is a testimony to the redemptive power of Christ. Not until eternity will they know the rich blessings and lessons with which they have graced my life.

I learned long ago that work in the area of sexual abuse is a foray into enemy territory. The wisdom and necessity of faithful prayer warriors have been indelibly imprinted on me. About twenty people committed to pray daily for me as I worked my way through this project. I recently saw one of them and was greeted with the question, "So, how is our book coming?" What a wonderful question that was, for it truly is *our* book. And again, not until eternity will the fruit of their faithfulness be made known.

I am exceedingly grateful to my associates for their prayers, their reading and editing of this material, and their support. Dr. Phil Henry, Dr. Ruth Palmer, and Dr. Barbara Shaffer, your humor, your questions, and your compassionate hearts delight and challenge always. I am grateful to God for the honor he has given me in knowing and working alongside each of you.

Isabelle Henard, my office manager, has carried on valiantly. Her love and support are always a gift. Her management of the phone and other "office stuff" has been invaluable.

The staff at Tyndale House has been a joy to work with. I am grateful to Ken Petersen for his vision for this book. Lynn Vanderzalm has given me steady encouragement and excellent insight. Working with her has been a delightful experience.

Dr. Gary Collins and Dr. Tim Clinton, both colleagues and friends, have not only encouraged me but also through the AACC have helped provide a forum for many of the ideas in this book. Their perennial call to both excellence and unity among Christian counselors spurs me on.

I owe Bev Ingelse, a faithful friend in many ways, a great debt. She gave me her home as a quiet place to write, reminded me to eat, prayed with me and for me, and managed my relationship with her computer. I, who can often get reticent people to talk about things they would rather not remember, can easily cause computers to forget what I told them to save.

As always, my husband, Ron, has been a support and an encouragement. He has cheerfully picked up some of my load on the home front, as well as enabling me to pursue my dreams in the professional arena. Our sons, Josh and Dan, are a great joy to me. Their zest for life, their gentle hearts, and their eagerness to learn are often just the antidote I need when the load gets heavy.

All of you, and many others unnamed, are part of my life and thus contributors to this work. I, and those who read it, are richer as a result.

PART ONE

Foundations to the Treatment of Sexual Abuse

1

Why I Write

Counseling Survivors of Sexual Abuse

When speaking on the topic of sexual abuse, I am often asked, "What are the experiences that formed the basis for your thinking about this subject?" It is a fair question to ask anyone who is presenting ideas on a given topic. I think the area of sexual abuse flows from or touches on so many larger topics that it is especially important to understand where someone is coming from as you listen to that person.

The thinking for this book has been formulated over a lifetime. On one very important and practical level, this is a book about the treatment of adult survivors of sexual abuse. I have treated survivors for over twenty years, and through my encounters with these courageous and wonderful people, I have learned many things. This is a topic that is without doubt very near and dear to my heart.

When I first began hearing from women in the 1970s about their experiences of being sexually abused, I was saddened and shocked. I had the privilege of growing up in an intact and healthy family. Though stories of the sexual abuse of little girls shook me to my core, it never occurred to me not to believe them. Often counselors were warned to not get "hooked" into believing hysterical women. I chose not to heed the advice.

At that time, the topic of sexual abuse was still very much under wraps. There was little to nothing about it in the books available on therapy and/or child development. Sexual abuse was not ever discussed in graduate school. There were no seminars, workshops, or articles available. I learned from my clients. They taught me what it was like to be molested as children, what it felt like to be adults with such memories, how dissociation "worked," what self-injury "gave" to them, and what they needed from me in order to begin to heal. They came to me for help, and I became their student. I made many mistakes. I missed a lot of clues. They suffered needlessly as a result. I owe them, as do my later clients, a great debt. In part, this book is a tribute to their courage and their willingness to teach me.

My clients and their determination to deal with the truth of their lives are part of what this book is all about. In addition, there have been three other life-changing influences that are evident both in my work and throughout this book. My understanding of and response to the suffering of others were profoundly shaped by my father's thirty-year battle with a debilitating illness. I learned from him that suffering *is*. His life taught me that health and wholeness are often beyond our control and certainly are not worth our worship. To live in this world is to confront suffering, both our own and other people's. At the same time, both of my parents taught me that though suffering is inevitable, we are not to respond to it passively. We are called to battle sin and its effects with both strength and courage. At my parents' feet, I learned the paradoxical lesson that sometimes the way to fight against sin and suffering is to wait. We destroy the dignity of others when we refuse to wait for them—whether they need to tie their own shoes or they are struggling to find words for the indescribable. We bestow honor on another when we consider him or her worth waiting for.

My father's life also taught me that though suffering is horrible and was never meant to be, there is a larger picture. While we are called to look suffering full in the face and confront it with courage and compassion, suffering is not to be our master. Whether we are the one in the bed of a nursing home, never to rise again, or the one tending to a client wracked with sobs over the loss of a child, our purpose is ever and always to glorify God. Yes, we are to fight against suffering, disease, and death, but sometimes they will appear to win. The Spirit of the Lord is upon us to bind and heal. However, ultimately the goal is not simply the healing, for even those who do experience healing will go on to suffer in yet other ways. We are to heal, bind up, and comfort *so that* God will be glorified (Isa. 61). Whatever the backdrop of a life, honor to the name of Jesus is the ultimate goal.

In the context of understanding that ultimate goal, my father's life also taught me that God uses brokenness. Brokenness does not lead inevitably to uselessness. God is the God of life, the One who redeems. Our faith teaches us that out of suffering, loss, and death, God brings life. No matter the extent of the brokenness, no matter the depth of the pit, the God of the impossible can beautify and use what appears useless to us. My father's life laid the foundation for my work with survivors.

I also owe a great debt to Elie Wiesel, survivor of the Holocaust and teller of tales. When I first began working with women who had been victims of incest, I searched desperately for writing that would help me help them. When I found nothing specific to the topic of incest helpful or available, I turned to the writings of those who had endured affliction and oppression. One of those was Elie Wiesel. I am indebted to him for helping me learn how trauma and atrocity affect human lives.

Wiesel grew up as a young boy in eastern Europe, where life was as secure as eastern European Jews knew it to be. Occupation by the German soldiers, confiscation of private property, the yellow star, and finally, deportation smashed his world. He found himself in one of the death camps, exiting a cattle car and watching as a lorry delivered a load of babies to the flames. Wiesel imposed a ten-year vow of silence on himself after his release, but he found that he could not stifle his need to express what he had experienced. Wiesel discovered that to be a survivor is not enough; one must also be a witness.

Elie Wiesel experienced the depths of human depravity. He does not dodge their ghastly revelations, and he does not let us do so. He challenges us to face life as it truly is in this dark world of ours. He demands that any voice we give to the truths of redemption must take into account the reality of such events as the Holocaust rather than be founded on a denial that the events occurred. We who call ourselves Christians blaspheme the name of Christ if we pretend that the evils of the Holocaust or the rape of little girls and boys are less than they truly are. Any redemption that fails to take such evil into account is no redemption at all.

Another truth that I learned from Wiesel is that though there are evils that defy description, one must still bear witness to them. Though language is inadequate for the task, Wiesel says that "not to transmit an experience is to betray it."[1] For a long time, however, I felt I did not have the right to speak. After all, I was not a survivor of sexual abuse. How could I dare stand up and say what it was like to be molested as a child? And who was I to tell abused people what would help them heal? It seemed arrogant and presumptuous.

Wiesel challenged my silence, for he suggests that though there is an appropriate silence when one is inadequate for a task, there is also a silence that is betrayal or a choice to ignore reality because it is too painful. To be silent is to abuse the victim again, to allow others to erase her trauma from their minds. And so I write—not because I know, but because I have listened. I write—not because I have words adequate to describe the suffering of little girls and boys raped by their fathers, mothers, uncles, or grandfathers, but because to be silent is to pretend and deny. I write—not because I have answers for why such suffering should exist, but because it is the truth of things as they are, and it is a truth that cries out to be spoken.

This book provides a place for me to tell the truth as I have seen it. It is certainly not the whole truth, for that could not be told. To speak of the rape of little girls and boys is also to speak of principalities, powers, rulers of the darkness of this world, unseen forces that defy human description. To write about incest is to write about the outworkings of an enemy beyond our comprehension. Yet I must write, and I do so for two reasons. One is for the many survivors I have known. Out of deep love for them and respect for their great courage, I write to provide them with yet another place to speak for themselves. It is my hope that through this book, the church of God will pay heed to what we are doing to our children and will rise up to cry out in earnest against such evil as well as to tend the wounds of those thus treated.

The second reason I must write is due to the fourth and most powerful influence in all that I do—I have met the Redeemer. He is a Man of Sorrows and intimate with grief. He was left alone, regarded with contempt. He is scarred for all eternity. His suffering has left its tracks across his face. His hands and feet carry marks of the violence done to him. He was afflicted, struck, crushed, stripped, and oppressed. Suffering does that, you know; it leaves its mark all over those who must endure.

I have not only met this Redeemer; I have seen his work. I have watched him comfort, bind up, set free, rebuild, and repair "the desolations of many generations" (Isa. 61:4, NASB). I have seen him tenderly choose the rejected, strengthen the weak, carry the broken, and destroy those who war against the soul. I have seen him do for survivors what he did for oppressed Israel: "All who took them captive have held them fast, they have refused to let them go. Their Redeemer is strong, the Lord of hosts is His name; He will vigorously plead their case, so that He may bring rest" (Jer. 50:33-34, NASB).

In knowing Christ and seeing his work, I have had the bittersweet privilege of bowing to his work of redemption in my own life and person. I have found that as I do so, he then wondrously stoops to use me as a worker of his work in others. It is *he* who is teaching me how to comfort, bind up, and set free. If there is any life and truth in this book, it is because of him. If there is any life and truth in the work I do, it is because of him. The more I know him and see his work, the more I become what Amy Carmichael refers to as "a worshipper at the feet."

So I pay tribute to those I have known, loved, and read, who have taught me priceless lessons: the survivors, my parents, and Elie Wiesel. Without them, the work that I do, and this book, would not be possible. Above all, I am eternally indebted to our Redeemer, Jesus Christ, whose own suffering has given me life so that I might give the same to others.

THE WITNESS

Elie Wiesel says that one who was not *there* can never truly understand it and one who *was* there can never communicate it. I was not there, and I acknowledge that I cannot fully understand what it is like to be little and abused. However, Wiesel offers two other possibilities. One is that though we must never attempt to speak *for* survivors and never attempt to speak *instead* of survivors, we can provide one more place where survivors can speak for themselves. And so I hope to use this book as a place where the suffering, the hard work of therapy, and the glories of redemption in the lives of survivors can be told.

The second possibility Wiesel offers is that one can take the role of a witness. To be a witness is to know by personal presence and perception what has occurred. I have been personally present for more than two decades in the suffering of many adults who were sexually abused as children. Therefore, I can give testimony. Proverbs 14:25 says, "A truthful witness saves lives" (NASB). It is my intent to speak truly about what I have seen over the past twenty-plus years. I long for that truth to bear the fruit of deliverance in the lives of both survivors and those who work with them.

Isaiah speaks of an "altar to the Lord in the heart of Egypt." He says that altar is "a sign and witness to the Lord Almighty in the land of Egypt. When they cry out to the Lord because of their oppressors, he will send them a savior and defender, and he will rescue them" (Isa. 19:19-20). In speaking truly about what I have seen, I offer it up to the Lord Almighty, in the land of the enemy, hoping the Lord will use it to point the way, for both counselors and clients alike, to the Savior and the Defender.

Wiesel says it is the role of the witness "to disturb, alert, awaken, to warn against indifference to injustice—any injustice—and above all against complacency about any need and any people."[2] May the story that follows disturb and awaken those who treat survivors, indeed the whole church, so that the result will be a response that fits both the truth of the suffering and the truth of the Redeemer.

2

Meeka's Story

※

W hat follows is a true story. It is a story that will shock and disturb many who read it. It will grieve all who are willing to enter in. Before you read it, it's important for you to know why I chose this particular story.

First, I believe this story is a powerful teacher. Darkness teaches us about the light. On the physical level, we all have experienced the contrast of emerging from a darkened room or theater into the brightness of a lighted room or the outdoors. Often the light has not changed; it was there before we entered the theater. But, having experienced and even gotten used to the darkness, we are startled by the light. The reality of the light and all that it means is intensified for us. We grasp the clarity of the light because of its contrast to the darkness we have just left.

On a spiritual level, I have found that God often uses the darkness to teach me about the light. By pointing this out, I do not mean to suggest that we should seek out darkness in order to appreciate the light better. That seems akin to sinning in order that grace might abound. As Paul says, "By no means!" (Rom. 6:2). However, the darkness and light do teach us that our Redeemer can and often does use what was intended for evil to give birth to good instead.

The following story and many others like it have increased both my understanding of and love for the light in two ways. When we see or hear about obvious manifestations of evil, we distance ourselves with feelings of shock, disgust, and superiority. We think that such things have little to say to us because they are so extreme. However, Scripture teaches us that sin is sin. One of the things that has startled me when reading the Gospels is an awareness that Jesus often expresses a very strong reaction to what you and I would deem "lesser" sins—hypocrisy, pride, self-centeredness. His fiercest language is used against the religious leaders for their arrogance (Matt. 12:34; John 8:42-47). Jesus' responses teach us how deceitful we are.

Jesus taught us that God is so utterly holy that he sees no difference between the evil of an arrogant heart and the evil described in the following story. Meeka's story boldly illustrates for us the nature of evil. The story dramatically demonstrates the capability of the human heart apart from God's restraining grace. I pray that as we read, we will not allow our shock or distress to blind us to the truth that our God is so holy that our "minor" sins are more offensive to his nature than Meeka's abusers' sins are offensive to us. May the story also remind us that nothing we encounter in our own lives or another's is beyond the reach of God's redemptive power.

Another way stories such as this have strengthened me to walk in the light and enabled others to do so as well comes from a principle any practitioner who has worked with psychosis understands. When we were students, many of us read about the various psychoses, but our studies did not automatically result in an astute awareness of psychosis in people. It is often only when we spend time on an inpatient ward with psychotics that we begin to recognize psychosis quickly. Not only that, but once we grasp what psychosis looks like, feels like, and sounds like, we find ourselves more adept at seeing the more subtle abnormalities in others. Understanding psychosis can often result in a clearer grasp not only of neurosis but also of normality.

I have found this same principle at work as I have studied sexual abuse. As people who were victims of chronic, violent sexual abuse teach me what it was like and how it affected them, I have become far more aware of the subtle effects present in others whose experience was, by comparison, less extreme. Strains of the same damaging effects to person and relationship are present, even though they are not as intense. In fact, I have seen many times that those who have never experienced any form of sexual abuse but who suffered profound neglect and emotional deprivation carry many of the same scars as survivors. Such clients will very often greatly minimize the impact of their childhood because, after all, they did not have anything like sexual abuse happen to them. Obviously the same conclusion is often reached by those whose experience of sexual abuse was "only" verbal or "only" physical.

If we allow it, the story that follows can be our teacher. It will teach us that sin, *any* sin, is an assault on God and on the person, and therefore, sin of any kind should disturb and grieve us. You also need to know that as disturbing as this story is, it is not even the whole story of what Meeka endured. If we allow it, this story will teach us that sin is so serious that *any* evil done to a developing child will violate that child. The story will fill us with compassion for those who come to us broken by the sins of others. If we let it, this story will put us on our knees and call us to examine our own hearts and lives, lest we should in any way be sinning against a holy God or one of his creatures. And finally, this story will cause us to stand in awe before God as we recognize the worthiness of the Lamb that was slain "to receive power and wealth and wisdom and strength and honor and glory and praise!" (Rev. 5:12).

****

My family grew up on a farm in South Dakota. Originally it was 275 acres, with much of it later sold, bringing it down to just 105 acres. We had numerous sheds, two large barns, a milk house, corn bins, and a silo. In one of the sheds were all our saws, tools, and workbenches, and the others held much of our large machinery.

I was one of twelve children. The order of children went boy-girl-boy-girl-girl-girl-boy-girl-boy-girl-boy-girl. I was the fifth child. If I had been a boy, it would have made sleeping arrangements, as well as many other things, much easier. The order of children would then have been boy-girl all the way down the line. That would have given us six girls and six boys instead of seven girls and five boys.

We lived about one and a half miles outside a small town with a population of just under five hundred. The town was known for being a Christian community. Considering that there were only five hundred people in the town, there were two large churches, one Presbyterian and one Catholic. Everyone in town went to church, and it was presumed that anybody who was anything came to both Sunday morning and Sunday evening services.

My parents did likewise. They were well respected in the community and very active in the life of the church. We would not think of skipping church. Someone was always there, even when the kids were real little. Once we children were considered old enough to sit still, we were taken to church, and we sat still.

My parents always seemed to be living at the poverty level. We could never get ahead, and the bills just seemed to continue to pile up. We had a huge garden every year and canned or froze much of its produce in order to provide food for the winter. We raised our own beef and made our own jams and butter. We were very independent and did not rely on any others to help us out. We could manage.

We had a large yard in which to play, and the kids in the family always spent much time outside. We had horses to ride and a pond that gave us our own skating rink in winter. We always had plenty of kittens and two or three dogs as part of our farm.

We worked together. We played together. We even did very well at playing baseball and basketball with teams made out of our family alone.

I rarely felt that I got enough attention because I was one of so many kids and was plastered somewhere in the middle of the family list. I longed to be held. Even as a very young child, I found ways to get those needed hugs. At the age of four, I would purposely fall down the stairs; I had found that when I fell down, someone would come and see if I was OK and hold me. Often it would be Mom, and that was what I wanted. I wanted a hug from Mom.

Poverty left its marks on the family. The more children who came along, the harder it became. By the time four children had been born, Mom and Dad had more than enough children and were already way behind in ever being able to support them adequately. They did not want more children. But soon I was on the way. Since abortions were out of the question, I was kept, but it was made clear that I had best be a boy if I was going to be born at all, for I would be needed to help care for the farm. Another girl would not be an asset to the family. They already had too many girls. In fact, a girl would be a liability. My parents did not love me; I was not wanted, yet there I was. I was part of this family even though they wished I was not.

The very day that I was taken home from the hospital the abuse began. My family tells the story that in protest to my being a girl, Dad would use the heels of my tiny feet to stub out his cigarettes.

We had a lot of different animals on our farm: cows, horses, dogs, cats, chickens, rabbits, and some pigs. We all spent a lot of time outside. We had a large yard, lots of buildings to be in or out of, behind or around. One of the buildings was a pretty cool playhouse. It had a roof, windows, a door—it really was a little house. I used to play in there a lot. I'd bring my dolly outside with me, and together we'd go into the playhouse. Sometimes I went in there just to be alone. Sometimes it felt as if it was a special hideout from everything else that went on. Sometimes the other kids played with me, and we'd play house.

One time I was in the playhouse all by myself. It was quiet. Daddy came and looked in the window and then knocked on the door. I told him he could come in. He sat down next to me, put his arm around me, and held me for a bit; then he went away. It was wonderful. Then one time when I was four years old, my daddy came and knocked on the door. I told him he could come in. He sat down next to me, pulled me onto his lap, and let me sit there for a moment. Then he changed, and he began to hurt me. He told me he loved me. He told me he cared. But then he took his hands and messed with my body. After he did this, I would no longer go to the playhouse by myself, for if I heard steps or the door, I would think it was him, and it would scare me inside.

My grandparents lived on another farm about ten miles or so from our place. Even when I was a tiny little kid, they were often called in as baby-sitters. Actually, we were brought over there to be baby-sat. I remember one time that I had been put to bed and had fallen asleep, but I woke up several hours later. I couldn't remember where I was. I called out for Mom and Dad, but nobody came to get me. I was so scared, and it was so dark. Grandpa came in and picked me up. He held me for a second and then laid me down on the bed and began to fuss with my body. He opened up his pants and played with his body as he also played with mine. This happened a couple of times, and every time I was brought upstairs, I would begin to get scared. It was usually my daddy who would drop me off at their house. When Daddy dropped me off there, I asked him not to. I didn't want to go there. I didn't want to stay at their house ever again. I would cry, but he wouldn't listen to me. It didn't matter. If he took me there, I would have to go and "obey."

It got to the point that whenever I went over there and heard a door bang or footsteps close by, it always put me on edge. I'd curl up in the corner of the room and hope they didn't find me. If they did, it usually meant more trouble. At times they would come in and start getting me ready to go someplace else—usually the basement.

Grandpa and Grandma used threats to keep us in line. They told us they would hide us in the cabinets and lock the doors if we didn't behave. That in itself wasn't so bad, except that they told us that rats and snakes lived in those cabinets. As a little tiny kid, I believed them.

Then came the first time that they did put me in the cabinet. They kicked me to get my legs inside the cabinet. They slammed the door, and I heard the lock being turned. I was glad that it was locked, but then I got terrified because of the rats and snakes. The truth was that there were lots of mice in the cabinets. My grandparents put me in there when I didn't do anything wrong. Sometimes when they'd come and unlock the cabinet and let me come out, they would take me to the table in the basement and make me lie on it and take off all my clothes. They would also take theirs off and make me play with their bodies, and they would play with mine.

When I got into school, I realized that I didn't fit in there either. My clothes were always handed down to me by my older sisters, and the kids would laugh at me because of it. It was hard to make friends there, and it just seemed to tell me that what I had already experienced at home was the way things were. I didn't fit. I wasn't wanted or loved.

All of us kids had to do our share of the chores around the house in order to make life work. Dad would be home when we'd get home from school, and he would call us all to help work. Basically, no matter how little we were, there was something that we could do to help make the farm work. Maybe it was a little pail instead of a big pail, but no matter what, we all had to help.

Dad would hand me my little pail, and off we'd go. I used to like doing it. It was "our time," a special time for the two of us. We'd milk the cows together. We milked some of them by hand, and I got to sit on his lap while we worked. He'd get me to try to milk the cow, but it was hard for me. My hands were too little. But some of the times on his lap were not fun. When he would point out the cow's udder and talk about Mommy's breasts, he would touch mine and tell me that someday mine would grow large enough for men to suck. He said it was good and right and that God made us that way. He also would put his hands in my panties, especially when I wore a dress. I began to not like being on his lap and didn't want to do chores with him. But he made me do it again and again.

As I'd sit on his lap, he would have me feel the pocket in his overalls. There was a lump at the edge of his pocket. He told me it was a special sucker just for me. I begged him for the sucker. I was four years old and loved suckers. I especially wanted a chocolate one. Finally he let me have the sucker. When he went to get it out of his pocket he instead pulled down his pants. His penis was the sucker he talked about.

I made a "fort" in the haymow. It was a place where I could hide and be alone. I had this kitten I really liked. I would lie there with the kitten on my belly, and it would purr, and I loved it. One day, Daddy found me hugging my kitten. He said it was *his* job to hug me, and if I told anyone about our "special times," he would kill my little kitten.

Daddy had his own special place in the barn where he liked to take me. No one could see us when we were there. Sometimes he would just hold me tight. Other times he would hold me first, then mess with my body, and then hold me again, telling me how extraspecial it was. Sometimes he would just send me there and then come after I had been there for a few minutes. When that happened, he expected me to "be ready" for him. That meant that my clothes had to be off so I would be ready for him to "play with me." I had to do whatever he told me to do. Many times that meant that he would put his penis or some other instruments in me. If I was "being good," then things went better. If I did not do things just as he wanted, he would pee on me. He even made me eat his excrement if I was not being good. But I found that as time went on, I could never be good enough. Often he would abuse me in all sorts of ways and then walk away, leaving me to "clean myself up" so I could go inside again.

Sometimes even on Sundays when we were at church, he would take me down to the boiler room and abuse me there. He told me that God told him to do this, that it was right, that it was what I needed so that I would know how to be a real woman. He told me that God told him to teach me about these things.

I used to cry into my pillow at night. I cried out for God to stop it. I remember that one day in Sunday school our teacher told us that if we'd pray, God would answer our prayers. And I prayed. I prayed hard. But the abuse never stopped. In fact, I'd even pray when he was doing it to me, but it wouldn't stop; it seemed to get worse. Who was God? He certainly wasn't a God of love, and he certainly didn't love me. He loved my daddy more, it seemed to me. Daddy always got what he wanted.

If I was being bad as a kid, my mother would tell me I'd have to wait for Daddy and he would discipline me. He'd take me out to the barn. He'd spank me—but also abuse me as part of it.

I always used to think that sometime—maybe the next time—things would be different, that Daddy would stop doing these things to me. I thought that maybe next time he would really love me. But it never seemed to change. One summer day when I was seven years old, I was working in the kitchen with my mommy. In my own way, I tried to tell Mommy that Daddy was hurting me. But Mommy did not care. She yelled at me for even thinking anything bad about Daddy and said she did not ever want to hear another word out of me. She just shrugged it off. She didn't love me. She didn't care what happened to me, and it destroyed me. No one cared. No one loved me. No one wanted me. I wanted to die. There was no longer any reason to hope, for if Mommy couldn't help, then who would?

Daddy had lots of games that he would play with us in the house, especially at night when he put us to bed. We'd play hide-and-seek with him. We'd hide under the sheets or behind the door or under the bed or in the closet. When he found us, we would get a whisker rub from him. I often tried to hide—really hide—from him because when he'd give me a whisker rub, he'd put his hands in my pants.

The abuse continued, and over time it got worse. The intensity of it grew. Even when I was sick, he would do it. He'd take me on "special errands" with him. This just gave him even more opportunity to abuse me.

Very early on, I suspected that I was pregnant. I was taken to a "special doctor" to find out if it was true. It was. When I was on my way back to this same doctor for an abortion, my dad stopped the car partway there and hit me numerous times in the stomach because I should not have gotten pregnant. I tried to run away, but he was too big and fast for me. At the doctor's office it became clear that my dad could not pay for the abortion. So I was "sold" to the doctor. While the doctor used my body, my dad stood and watched with a smirk on his face.

Later on there was a group of men that always took turns with me. While it happened, I watched them hand the money to my dad. Daddy let them use my body so that he could pay our bills.

The abuse was very severe, and over a period of time I aborted or birthed and lost four babies. This has left me completely devastated. This, along with things my daddy always told me, convinced me that I was totally worthless. I had no hope for anything anymore. My life was dead. I left home when I was seventeen years old. At times I had to return home, and even at those times the abuse would continue.

I never had people I'd really call friends. As I tried to find some friends in school, I ended up hanging around with the other kids who had no one to be with. We were often laughed at and ridiculed. It made sense to me that that should happen. Daddy told me that I was no good, not worth anything, and all I would ever have to offer to anyone was sex. But even sex wasn't good enough.

In college I found men to be with, but the use of my body was always the focus. After a night or so, they'd be gone as well. I also found a woman to love. Sex with her was everything, but over time that also ended. Nothing remained. Nothing was true.

I graduated from college, established myself in a career, and in the eyes of those around me, I became successful and competent in what I did. But periodically I'd find myself in and out of counselors' offices. Something troubled my life. But nothing seemed to generate significant changes in my life. Nothing dramatic was wrong, but not everything seemed right.

In the mid-1980s I was part of an inner-city evangelistic effort in California. One day as we were on the streets, I became engaged in a conversation with a young woman who asked me, "How do I forgive someone who has raped me?" I was dumbfounded and felt extremely inadequate to answer such a question. But I was *more* shocked and troubled by the answer I gave her: "It is one of the most difficult things you will ever have to do. I know, for I too have been raped."

I was shocked by my answer, for I had never been "raped," or so I thought. Over the next few days, I was overcome with one memory after another of my own past and the abuse that I had suffered. At that point, my entire life seemed to fall apart. I cried all the time. I couldn't focus on work. I didn't want to go anywhere. I didn't want to remember anything anymore, although it was right in front of me all the time. I tried to push it all away, as I had when I was a kid. I tried again to "put it in the box and shelve it," but it seemed that the box kept falling off the shelf and was spilling all over the place. I attempted to deny it all: It didn't happen. He didn't do it. It couldn't have happened. At that point in my life, everything blew up. Nothing was the same. Nothing and no one could be trusted. I wondered who I really was. I didn't know if I could go on. How could I make it? Life didn't seem worth living anymore.

****

Some of you are disturbed by this story. Perhaps some of you want to say that such a thing cannot be true or at least that it is highly unlikely. Not only is this story completely true, but it is only half the story. Some of it is too overwhelming to put into print.

Amy Carmichael expressed it eloquently when she spoke of the little Indian girls whom she rescued from the Hindu temples: "Those who know the truth of these things will know that we have understated it, carefully toned it down perforce, because it cannot be written in full. It could neither be published nor read. It cannot be written or published or read, but oh, it had to be lived! *And what you may not even hear, had to be endured by little girls"* (emphasis hers).[1]

Meeka's experience may be more extreme than the experience of the people who come to you for help, or it may be mild compared to some of the stories your clients have shared with you. As I suggested in the initial paragraphs of this chapter, though the intensity of the abuse that has marked our clients certainly matters, the fact that they were abused at all is more the point. Let us allow Meeka's story—and the stories of all our clients—to teach us about darkness and the light, about how sin and trauma affect people, and about the evil in our own hearts. You will not be left with what you have just read. Chapter 9 will share more of Meeka's story and demonstrate God's awesome power to redeem us from the darkness and restore us to the light.

The God we worship, the God of truth, has said that "the whole world lies in the power of the evil one" (1 John 5:19, NASB). If we believe what he says, then it seems to me that Meeka's story should not shock us. Rather, we should be surprised that such stories are not far more common.

Keep in mind also that while the story is both true and understated, John goes on to say, "And we know that the Son of God has come" (1 John 5:20, NASB). It is because of this truth that Meeka's life is now a redeemed life. It is because of this truth that this book has been written. To work with sexual abuse is to face the power of the evil one. To know the God of truth is to bear witness to the fact that the Son of God has come and redemption is at hand!

3

Understanding the Nature
of Personhood

This is a book about the treatment of adult survivors of childhood sexual abuse. I suspect that most people, upon picking
up such a book, will immediately expect to find themselves reading
a description of sexual abuse and recommendations for treatment.
Obviously, such expectations are justified, and I hope they will be
met. However, before defining the problem and giving an effective
response to it, we first need to look at the four foundational components our subject suggests to us.

First, this is a book about adult survivors, which means we must
have some basic understanding of personhood if our treatment is to
be helpful. Second, this is a book about treatment, and that suggests
that we must lay the groundwork for an understanding of therapy.
Third, we are considering sexual abuse, which is first and foremost
a trauma. Any treatment approach that is not predicated on a basic
comprehension of the nature of trauma and what it does to human
beings will be ineffective and possibly harmful. Finally, we are
dis~- cussing something that happened in childhood. Therefore, we
need to grasp the experience and development of a child if we are to
be clear regarding the impact of that suffering.

PERSON

We will begin our discussion by first considering the nature of persons as they were created to be. The shattering of something is better understood when a picture of its original wholeness is seen. You would have a greater appreciation of someone's sadness regarding the destruction of a Ming vase if you had seen the vase in its original beauty and known its history. The depth of our brokenness as people can be grasped only in the light of our created wholeness.

We are told in Genesis 1:26-28: "Then God said, 'Let us make man in our image, in our likeness....' So God created man in his own image, in the image of God he created him; male and female he created them. God blessed them and said to them, 'Be fruitful and increase in number; fill the earth and subdue it. Rule over the fish of the sea and the birds of the air and over every living creature that moves on the ground.'_" Many volumes have been written about the image of God in mankind. For the purposes of our study of sexual abuse and its effects, I would like to consider three aspects of that image: voice, relationship, and power.

Voice

We learn through the existence of Scripture itself and through the entrance of the Son of God into time that it is the very nature of God to speak, to communicate his thoughts—his very self—to others. Jesus, in being called the Word, suggests that self-expression is inherent in the Godhead. God is forever seeking to speak himself into his creation. Again and again in Genesis 1 we read, "And God said..." By nature, God is perpetually articulate. The psalmist tells us that "the voice of the Lord is powerful...is majestic...strikes with flashes of lightning...shakes the desert" (Ps. 29:4-8). The voice of God *is*. We are created in the image of one whose voice has not been silent since the dawn of Creation. What does it mean to be created in the image of one who speaks? It means that you and I as the created ones have also been given voice. We need to understand what our voices were meant to be if we are to comprehend their loss. The concept of voice is defined for us in Scripture: "God, after He spoke long ago to the fathers in the prophets in many portions and in many ways, in these last days has spoken to us in His Son...[who is] the exact representation of His nature" (Heb. 1:1-3, NASB).

The second person of the Godhead is the Word. He is God speaking, and he is God speaking in the flesh. The person of Christ is one who exactly represents God and yet is one whom you and I can understand. "No man has seen God at any time; the only begotten God...He has explained Him" (John 1:18, NASB).

Voice is that which articulates personhood. It is the exact representation of the person. It is the person speaking himself or herself into the world. Voice explains the person to others in terms that can be understood. Voice is an extension of self.

You and I are created in the image of God, who is eternally speaking. God speaks; we speak. God's word makes him accessible; our word makes us accessible. God's word creates; our word creates. God's Word explains himself to us; our word explains ourself to others. God's essence is found in the Word; our essence is expressed in our voice. To be in the image of God is to have a voice and to speak that voice out into the world. Anything that distorts the voice of God results in the destruction of person. Anything that silences voice destroys the image of God in human beings. Speaking out of his suffering of affliction, the psalmist says in Psalm 88 that one of the results was, "I am shut up, and I cannot come forth" (Ps. 88:8, KJV). We were originally created to hear the voice of God and out of that unhindered hearing, to speak our own voice out into the world.

The Fall brought about the destruction of voice. The word of God was distorted, and the distortion was believed. Humanity was shattered, and part of that shattering was evidenced in the voice. A failure to listen to the voice of God resulted in hiding, lies, secrecy, and silence. And so it continues; whenever a human being refuses to heed the voice of God, the result is hiding, lies, secrecy, and silence in one's own life, as well as in the lives of others. Oppression, cruelty, violence, and the sexual abuse of a child silence the voice of one created in the image of the God who speaks.

Relationship

A second aspect of God's image that is apparent in the Creation story is relationship: "Then God said, 'Let *us* make man in *our* image, in *our* likeness" (Gen. 1:26, italics added). From the very beginning, we see that relationship is part of who God is. God speaks of himself as someone who is eternally relating. Since he made us to be like him, we can assume that we too are relational.

God has given us a picture of the perfect relationship. It is illustrated for us in the relationship between the Father and the Son. Two components to that perfect relationship are important to our understanding of the nature of persons and how trauma affects them. First, Jesus knew the Father and was known by him (reciprocal knowledge). Second, Jesus loved the Father and was loved by him (reciprocal love). In essence, then, relationship as it was intended to be includes both a reciprocal knowing and a reciprocal loving.

Jesus knew the Father and was known by him. To know others means to see them clearly for who they are, to know them in truth. To know others means we possess correct information about them. To know others also carries the idea of understanding them. It means that we have such a sense of their essence that we can predict their responses and feelings to different events. We know their mind and their heart.

Jesus knew the Father. He had no doubt about who the Father was. He had grasped his essence, his heart. He had no confused ideas, no misperceptions, no half-truths. What he knew about the Father and spoke about the Father was in perfect alignment with who the Father is.

Jesus was also known by the Father. He says in John 10:15, "The Father knows me." There is reciprocity in the relationship. Each is fully accessible to the other. Neither is removed, hidden, disguised from, or distorted by the other. There are no corners or crevices in one that are not known by the other. Each is responded to in truth or according to the reality of who he is. The Father is ever the Father—holy, mighty, powerful, just, loving, and merciful. The Son is ever the Son—he does nothing without the Father, he is obedient to the Father, he loves the Father, and he is secure in the unchanging nature of the Father.

Jesus also loved the Father and was loved by him. He tells us in John 14:31 that "the world must learn that I love the Father." He dem~- onstrated his love for the Father by always doing what the Father commanded. He knew what was in the heart of the Father and delighted to fulfill it. Knowing who the Father was in truth enabled him to love the Father freely. If we do not know people in truth, then we fail to love *them;* instead we love something we imagine them to be. It was love for the Father that motivated Jesus' every thought and action. He never did anything that was not grounded in love for the Father. The life of Jesus was a living demonstration of his love for the Father.

The Father also loved the Son. Jesus says in his prayer to the Father, "You loved me before the creation of the world" (John 17:24). The Father loved the Son before the dawn of time. The Father loved the Son perfectly as he stood on the edge of heaven and bid the Son farewell. The Father loved him as the Son sweat great drops of blood in Gethsemane. The Father loved the Son flaw-lessly as he watched him die at Calvary. There was never a time or place where the Father and the Son did not perfectly love each other. Neither ever acted in a way that contradicted their love for one another.

As creatures made in the image of God, we were intended to have a voice that speaks out into the world, and we were meant to live in relationship as those who are known and loved. The Fall, that awful choice to act against the voice of God and in contradiction to our relationship to him, not only silenced voice but also shattered relationship. The first response of humankind to sin was to feel so afraid and full of shame that hiding and covering seemed the only recourse. The experience of knowing and being known, loving and being loved, was destroyed.

Power

The third aspect of personhood, or of the image of God in mankind, is seen in the fact that God gave human beings power to influence people and events. When God first blessed the creatures he had made, his original command to them was to "be fruitful...subdue [the earth]...rule over...every living creature" (Gen. 1:28). We were to hear and speak, to know and be known, to love and be loved. We were also intended to have an impact on the world and each other. We were meant to have influence, to regulate, to create, to govern. We were given significance. We were intended to live in a way that would let the world know we had been here. God meant for us to leave our mark. We were not meant to be invisible, ineffective, or helpless people. In his creation of us, he had left his stamp on the world and on his creatures. In being like him, we too were to have an impact on the world and the people around us.

To be created in the image of God is to have a voice, to be in relationship, and to have power or impact. All three aspects of personhood are fully experienced only when we live as creatures rightly related to God. All three were shattered by the Fall. The source of the destruction of our personhood was God's archenemy, who is the counterfeit of all God intended us to be. Jesus gives us a vivid description of that enemy in John 8:44: "You are of your father the devil, and you want to do the desires of your father. He was a murderer from the beginning, and does not stand in the truth, because there is no truth in him. Whenever he speaks a lie, he speaks from his own nature; for he is a liar, and the father of lies" (NASB).

Satan sought what was forbidden: "I will make myself like the Most High" (Isa. 14:14). Personhood is shattered whenever we seek what usurps God or is forbidden by him. To seek to occupy the place of God is twisting power and using it for one's own ends. The outcome is the destruction of self and others.

Satan is a murderer. He is the destroyer of relationship. He is a hater rather than a lover. Personhood is destroyed whenever we fail to preserve relationship in love and in truth. To fail to love is to destroy relationship, to murder.

Satan is a deceiver, a deserter of what is good and true. He is a liar, a silencer of truth. Personhood is fractured, marred, whenever we deceive or distort. Deceiving, calling evil good, and manipulating the truth all silence voice.

When Adam and Eve refused to heed God's voice, ceased being grounded in a relationship with God, and attempted to wrest God's power for themselves, personhood was damaged. Voice was silenced and distorted. Relationship became broken, and humans were alienated. Power, originally meant as a force for good, became destructive and injurious. Again and again throughout history, whenever one human being acts toward another in a way that is not rooted in the truth of God, the same results occur: silence, isolation, and helplessness. This devastation can occur in milder forms, as when one person speaks sharply or critically to another. We have all known the experience of being rendered silent in the face of a cutting remark. Severe destruction occurs whenever one human perpetrates an atrocity against another. It is here, in our understanding of the nature of personhood, that we can begin to grasp the evil perpetrated in the life of a human being when trauma occurs. Trauma is, by definition, an injury done to personhood.

4

Understanding the Nature of Therapy

Therapy is first and foremost a relationship. It is a particular kind of relationship carried out in a specific context. Like all relationships, it involves two people's joining together, connecting for a particular purpose. As they interact, these two people will have an impact on each other. The Latin word for "relate" is referre, which literally means "to bear back." Relationship is interactive in nature, with each person continually bearing something back and forth. Both reciprocity and impact are involved.

Given our previous discussion of personhood, we can say that the therapeutic relationship is, in part, about knowing and loving another in truth. Though the nature of therapy is such that very specific, necessary, and helpful guidelines are laid down regarding the extent of the knowing and the loving, both are still facets of the relationship. The person of the therapist becomes known to the client. If therapy is to be helpful, the person of the therapist must be found to be faithful, safe, and truthful. If these qualities are not demonstrated, the therapeutic relationship fails to be a place where the client can bring the truth about herself. She is often bringing truth that she fears to express or even face in the context of ordinary relationships. The personal "knowing" that the client needs to do, or the facing of the unspeakable, can occur only in the context of safety.

Few discussions of therapy talk about loving the client. Words like *care, empathy,* and *concern* are often used, but love is not generally considered a necessary component to good therapy. However, as those who know Christ, you and I are called to love. It is not an option, and it is not to be excluded from the therapy room. After all, how can those who do not know our Lord see how loving he is when their conception of him is so marred by trauma? They will see by looking at us. Whenever there is a flaw in our loving, we make it harder for them to see and apprehend his great love. The way of love is laid out for us in 1 Corinthians 13, and the qualities described there will serve only to enhance therapy. What but a *patient* love can sit faithfully with the scars of trauma? A love that *does not seek its own* is crucial. Those who have been abused have been cruelly used to meet the needs of their abusers, often the very people who were meant to teach them the way of love. Love *does not take into account a wrong suffered.* How often therapy involves acting out as clients bring into the relationship the worst parts of themselves and struggle with them there! Love *protects, hopes, perseveres.* Such qualities, demonstrated faithfully, are vital to effective therapy.

Voice is obviously a vital component of therapy; the expression of self by both therapists and clients is necessary if healing is to occur. As therapists speak their "self" out into the relationship, they not only share their self but also model for clients how to do the same. At the same time, therapists are helping both cognitively and emotionally to create a healing environment.

We said earlier that God gave us voice for the purpose of creating, governing, and articulating. To be shut up is to be less than God intended. Voice can be expressed in many ways. It is simply thoughts, words, and feelings articulated in some form. That expression can be spoken, written, painted, sung, or danced. It is some representation of the person who sits before us. In many ways, therapy is simply the voice of one person calling out to another, urging that person to give expression to her self.

Therapy is a relationship that continually draws out the voice of another. To have the capacity to draw out the voice of one who has been silenced for many years is to have a great deal of power. We might define power as an ability to produce certain desired effects. As the ones who can help unleash another's voice and bring to the relationship components that foster healing, therapists have a great deal of power.

On the other hand, to have been silenced means to feel powerless. Clients' experiences of themselves as powerless have been deeply in~grained by the abuse. People who have continuously been acted upon in harmful ways often assume a vulnerable, receptive mode and thus are set up for others to abuse the power they have over them. Clients enter therapy looking for help. They see therapists as the ones who have the power to help. Clients see themselves as those who have no choice and to whom things are done. Clients see therapists as the ones who determine the relationship, set boundaries, and have greater knowledge. It is a very short step from these components to an abuse of power. Obviously, the responsibility rests on therapists to use power only for clients' good and for the purpose of helping clients find their own voice and exercise their God-given power.

If we see therapy as a relationship that is to foster the expression of God-given voice and the exercise of God-given power, we clearly have a potentially powerful tool that can be used for good or evil. Relationships can bring great harm to others. Voices can be silenced or used to speak lies. Power can so easily be a force for evil. What is to govern such a tool so that those of us who wield it will not cause destruction when we are meant to bring life?

I believe that unless therapy is both incarnational and redemptive, in process and in purpose, we who call ourselves counselors will fail to bring to our clients true life as embodied in the person of Christ. What do I mean when I speak of therapy as needing to be both incarnational and redemptive?

Healing, or life, cannot occur in isolation. We see this from the record of the beginning of time. The triune God, who *is* life, is eternally relating. This God said, "It is not good for the man to be alone" (Gen. 2:18). Relationship was central to the creation of all things.

We are in our very essence relational. As creatures, our life depends on keeping our relationship to God in its proper place. When that relationship is no longer central, the result is death.

When relationship was originally broken by Adam and Eve's sin, God opened the way to restoration by becoming like us. In becoming flesh and blood, God entered into not only our world but also our life experience. He walked alongside; he touched; he wept; he fed; he grieved. He came as close to us as one can ever come in relationship—he got inside our skin.

When Jesus came to restore relationship, he was called the Word. He was God speaking, explaining himself to his creatures in terms they could understand. He was also the Truth. God is a God of integrity; he cannot speak other than who he is. His words are always in harmony with his character. Whatever he demonstrated in Jesus is a true representation of God. He cannot lie, pretend, or deceive. So Jesus is God in the flesh, God relating and God speaking. He came in such a manner because you and I as creatures need skin and words in order for healing, for life, to occur.

Jesus incarnate is also God's power unleashed: "I came that they might have life" (John 10:10, NASB). There is no power greater than the power to create life. Mankind has for years sought such power without success. We cannot create life. At best, we can only bear the life that is created by Another. Jesus is the Life Giver, and his power cannot be surpassed. His is the power that conquered death and hell. His is the power that can take a life shattered beyond recognition by evil and abuse and restore it so that it reflects his beauty.

Jesus is God's power demonstrated in a surprising way, however. On the one hand, all the forces of hell must obey his command. On the other hand, he is a baby—dependent, vulnerable, and in need of protection from evil men. He who came as the Word of God, to live in relationship with his creatures and to give the power of life to all who will come, did so in a mysterious way. The culmination of this great mystery is seen in the Cross of Christ, the center point of all redemption. It is on the cross that we see the voice of the Word unanswered and eventually silenced in death. It is on the cross that we see a perfect relationship shattered and broken as the Father abandoned the Son. And it is on the cross that we see the awesome power of heaven restrained while God the Son died and hell seemingly won. The Incarnation involved both the exercise of incomprehensible power and, simultaneously, great restraint of that power. Jesus was God storming the gates of hell even while he bowed himself to our finiteness and brokenness.

As believers, we are called to live out the mystery of the Incarnation. Jesus became incarnate for the purpose of explaining the Father to others. Our lives, too, are to explain the character of the Father. The essence of the Incarnation was the bringing down into flesh-and-blood actualities the very nature of God himself. We, too, in our very persons, are to be the message of who God is, even while we bend to bear the burdens of others and enter into their life experience. Certainly that involves speaking what is true, but it is far greater than merely putting truth into words. To live incarnationally means that *all* of life, public and private, is a living illustration of God himself. To reduce life or therapy to a mere verbalization of truth is to fall far short of our calling as Christians. Incarnational therapy means that the person of the therapist outside the counseling room and unknown to the client is as important as the words spoken during the therapy hour. Living incarnationally also means entering into the fellowship of Christ's sufferings as we who are flesh and blood move into the anguish and darkness of others' lives. It is not simply that we tell the truth about a life (though that is part of it) but that we, like him, enter into the humanity of others. To demonstrate who God is means to be conformed to the image of his Son in all things. Such concepts will be considered in greater detail when we discuss the person of the therapist in a later section. For now, let us simply say that anything the therapist does or says that communicates less than the truth of who God is, is a failure to live incarnationally.

The Incarnation, God in the flesh, occurred for the purpose of accomplishing redemption. Jesus came in order to explain the Father, but he also came for the purpose of buying back that which was lost. He came to restore what had been broken, to bring life out of death, light instead of darkness. The Incarnation brought the presence of God to bear on every evil, every sickness, every wound for the purpose of making all things new. The purpose of God is ever the same—we are to live incarnationally so that through us the life of God might buy back that which is lost.

One of the truths we learn from the beginning of time is that life begets after its own likeness. God created us in his image. That makes humans both image bearers and image carriers. The principle was demonstrated when God said living creatures were to produce after their own kinds. This principle is seen again when God says he visits "the iniquity of the fathers on the children, on the third and the fourth generations" (Exod. 20:5,NASB). We produce in others what we are, and simultaneously, we bear the image of the one who owns us. Redemption is God's bearing the sin and death that mankind has produced and reproduced, in order once again to create humankind after his own likeness. The Incarnation was for the purpose of redeeming human beings so that they might reflect once again the image of God.

Therapy with survivors of sexual abuse means working with those who carry the destructive image of the perpetrator in their very person. The therapist has the privilege of bringing the presence of God to bear on the results of the evil that was done so that all things might be made new. Therapy then becomes the working out of redemption in a life shattered and scarred by evil. As therapists enter into the life experience of their clients, bearing the image of the Lord Jesus Christ in their person, they will see the work of redemption unfold. And as therapists bow to the working out of redemption in their own lives, they will find that the life of God in them begets after its own likeness in their clients.

5

Understanding the Nature of Trauma

To experience an atrocity is to live the unspeakable. It is unspeakable first because its horrific nature is so staggering that words are woefully inadequate to communicate what has happened. Second, words fail because such an experience silences, isolates, and renders powerless. How is it possible, then, for one who has been shut up, alienated, and made helpless to speak, when the very nature of the monstrous event renders such speech impossible? The paradox, of course, is that in order to heal at all from such violence, one must learn to speak the unspeakable. What is too terrifying to hold for long moments in the mind must be remembered and reflected upon. That which is utterly impossible to put into words must finally be spoken about again and again. Not only must the indescribable be described, but that which so powerfully isolates one human being from others must be uttered within the context of relationship if healing is ever to occur. Why is that? It is because those things that the atrocity crushed—voice, connection, and power—are the essence of person-hood. If they are not restored, then the one who has been so horribly crushed remains silent, disconnected, and helpless—a grievous distortion of the image of God in humanity.

Human beings commit many atrocious acts against other human beings. One of the most horrible and unspeakable of these is the sexual abuse of a child. To do violence to a child in any way is to do a great evil. A child is by definition unformed, developing. The sexual abuse of children shatters and violates every aspect of their being—their world, their self, their faith, and their future. To be small, vulnerable, and dependent in a world of big people who are meant to give protection and care, and then to find oneself violated in body, mind, and soul is to undergo an unspeakable trauma. To experience repeated trauma while in the process of developing is to be shaped, imprinted, by terror and fear rather than by love and safety. Needless to say, the scars run deep.

The treatment of such scars, the healing of such wounds, requires a knowledge of the nature of trauma and its consequences as well as an understanding of the development of the child. Repeated trauma perpetrated against a child has a different impact from trauma experienced by an already formed adult. Repeated trauma in adult life attacks personality structures already formed and often erodes them. The same experience in childhood has the power to shape in sad and twisted ways the developing potential of the child. Because of the abusive nature of the environment, the child is forced to adapt in ways that are often maladaptive in the larger world. Treatment of such entrenched and long-standing responses to life will be ineffective unless the fact that the abuse occurred to an immature child is kept ever present in the therapist's mind.

TRAUMA

Trauma involves "intense fear, helplessness, loss of control, and threat of annihilation."[1] Such fear, helplessness, and the threat of nonexistence silence persons, alienate them, and render them powerless. The rape of a child is a violent injury to personhood. It is a wound that reverberates throughout the core of a person, often throughout the years.

Judith Herman, in her book *Trauma and Recovery,* says, "Traumatic events are extraordinary, not because they occur rarely, but rather because they overwhelm the ordinary human adaptations to life."[2] When one is faced with pain and suffering, a normal human response is to call for help. The repeated sexual abuse of a child, so frequently accompanied with threats to life and well-being, renders the child speechless. And even those who do attempt to speak often find their hearers unable or unwilling to hear because the consequences of the message are far too devastating.

A second adaptation to suffering and pain is to find solace and comfort in relationship. When we grieve the death of a loved one, we seek comfort in those people who know and love us. The comfort found in such relationships serves as a balm for our wounded spirit. The rape of a child, particularly when it occurs within the nuclear family, very often occurs in a context of neglect and emotional deprivation. The child usually lives within a network of relationships that are in reality only pretense, for the child is not truly known or truly loved. Safety and comfort in the strong arms of another are not accessible. The child is an accepted member of the family system only as long as she allows herself to be abused by one and pretends nothing is wrong for another.

A third possible response to terrible pain is to fight against it. When we are attacked, we often survive by attacking in return or, at the very least, by fleeing to protect ourselves. Our attention and perceptions are heightened as we go into a state of alert. We are mobilized to fight or flee whenever we sense danger to our person. To be a child who is sexually abused is to find one's actions to be of no avail. The child is small; the abuser is big. The child's knowledge is limited; the perpetrator's knowledge is vast by comparison. The child is frail; the abuser is strong. The child's credibility is questionable, for what do children know? The abuser's credibility is high, for deceit has become a way of life.

The repeated molestation of a child is an evil perpetrated against personhood. It is an assault on the core of God's work in making us male and female. It is violence done to the creation of God, for it silences, isolates, and renders the person helpless. Sexual abuse takes the image of God in a human being and smashes it. The rape of a child takes two arenas where God intended his image, his character, to be reflected and demonstrated—the individual and the family—and hideously distorts what was meant to be beautiful. Such evil must cause a shudder to run through the heart of God. Any minimization of an evil such as this reflects a failure to grasp what God intended when he created us in his own image. Any healing response to such evil will be effective only insofar as these truths are understood. We are not talking about surface wounds when we speak of the rape of a child; we are talking about personhood wounds.

When personhood is shattered and actions become meaningless, a traumatic reaction occurs. The child is unable to stop or escape the abuse, and so the responses that were meant to protect and defend become maladaptive. Profound changes occur in emotion, cognition, memory, and physiology. In addition, those aspects of the self that were meant to function in a unified manner become segregated one from the other. Normally, in a state of alert everything works in a coordinated manner so the person is protected. However, when a person is overwhelmed by fear and helplessness, functions such as hyperarousal, heightened perception, and aggressive impulses can become disconnected from their source and can seem to take on a life of their own. The result of such trauma has come to be known as post-traumatic stress disorder.

POST-TRAUMATIC STRESS DISORDER

Post-traumatic stress disorder is defined in the *Diagnostic and Statistical Manual of Mental Disorders IV* as "the development of characteristic symptoms following exposure to an extreme traumatic stressor involving direct personal experience of an event that involves actual or threatened death or serious injury, or other threat to one's physical integrity; or witnessing an event that involves death, injury, or a threat to the physical integrity of another person; or learning about unexpected or violent death, serious harm or threat of death or injury experienced by a family member or other close associate. The person's response to the event must involve intense fear, helplessness, or horror (or in children, the response must involve disorganized or agitated behavior)."[3]

To qualify for the diagnosis of post-traumatic stress disorder one must

1. continue reexperiencing the trauma through such things as intrusive recollections, nightmares, flashbacks (recurrent sensory memories wherein one feels as if the event is occurring in the present), and psychological and physiological distress when exposed to internal or external cues reminiscent of the trauma.

2. experience a "numbing of general responsiveness" to or avoidance of stimuli associated with the trauma, such as withdrawal, restricted affect, dissociation, amnesia, and loss of interest in daily activities.

3. experience ongoing symptoms of increased arousal, such as sleep disturbances, difficulty concentrating, hypervigilance, anger outbursts, and an exaggerated startle response.[4]

Let us consider the foregoing diagnostic criteria based on the story of Meeka.

AN EXTREME TRAUMATIC STRESSOR

Meeka is four years old, and she likes ice cream and kitty cats. She wishes she were bigger because when you're bigger, you get to go to school. She used to like to play outside by herself near the shed. It was fun to sit in the sun and pet her kitty. She used to like bedtime, too. It was a quiet time to snuggle down under the covers.

Daddy changed all that. Now Meeka watches to see if he is there before she goes outside. When she gets into bed at night, she feels afraid and lies there listening, always listening for footsteps. Often she wraps her covers around her in mummylike fashion in an attempt to provide protection for herself. But a four-year-old is little, and Daddy is very big. Try as she might, she cannot find a way to get away from him. He confuses her and frightens her. He touches her and tells her it's their secret and she is not to tell anyone, not even Mommy. Sometimes the things he does hurt her. He puts things inside her. She doesn't understand, and she wants it to stop. She tells him, but he says this is what fathers do for their daughters and it's for her good. He says he will kill her kitty if she tells.

He also says it's her fault for leading him on. What does that mean? One night she tries sleeping in her closet, but he always finds her. Nothing she tries works.

Sometimes she thinks about telling Mommy, but she feels afraid. Daddy said not to and said he would punish her if she didn't obey. When Daddy punishes, he hurts her. Maybe Mommy knows anyway. She always tells her to run and be with Daddy. Mommy doesn't seem to have much time for her. She always has "more important" things on her mind. One time Mommy caught Daddy in her room late at night, but he said Meeka had had a nightmare and that he was calming her down. Mommy believed him.

Now when Daddy hurts her, she has begun to pretend she is real little and can hide under the flowers in her wallpaper. It's funny because she feels as if she's watching herself from far away. She digs her fingernails into her palms and sometimes pulls her hair so hard that it comes out. The pain from those things takes her mind away from what Daddy is doing. Sometimes after Daddy leaves and everything hurts, she talks to her "friend." Mommy gets upset and tells her to stop because her "friend" isn't real, just pretend. Mommy doesn't seem to understand that her friend is the only one she can talk to about Daddy and that her friend is very comforting to her.

Daddy seems to get more and more angry, even when she tries hard to do just what he says so he won't be mad. He calls her bad names and tells her how wicked she is for making him do this. Doesn't he understand that she doesn't want him to do this? What could she possibly be doing to make him do these things? Then, after she does just what he wants so he won't get mad, he gets mad anyway. It just doesn't make any sense. *Nothing* she can think of is successful in stopping it.

Meeka's rape is certainly "an extreme traumatic stressor involving direct personal experience of an event that involves actual or threatened death or serious injury or other threat to one's physical integrity." Intense fear, helplessness, and horror are clearly responses to such abuse. The child's voice is silenced, relationships are shattered, and she is rendered utterly helpless. The integrity and wholeness of her body, her mind, and her soul are smashed.

Meeka's world is no longer secure. Any illusion of security or hope for safety is shattered if the trauma is repeated enough times. Every attempt to forestall the unremitting terror is useless. Being good, being bad, hiding, lying, looking pretty, getting dirty, praying—none of it seems to make any difference. The terror comes again and again like the waves of the sea. It is unstoppable.

Any budding faith Meeka had is destroyed. Repeatedly she begs God to keep her safe. Repeatedly he appears impotent to do so, or perhaps he doesn't care. She concludes that he is not there, that he is powerless or cruel, or that she is not worth loving (a likely conclusion, since Daddy finds it so).

Meeka's self is shattered. To other people her thoughts are irrelevant, her feelings do not matter, and her words are meaningless. Any expression of her true self must be done in secret because there is no place where such expression is valued or given credibility. She cannot say she doesn't want the abuse and be heard. She cannot tell anyone she is being abused and have it matter. Who she is in truth is not acknowledged. She is reduced to pretense.

Any hope and future are also destroyed for Meeka. Potential is part of the very essence of children. They carry within them the hope for the future, the potential for new life and new discoveries. What might have been will never be in this child. In Latin, *victima* is "an animal offered in sacrifice." Truly, a child victim of sexual abuse is a person offered up to appease the greed of the idol being worshiped—the self, the "I" of the perpetrator.

REEXPERIENCING THE TRAUMA

When Meeka grows up, she will find her past continually intruding on her present. She will find the trauma repeatedly interrupting her life. It will feel as if both present and future have been swallowed up by the past. It will break in without warning, in flashbacks when she is awake and as nightmares when she is asleep. Triggers in the form of smells or sounds can evoke memories that return with all the emotional force and physiological responses that accompanied the original event. Her dreams will often consist of fragments of real memories so that, in the words of one woman,

"I'm afraid to sleep because it just means he will come after me again and again." Even those nightmares that are not remnants of actual memories will carry in them the extreme feelings of fear and helplessness, replayed over and over again.

Sometimes the trauma is experienced repeatedly in the form of reenactments. These can take the form of risk-taking behavior, self-destructive choices such as alcohol and drug abuse, battering relationships, prostitution, or self-mutilation. There is a driven quality about these reenactments, as if the survivor is attempting repeatedly to find a way to master the unmasterable. All of these aspects of reexperiencing the original trauma tend to carry with them the emotional intensity of the horror suffered as a child. Because of this, the survivor is constantly feeling overwhelmed by helplessness and fear, living in a perpetual state of trauma. She continues throughout life to experience herself as silent, isolated, and helpless. She experiences herself as forever unable to escape the unspeakable.

NUMBING OF GENERAL RESPONSIVENESS

Meeka will find herself perpetually withdrawing from others despite a longing for intimacy. She will often feel detached from others, distant and different. Her range of emotions will be severely restricted, and when people ask her how she feels, she will often respond with a nondescriptive term such as *upset.*

As a child who was repeatedly abused and helpless to stop it, she learned psychological ways of "going away." Survivors speak of "zoning out," "going inside themselves," "distancing," or "blanking out." Because nothing else worked, this defense often generalizes to all aversive and anxiety-provoking experiences in later life. The most dramatic form of this "going away" is dissociation, defined as "a disruption in the usually integrated functions of consciousness, memory, identity or perception of the environment."[5] Whenever a memory or current event containing abusive elements occurs, the survivor may resort to dissociation as a way of removing herself from what she fears. Those survivors who are not adept at dissociation will often use alcohol or drugs or food in order to numb themselves.

Another outcome of the trauma of sexual abuse is that the survivor may be experiencing depression. Her withdrawal, restricted affect, and loss of interest in daily activities may all indicate a depressive disorder. Theories of the etiology of depression stress a variety of factors, including early loss and abandonment, self-blaming cognitions developed in childhood, and chronic experiences of helplessness when faced with aversive conditions. Obviously, all of these factors are relevant to the experience of sexual-abuse victims. It is, in fact, not unusual for survivors to present themselves for treatment of depression rather than for treatment for incest.

ONGOING SYMPTOMS OF INCREASED AROUSAL

Meeka is very likely to find herself hounded by ongoing physiological disturbances long after the abuse has ceased. She will startle easily, sleep poorly, and react with irritation to small hassles. Though the stressor that originally caused the physiological responses has long since ceased, the state of hyperarousal often persists. She may take longer to fall asleep than most people, sleep restlessly, experience nightmares, and find herself awake in the middle of the night or very early in the morning. Her fears and sense of helplessness are often heightened at night; the abuse may have frequently occurred at night, and the sleeping state is felt to be more vulnerable. Nightmares only increase her fears and tension (states clearly counterproductive to rest) because to sleep is to be "found" yet again by the perpetrator.[6]

Many survivors find it very difficult to concentrate. They are often hypervigilant, constantly watching for signs of danger. A mind that is ever watchful over the surrounding environment is not free to focus intently on one particular subject lest such concentration lead to missing a signal of danger.

Sleep is not the only bodily state that is disrupted by chronic hyperarousal. While growing up, the child-victim's body was not her own but rather was used at the whim of her abuser. His use of her was often totally unpredictable, keeping her constantly in a state of alertness, or the abuse occurred regularly during those times we normally think of as comforting, such as bedtime, mealtime, bath time. This can lead to chronic sleep disturbances, eating disorders, gastrointestinal problems, self-injurious behavior, and disturbed sexual arousal, e.g., inability to feel safe in loving sexual relationships or arousal that occurs in the context of pain.

An understanding of the above responses to an extreme traumatic stressor is vital. Too often the survivor is seen by herself and others as "nuts," "crazy," or "weird," unless her responses are understood within the context of trauma. A traumatic stress reaction consists of *natural* emotions and behaviors in response to catastrophe, its immediate aftermath, or memories of it. These reactions can occur anytime after the trauma, even decades later. The coping strategies that victims use can be understood only within the context of the abuse of a child. The importance of context was made very clear to me many years ago when I was visiting the home of a Holocaust survivor. The woman's home was within the city limits of a large metropolitan area. Every time a police or ambulance siren sounded, she became terrified and ran and hid in a closet or under the bed. To put yourself in a closet at the sound of a far-off siren is strange behavior indeed—outside of the context of possibly being sent to a death camp. Within that context, it makes perfect sense. Unless we as therapists have a good grasp of the effects of trauma, we run the risk of misunderstanding the symptoms our clients present and, hence, responding inappropriately or in damaging ways.

6

Understanding the Nature of Child Development

The trauma of sexual abuse has far-reaching effects in the life of an adult. Chronic abuse in the life of a developing child has consequences that are even more profound because the experience of abuse is woven throughout the development of the self. The traumatized child grows up in a family in which normal caretaking relationships are severely disrupted. The primary relationships that are meant to teach us about ourselves and others in nurturing ways end up forcing the child to erect defensive barriers that profoundly alter the developing self. Trauma shapes every facet of the self. The child will feel the impact of trauma physiologically, affectively, cognitively, and spiritually.

Human beings are indeed "fearfully and wonderfully made" (Ps. 139:14). The handiwork of the God of the universe is by no means simple or easily understood. For all our efforts, we still struggle to grasp the inner workings of the body, the mind, and the heart of humanity. Our complexity is beyond our comprehension. To take such a complex creature, one who was meant for God and is destroyed by sin, and attempt to understand how the development of that creature can be affected by hideous trauma is to attempt the impossible. Yet it must be done to some degree. To fail to do so is to minimize the glory of God's handiwork as well as the depth of the sin committed against that handiwork. To fail to do so is to risk falling into disrespectful, superficial, Band-Aid approaches to the victims who sit before us.

We will consider the impact of chronic sexual abuse on a developing child first by looking at Erikson's stages and their tasks; second, by exploring how the defenses children typically use against overwhelming trauma also affect the development of the self; and third, by reviewing what trauma does to voice, relationship, and power.

ERIKSON'S STAGES

In order to evaluate the impact of chronic sexual abuse, it is essential to understand the intellectual, verbal, and emotional development that is normal for a child at the age at which the trauma occurred. Not only is the impact of the trauma dependent on the child's age, but the form that the memory of the trauma takes is also dependent on the child's age.

Erik Erikson, deemed the father of developmental psychology, divided the life cycle into eight psychosocial stages. Each successive stage is concerned with a particular crisis the child must resolve in his or her quest for identity before moving on to the next stage. If the childhood crises are not handled satisfactorily, the person then continues to fight early battles later in life. Erikson believed that each stage builds on the previous stages and also influences later stages. We will use Erikson's stages not as absolute or scientifically proven stages but rather as a schema to help us grasp how sexual abuse might affect a developing child. As always throughout this book, all examples are true.

Stage 1: Trust versus Mistrust (Infancy: Birth to One Year)

In this stage, the infant's basic task is to develop a relationship with someone who can be trusted to meet his or her needs. If the balance is weighted toward trust, the child will have a better chance of weathering later crises. Infants with an attitude of trust find that their parents will feed them when they are hungry and comfort them when they are in pain or afraid.

Example of trauma: Sara grew up knowing she was not wanted. The story was repeatedly told that her father used to refuse her mother access to Sara's room for hours and sometimes for two days at a time. "I never wanted that child anyway."

Stage 2: Autonomy versus Shame and Doubt (Early Childhood: Two to Three Years)

The child's focus in this stage is the need to establish that it is acceptable to be a separate person with some degree of control over himself or herself. At the same time, autonomy increases anxiety over separation and the risk of failure. Shame and doubt occur if basic trust was never established or if one's attempts at independence are overcontrolled, ridiculed, or punished.

Example of trauma: Sara's father dominated the home with his rage. If her mother was not quick enough in responding to Sara's toilet-training needs, any accident was handled by the father's taking the child and shoving her face into the toilet bowl into which he had put the feces. Her mother did nothing.

Stage 3: Initiative versus Guilt (Preschool: Four to Five Years)

In this stage the child needs to be encouraged to make as many choices as possible. The basic task is that of establishing competence and initiative. The child takes initiative by curiously investigating everything, talking incessantly, and constantly moving.

Example of trauma: Sara was frightened and spoke little. She was rarely allowed outside the premises and so did not develop peer relationships. She was required to stay either in her bed or in her room for hours at a time so as not to "get in Daddy's way." When Daddy was not home, she was allowed the run of the house untended, often having to make her own meals. Any sign of mess left on the kitchen counters (which she was too short to see without a chair) was severely punished.

Stage 4: Industry versus Inferiority (School Age: Six Years to Puberty)

Middle childhood is about making things and entering the world of knowledge and work. The child strives to make things well and to gain recognition and praise for personal accomplishments. When the child is successful, he or she feels competent. Failure brings a sense of inferiority, a feeling of worthlessness.

Example of trauma: Sara liked school because it provided an escape from home. She was bright and periodically could perform well, depending on what was happening at home. It was during these years that her father's abuse became sexual as well as physical, and the resulting pain in her body often kept her from being able to hear what the teacher was saying. Whenever her grades reflected this, her parents would punish her for being stupid. The downside of school was peer relationships. Sara had little to no experience with peer relationships and was often sent to school unkempt and/or dirty. Her appearance combined with her social awkwardness resulted in teasing and isolation.

Stage 5: Identity versus Identity Confusion (Adolescence)

All of the previous stages have contributed to the child's developing identity. In the fifth stage, however, this concern reaches a climax. Adolescents are attempting to determine who they are apart from their parents. Rapid physiological changes make their bodies feel unfamiliar. They can feel very confused about who they are during this time of trying to develop a clear sense of self.

Example of trauma: Sara's father's sexual abuse intensified during this time and was more frequently laced with episodes of violence. She sometimes found her body responding to the things he did, which only confirmed in her mind that something was terribly wrong with her because she obviously liked what he did and was somehow making him act in this way. His hatred for her seemed only to increase. It reached its height when he discovered she was pregnant. He beat her badly in an attempt to force a miscarriage. When that did not occur, he took her to a doctor, who performed an abortion in spite of her pleas against it. Her mother was silent.

Sara managed to graduate from high school and left home at the age of eighteen, an alcoholic and daily pot smoker. She found a minimum-wage job and a man to live with. He beat her severely and threw her out when she became pregnant.

Stage 6: Intimacy and Solidarity versus Isolation (Young Adulthood)

If young adults emerge reasonably healthy from stage 5, then they anticipate forming intimate relationships with others without the fear of their own sense of identity being threatened.

Example of trauma: Obviously, Sara has not had the privilege of developing confidence in her own identity. Her attempts at intimacy fail, and she hides her pain and loneliness in drugs and alcohol. She finds herself on welfare, highly promiscuous, attempting to parent a child, and full of increasing despair. At the age of twenty-three, life seems hopeless, and she takes an overdose.

Stage 7: Generativity versus Stagnation and Self-Absorption (Middle Age)

This stage focuses on an interest in guiding the next generation through child rearing or creative, productive endeavors.

Example of trauma: It is clear that a person as traumatized as Sara cannot be anything other than self-absorbed. She will be unable to parent the next generation effectively. Her life will be lived out on the level of survival, not productivity. She will continue this way unless she is able to get long-term and effective help to work through the severe damage done to her person.

Stage 8: Integrity versus Despair (Late Adulthood)

When a person has the privilege of progressing through life with reasonably healthy relationships, this final stage brings a sense of completeness and the feeling that a worthwhile life has been lived. If not, the person is left with despair—regret, fear, and self-loathing.

Example of trauma: Without radical intervention and the grace of God, Sara will end her life full of despair, believing that she was indeed what her parents taught her she was—worthless, unlovable, and hopeless.

Certainly abuse occurs along a continuum of severity, and Sara's case is toward the more severe end of the scale. However, one can clearly see that chronic sexual abuse of any degree will massively influence children's development. It will interfere with and derail the learning of the basic tasks of life as well as profoundly influence children's beliefs about themselves and their relationships with others, including God.

DEFENSES AGAINST DEVELOPMENTAL TRAUMA

Childhood trauma clearly impinges on the development of the self. When children are threatened by physical and sexual events that are removed from any possibility of resolution, they must find other ways of protecting themselves. The normal avenues of communicating with the caretakers in their lives about the trauma and having them respond in protective, modulating ways are not accessible in a familial climate of ongoing abuse. Children are left on their own to manage the unmanageable.

It is obvious from the above discussion that the traumatic stressor shapes the development of the self. I believe that the internal defenses erected against the stressor also shape development. Because children are cognitively and emotionally immature, their defense capacities are limited. In the face of chronic physical and/or sexual abuse, children usually resort to varying combinations of three defenses: repression, denial, and dissociation.

One of the things that occurs in healthy development is a sense of coherence or integrity to the self. We see this early on when infants first begin to discover their fingers and eventually progress to an awareness that those wiggly things actually belong to them. What children do on a physiological level, they also do on a cognitive and affective level. They learn that their thoughts belong to them and cannot be "heard" by anyone else. They learn that their feelings belong to them and that they have control over how to express them and to whom. In an atmosphere of acceptance and discovery, children learn "what is me and what is not me."

The experience of chronic trauma shatters that process of discovery. The child's feelings and thoughts in response to the abuse are so overwhelming that the child will sacrifice a sense of coherence for the sake of survival. In essence the child says, "I cannot live with these feelings and survive, so I will make them 'not mine.'_" Survival is gained, but such defenses also inflict great loss on the developing self. What is lost is a sense of wholeness, of being real, of being spontaneous and aware of one's own inner workings. In essence, what is lost is the integrity of the self.

Repression is probably the defense that is least disruptive to the developing self. Essentially, when utilizing the unconscious mechanism of repression, the person is saying, "I forget that this happened." To remove something from one's reality by repression is to put it away basically intact. It is a way of keeping the trauma at a distance. It is the least fragmenting of the three defenses mentioned. In cases of severe and ongoing trauma, repression alone is generally an insufficient defense. The child usually needs to employ denial and dissociation as well.

Denial is essentially saying, "This is not happening." To deny what is real requires perceptual distortion and impaired reality testing. When the child senses impending danger, she may quickly slide into a state of denial, telling herself, "What I sense is not real." Unfortunately, denial puts the victim in danger of retraumatization because she has schooled herself to fail to recognize those signs that in any way remind her of the original trauma. Her automatic response to such clues is, "This is not happening." As a result of denial, the child loses continuity in her experience and learns to ignore aspects of herself that are, in fact, vital to her well-being.

Dissociation is the third defense. Here the child says, "This is not happening to me." Or perhaps she takes it a step further and says, "This is happening to someone else." Of the three defenses, the use of dissociation has the most serious consequences. In order to dissociate, the child must (1) alter her thinking, (2) disrupt her sense of time, (3) alter her body image, (4) distort her perceptions, (5) experience a loss of control, (6) alter her emotional responses, (7) change the meaning of things, and (8) become hypersuggestible.[1] The self of the child becomes fragmented, and those fragments often become totally inaccessible to her. She is no longer her "self" in any coherent sense of the word.

When a child's sense of self must develop in the context of ongoing abuse and sexual stimulation, the child will be unable to develop a coherent sense of self, stable capacities for trust, and the ability to modulate her own feelings. She will instead develop a fragmented sense of self, an inability to trust because of the unpredictable and irrational shifts in her environment, and she will experience her emotions as overwhelming, chaotic, and frightening.

THE IMPACT OF TRAUMA ON PERSONHOOD

Earlier we noted three aspects of the image of God in human beings: voice, relationship, and power. The Fall was a cataclysmic event that grossly distorted that image in all of mankind. The trauma of chronic sexual abuse in the life of a child is also a cataclysmic event that further mars what God intended that person to be. Ongoing trauma means that adults who were meant by God to nurture his life in their child instead use their own capacities for voice, relationship, and power to destroy. Jesus said that stumbling blocks are inevitable in this dark world, "but woe to the man through whom they come!" (Matt. 18:7). The destruction that abuse brings in the life of a child has the judgment of God on it. It is also the antithesis of Jesus' teaching that we are not even to "look down on" little ones (Matt. 18:10) or do anything to hinder them from coming to him (Mark 10:14).

We defined *voice* as that which articulates personhood. It is the person speaking himself or herself out into the world in truth. It explains the person to others in ways that can be heard and understood. We were not meant to live in silence. In Psalm 39:2, David speaks of his silence as resulting in an agonizing increase in his sorrow. He says later in Psalm 94:17, "If the Lord had not been my help, my soul would soon have dwelt in the abode of silence" (NASB). Silence is the place of no words, no communion, no music, no sound.

To live with chronic abuse is to live in silence, to be shut up. The voice of one so abused has been crushed. The victim is made inarticulate by intense fear. She is silenced by the deafness of others. What is the point of speaking when no one will listen? She is shut up by the threat of abandonment, which will surely come if the truth is told. She lives in a world where voices lie, distort, and deceive. She can survive in such a world only if she too learns how to lie, distort, and deceive. So she lies to herself and distorts the truth of her life in order to survive. She deceives herself and others, pretending she is really all right, when, in fact, she is dying inside. As the years go by, her voice is less and less a representation of her real self, until she finally reaches the place where she can no longer even hear herself.

We defined person as *relational,* that state of knowing and being known, loving and being loved. Just as we were not meant to live in silence, we were not meant to live in isolation. Scripture portrays the idea of being forsaken as a desolate and alarming state. Again and again God reassures his people that he will not forsake them. The scream of the Son of God rent the universe when he found himself forsaken. We are told from the beginning that "it is not good for the man to be alone" (Gen. 2:18). "Two are better than one....For if either of them falls, the one will lift up his companion" (Eccles. 4:9-10, NASB). The whole concept of the church is that of body, community, parts working together to support and sustain.

Ongoing sexual abuse requires the child to live alone. She is isolated because she cannot "tell." She is alone because no one comes to comfort. She is forsaken by those who were meant to sustain. She is not known in truth, for the fact that she is a little girl being abused is rejected and denied. She is not loved; to love is to protect and preserve, but she is being harmed and destroyed. Though the pretense of relationship may exist for the outside world, it is just that—a pretense.

Relationship, or attachment, as psychiatrist John Bowlby called it, provides the basis for our sense of security and safety in the world.

He states, "A central feature of my concept of parenting is the provision by both parents of a secure base from which a child or adolescent can make sorties into the outside world and to which he can return knowing for sure that he will be welcomed when he gets there, nourished physically and emotionally, comforted if distressed, reassured if frightened."[2] The chronically abused child not only lacks a "secure base" but also faces in that base a climate of pervasive terror and danger. Relationship has become a house of horrors.

The third characteristic of personhood is *power,* the ability to produce desired effects. The infant experiences her power when she cries, and the result is food and the presence of a parent. She feels powerful when she finds she can push against a toy in her crib and make it go round and round. God designed us to have an impact on our world, to create, to have influence. The very fact that God gave us the choice to obey or disobey granted humanity power we could not manage unless we maintained our place as dependent creatures. We failed to do so, and the consequences have been devastating.

When a child lives with unpredictable, terrifying, and relentless abuse, she experiences herself as perpetually powerless. Such phrases as "it doesn't matter" and "forget it" are frequent comments among survivors and are usually said with a shrug of the shoulders. They have learned that what matters to them does not matter to others. Who they truly were was invisible in the home, for no response was given to the abuse. Every effort they made to stop the abuse was ineffective. No matter what they did or said, it came again and again. They perceive themselves either as having no impact on the people around them or as extremely powerful in a lethal way; they define themselves—or have had others define them—as the source of the evil that was done. Power, like voice and relationship, has been destroyed, marred beyond recognition.

As seen in her story, Meeka lived daily with repeated trauma to her personhood. The tending of such wounds, the healing of such devastation, is neither easy nor quick. It is a long, hard journey out of darkness into light. It is a journey that will require much of both client and therapist. The descent into the darkness is costly. We can, however, offer a sure and steadfast hope, for the Redeemer has come!

7

Definitions, Frequency, and Family Dynamics

The central experiences of childhood trauma are silence, isolation, and helplessness. Healing, then, must involve a restoration of voice, safe connection, and rightful power. Such healing cannot occur in isolation but rather must take place within the context of relationship. The survivor's capacities to speak herself out into the world, to trust, and to experience herself as competent will develop only in relationship. The original damage to those capacities occurred in relationship; the mending of those capacities must also take place in relationship.

The therapy relationship is one of the arenas in which healing of sexual abuse often occurs. I would hope that it will not be the only relationship, for it is my experience that survivors who have a strong support system and/or are involved in a loving church community find the road to healing less overwhelming. However, the therapy relationship is unique in many respects and needs to be elaborated in detail. Before we discuss that process and the three phases that are involved, we will consider the following: a definition of terms, the frequency of occurrence, family dynamics, and the severity of effects, followed by a chapter on the symptoms and aftereffects of childhood sexual abuse.

DEFINITION OF TERMS

Sexual abuse of a child occurs whenever a child is sexually exploited by an older person for the satisfaction of the abuser's needs. It consists of any sexual activity—verbal, visual, or physical—engaged in without consent. The child is considered unable to consent due to developmental immaturity and an inability to understand sexual behavior. Incestuous behavior is illegal in all fifty states.

Verbal sexual abuse can include sexual threats, sexual comments about the child's body, lewd remarks, harassment, or suggestive comments.

Visual sexual abuse includes the viewing of pornographic material, exhibitionism, and voyeurism.

Physical sexual abuse includes intercourse, cunnilingus, fellatio, sodomy, digital penetration, masturbation in front of the child or masturbation of the adult by the child, fondling of the breasts and genitals, and exposure of the child's body to others. These may be performed on the child, or the child may be forced to perform any or all of the above.

Clearly, child sexual abuse involves a wide range of behaviors, alone or in combination. It is important to note that not all of the above examples are legally considered incest, though therapeutically they may be. One of the most crucial factors in our understanding of child sexual abuse is that it occurs in the context of a relationship with an adult from whom the child had every reason to expect protection, warmth, and care. In most cases, the abuse is perpetrated by an adult who has ready access to the child by virtue of authority or kinship. Most child sexual abuse is perpetrated by a family member or someone known to the child.

FREQUENCY OF OCCURRENCE

It is estimated that 20 to 40 percent of the female population experiences sexual abuse sometime before the age of eighteen. Estimates for males are usually approximately one in six.[1]

Incest can be a onetime occurrence for some people and span many years for others. For some it occurs more than once a day. Some women become so passive and hopeless that the incestuous relationship continues into adulthood (e.g., every time a twenty-four-year-old goes home for vacation).

The average age of the child when abuse begins is between six and twelve. Studies typically report that for a smaller sample the abuse begins before the age of six. It is unclear how underreported early abuse might be. Abuse that occurs at a very young age, that is forceful, and that is repeated seems to be stored in a way that allows it to be "forgotten" by the adult survivor. Some statistics suggest that young girls are more frequently targets of sexual abuse, whereas young boys are targets of physical abuse. This appears to reverse as children approach adolescence.

The majority of abusers of both male and female victims are male. Most perpetrators are considerably older than their victims. In some states, an age difference of five years is required in order for the activity to be classified as sexual abuse. However, other factors, such as physical size and the maturity of the individuals involved, clearly suggest that what others prefer to call "sex play" is, in fact, abuse.[2]

FAMILY DYNAMICS

Incest does not occur in a vacuum. We might, in fact, call it a family affair. Though the abuse may never be acknowledged or discussed in any way, the occurrence of incest in the home affects all the members of that home. Needless to say, incest is not a function of a healthy home. It is important to note that it is not known how much of the traumatic stress reaction or emotional disturbance is caused by the sexual act of incest and how much is caused by the unhealthy, emotionally deprived, neglect-filled home environment that fosters incestuous activity.

When a marriage is healthy and provides a good, safe environment for children, there exists a respect for all members of the family, clear boundaries, reasonable expectations, and empathy. Parents are the parents, and children are free to be the children.

The members of the family get their needs met appropriately. There is a certain fluidity in roles and rules even while accountability is required.

In those families where incest occurs, there is often a very disturbed marital relationship. Spouses often have little or nothing in common, and there is a great chasm of emotional distance between the two people. The spouses have very poor communication and conflict-resolution skills. They are unable to meet each other's needs for affection, nurturance, and companionship. Because they cannot communicate effectively, the partners are unable to function as an effective parental team. As a result, children are often cast in adult roles. They are often required to act as go-betweens, hear grievances against the other parent, or meet adult needs.

Current writings suggest that those families in which incest occurs fall into one of three categories.[3] In the first type, the father is the dominant figure. He tends to be very authoritarian, making all the family's decisions. The wife is devalued, as are all females. The wives usually grew up in homes where women were denigrated. Often they are themselves survivors of past physical or sexual abuse. They are silent, fearful, and emotionally distant. The fathers in such families are often enraged at the birth of *another* daughter. As was noted in the story in chapter 2, one child was "welcomed" home by a father who consistently stubbed out his cigarettes on her infant heels because she had the audacity to be another female. Frequently these fathers are also alcoholics. Their drinking triggers episodes of violence and/or sexual abuse.

I have also found that stepfamilies that are male dominant seem to have a higher incidence of incest. Often, men in these families initially appear to be rescuers for those who are economically struggling and emotionally starved. However, once they have gained entrance to the family, they use such vulnerability to their advantage and end up functioning as predators rather than rescuers.[4]

A second type of incest family is the mother-dominant family. In these homes, the wives rule. The husband works, hands over his paycheck, and has little or nothing to do with running the home or raising the children. These are men with shattered egos, a deep sense of inadequacy, and frequently their own history of victimization. Sometimes their own molestation has left them feeling so inadequate that they are incapable of intimacy with another adult. They prefer sex with children, compulsive masturbation, and/or pornography. The mothers in this system often despise their husbands for being weak. They themselves are totally self-absorbed and pay no attention to their children's needs. Their children exist to serve their needs.

The final type of system in which incest is found is the chaotic or disorganized family. These homes are characterized by neglect and abandonment. They are often homes that would be condemned by the local health department if reported. The parents abdicate their authority and responsibility to the children. The older children parent themselves and their younger siblings. This family structure is not uncommon in homes where both parents abuse alcohol and/or drugs.

My experience suggests two other possible configurations, which are basically variations on the above themes. One of these is the male-dominant home where the mother is self-absorbed and narcissistic rather than characteristically battered and silent. These mothers do nothing to intervene for their children, even when the abuse is brought to their attention, because they engage in nothing except care for themselves. As one mother told me years ago: "I really can't be bothered with such little things when I have so many important things in my life to worry about." One client described such a mother: "No matter what happens, it's always about Mother. There's never room on the plate for anyone else." I have also found that this kind of narcissism seems to be characteristic of those mothers who sexually abuse their children. There seems to be no awareness that mothers are to care for children; rather, children are given to "service" the mother in many ways.

A second variation I have found is a household that seems to alternate between being female-dominated and chaotic. The mother carries the entire responsibility for the home on her shoulders, eventually collapses from the weight, totally abdicates, and turns over the running of the household to a daughter. The child must then pick up the mother's load, often at a very young age, like three or four. I had a client who described how her "strong" mother would suddenly disappear into a darkened bedroom for weeks at a time, during which time my client, then four, was expected to take care of her eighteen-month-old sister, keep the house in order, find food (often from the trash next door), and service her father. Then, without warning, the mother would reappear and take charge until the next collapse.

Incestuous families generally fall into one of three categories: male-dominant, female-dominant, or chaotic. All of these family systems have poor boundaries, disturbed marital relationships, and children functioning in adult roles. Obviously, even without the occurrence of incest, such family systems would profoundly affect the developing child. Add the violence and confusion of sexual abuse to that surrounding chaos and neglect, and it is clear that such an environment would leave its mark on the identity, memory, cognition, and physiology of the growing child.

SEVERITY OF EFFECTS

The severity of a person's reaction to sexual abuse depends on many different factors. It is important to note that not all sexual abuse is traumatic (that is, having long-term impact). I have certainly seen men and women who have experienced some form of sexual abuse and who do not in any way meet the diagnostic criteria for post-traumatic stress disorder. You will find throughout the book that I will repeatedly emphasize the importance of considering each case individually. If we do not, we run the risk of classifying and categorizing people in erroneous ways, potentially doing great harm. To assume that everyone who has ever been sexually abused is therefore traumatized is presumptuous and will lead to an insistence that certain effects are present when, in fact, they are not. Many factors are involved in determining the severity of both the abuse and a person's response to it. That means that two people can live through similar experiences of abuse with quite different responses. That also should mean that when we hear a familiar story, we will not think, *Oh, I have heard this before, and therefore I know that the following effects are present in this person's life.*

Such thinking has often led therapists to misdiagnose their clients. It also gives the client yet another experience of not being heard, a repetition of one of the major components of abuse.

However, several characteristics suggest that the abuse will have a more severe effect on the victim. Abuse that occurred more frequently and is of longer duration is potentially more harmful. The more closely related the perpetrator and the victim are, the greater the damage will be. Similarly, the wider the age difference between the perpetrator and the victim, the greater the damage will be. Hence, women who have been abused by a mother or father generally sustain greater injury. It is also thought that abuse perpetrated by a male is more harmful than that perpetrated by a female. I do not know if that is so. I have seen devastating consequences in the lives of people whose mothers were their perpetrators. Sexual abuse involving penetration of any kind is considered more harmful. Abuse that was sadistic or violent in nature is more harmful. Women who perceive themselves as having responded passively or willingly tend to engage in greater self-blame. Those whose bodies responded sexually generally carry tremendous guilt. Disclosed abuse that receives no help has more potential for damage. Negative parental reactions (punishment, accusations, disbelief, or denial) and either ineffective or stigmatizing institutional responses are also very injurious.[5]

8

Symptoms and Aftereffects of Childhood Sexual Abuse

The long-term effects of child sexual abuse can be quite extensive. As noted in our discussion on child development, chronic
trauma can have a profound impact on maturation. The majority of
victims have little chance to get help in ending the abuse, and so the
immediate effects go untreated, continuing to shape the developing
child and the adult she becomes.

Before listing the symptoms and aftereffects of childhood
sexual abuse, two warnings are crucial. As was mentioned earlier,
although incest has negative ramifications, the severity of these is
mediated not only by such factors as the duration and frequency
of the incest and the child's relationship to the perpetrator but also
by other environmental factors—personality variables, family
dynamics, and other authority figures in the child's life. Not all
children respond to sexual abuse in the same way, even when the
experience of abuse is similar. It is absolutely necessary to assess
and diagnose each case individually. The client must be the one to
tell the therapist about the impact of the abuse. The therapist is not
to read a list of aftereffects and then tell the client what his or her
experience is.

A second warning concerns the fact that we are considering a list of *possible* responses to childhood sexual abuse. It is vital to recognize that this list consists of *indicators,* not proof that sexual abuse occurred. It would be very poor clinical judgment to assume that because a given client exhibits a conglomerate of possible aftereffects, it is then proof that he or she was sexually abused as a child. Symptoms such as these could reflect numerous other causes (e.g., witnessing ongoing violence in the home).

Long-term aftereffects of childhood sexual abuse are chronic symptoms that continue into adulthood. They may remit and appear somewhat sporadically, as if they have a mind of their own. They can potentially interfere with every area of the survivor's life.

The emotional aftereffects may include anxiety attacks, phobias (such as fear of small spaces), depression and suicidal ideation, despair and hopelessness, pervasive dissatisfaction with life, emotional paralysis or numbness, anger difficulties, and deep grief.

There can be many somatic effects of childhood abuse, such as migraine headaches, muscular tension, temporomandibular joint (TMJ) problems, gastrointestinal problems, anorexia, bulimia, compulsive overeating, and skin problems (anxious scratching or picking at the skin).

EMOTIONAL AFTEREFFECTS

Self-perceptions are often shaped by the abuse. Many survivors carry a deep sense of shame and are full of both self-blame and self-loathing. On a very deep level, many survivors assume that the abuse occurred because of some innate badness within them as persons. Survivors also see themselves as powerless to make good things happen or bad things stop; at the same time, they see themselves as having excessive power to cause bad or evil in the lives of others. They will often use words like *worthless, trash,* or *garbage* when referring to themselves. One client of mine used to refer to her attempts to find a way "to drain the bad" out of herself (which she did by cutting and heavy use of laxatives). In her mind, it was her inability to do so that resulted in the abuse.

Body image is also damaged by the abuse. Clients may have a distorted body image, seeing themselves as "too fat" or "too thin," when neither is objectively true. The body may be seen as "bad" and always in need of control and/or punishment. For others, the body is the only aspect of their person that is of value; hence, every relationship includes a sexual component.

Problems from the abuse reverberate throughout other relationships. Many survivors have a deep fear of intimacy and commitment while they simultaneously long for closeness. This ambivalence causes a push-pull effect that vacillates between idealizing and devaluing others. Some survivors have a long history of multiple short relationships. Others end up in relationships that seem to be reenactments of the past abuse, i.e., that are abusive in some way. Many times, survivors who are parenting are fearful of abusing their own children. I have listened to several men and women who were terrified that they had abused their children when they were small and simply had no memory of it. Such thoughts are torturous.

Adult survivors find it very difficult to trust others and often need to be in control relationally in order to feel safe. Because they were betrayed and used by people who should have protected them, they end up fearing and mistrusting others. They often have a sense of danger and increasing fear as closeness develops in a relationship. Feelings of isolation and being "different" are common. Some cope with their fears by becoming overdependent and submissive in relationships; others cope by becoming controlling and rigid.

PHYSICAL AFTEREFFECTS

It is common for survivors to reveal self-destructive tendencies. Addictions to alcohol, food, spending, drugs, and sex are prevalent. These addictive behaviors are often used to comfort and self-soothe whenever the survivor is overwhelmed by anxiety or other painful feelings. Suicidal ideation and/or attempts may be recurring. Self-mutilation, a behavior that causes the survivor extreme shame, is common. Burning, cutting, self-bruising, biting, sticking oneself with pins, scratching, and beating oneself about the head can occur.

Sometimes self-mutilating behaviors are engaged in as a way of relieving tension and anxiety. Sometimes they arise out of overwhelming self-loathing. It is a way of punishing one who is so loathsome. Other times, self-mutilation appears to be a reenactment of the previous abuse, an ongoing attempt to master what was unstoppable.

Many survivors talk about using self-injury in order to "feel alive" or as a major jolt to the body that results in quieting raging anxiety and fear. Such attacks on the body are more common among those who were repeatedly abused in early childhood. Those who inflict injury on themselves describe the process as beginning with overwhelming agitation and anxiety followed by a drive to attack themselves in some fashion. A dissociative state ensues, so the injuries initially seem to produce no pain, almost as if an anesthesia had been given. At some point in the attack, a sense of calm is produced, and so the attack ceases. The process is very similar to the experience of the abuse in childhood. Survivors often talk about a buildup of anxiety and agitation as they sensed the abuser hinting at or showing signs of what was to come. The feelings became unbearable as the perpetrator approached and began the abuse. The victim "removed" herself by the process of dissociation so that she did not have to feel the pain. She "returned" when the abuse was over, and quiet followed. This became the regulatory cycle of her life, and so it continues.

Sexual dysfunctions can have their roots in childhood sexual abuse. Survivors may have an aversion to sex, experience desire disorders, arousal disorders, or orgasmic difficulties. Some survivors are confused about their sexual orientation. On the other end of the continuum are those who show a compulsive interest in sex. This can be seen in the pursuit of multiple partners, compulsive masturbation, the desire for sadomasochistic sex, and prostitution. Those who are driven to a compulsive use of sex often do so in a fashion similar to self-mutilation. When agitation and anxiety rise, sex is felt to be absolutely necessary. It is sought and engaged in, in some kind of dissociative state, followed by quiet. The belief behind the behavior is, "I cannot be quiet unless I have sex (and/or pain)."

SPIRITUAL AFTEREFFECTS

The sexual violation of a child can have many spiritual effects. A distorted image of God coupled with a distorted image of the self creates several barriers to experiencing God's love and grace. When children are betrayed by those who were supposed to protect and love them, they find it very difficult to grasp that God loves them. Such hideous disruption of the family, making home a dangerous place, interferes with his or her sense of safety and belonging in a community of believers. God is often perceived to be punitive, an impossible taskmaster, capricious, impotent, indifferent, or dead. In the movie *Forrest Gump,* Jenny kneels down in a cornfield, asking God to please make her a bird so she can fly away. While she is praying, her drunken, sexually abusive father comes in pursuit. God does not make her into a bird, and she is left to her father. It does not take much imagination to understand what children learn through such experiences. To tell them that Scripture teaches truths that are different from their experience often has the same effect as attempting to describe the color green to one who has been blind from birth. It simply does not register.

As we read in Meeka's story, some children are even abused in God's name. Often they are told that it is God's will for them to submit to the abuse, for after all, God says children should obey their parents. One client I worked with was required nightly to kneel down beside her bed with her father to say her prayers. He would then help her into bed and proceed to molest her, telling her how wicked she was for making him do such things just after praying.

Elie Wiesel, one of the foremost writers about the Holocaust, states the problem eloquently. Throughout his books he tells the reader not to assume that it is a consolation to believe that God is still alive. Rather than being the solution, saying "God is alive" simply states the problem. He struggles again and again with what he describes as two irreconcilable realities—the reality of God and the reality of Auschwitz. Each seems to cancel out the other, yet neither will disappear. Either alone could be managed, you see— Auschwitz and no God, or God and no Auschwitz. But together? Auschwitz *and* God?[1]

For many survivors of childhood sexual abuse, the same two irreconcilable realities exist: the reality of a God who says he is loving and a refuge for the weak, and the reality of the ongoing sexual violation of a child. Each seems to cancel out the other, yet both exist. Again, the human mind can manage either alternative—the sexual abuse of a child and no God, or God and protection from sexual abuse. What is one to do with the rape of a child *and* the reality of God? The dilemma is not easily solved.

Another impact in the spiritual realm has its roots in the alienation and helplessness the victim experienced as a child. Bessel van der Kolk, director of the Trauma Center at Human Resources Institute Hospital in Massachusetts, refers to what he terms a "disorder of hope" in adults who were repeatedly traumatized as children.[2] Hope is the feeling, indeed the confidence, that what is desired is truly possible. To be repeatedly abused at the hands of one's caretaker and to be helpless to stop it is to experience the death of hope. Hope is something to be avoided, denied, for to feel hope is to be crushed yet again. Hope, then, in God himself or in his ability to redeem what has been destroyed is not only inconceivable, it is felt to be dangerous.

SUMMARY

We have stated that chronic sexual abuse of a child is more than likely a trauma that shapes the child's development. Such abuse has tentacles that reach throughout the adult life of the victim, often into every major area of her life, contaminating, disturbing, and destroying. The severity and extent of the destruction varies from individual to individual. Though the symptoms and aftereffects listed above are not uniform for all survivors, they need to be recognized as part of the possible impact of incest. As we move on to consider a treatment format, we must be sure that we respond to both the original trauma and its aftereffects if our approach is to be effective.

9

Meeka's Story Continued

E ven though I had to walk down the driveway to the therapist's office, it seemed to be an extremely long and uphill climb. Just taking that first step of walking into the office seemed to highlight the extreme struggles inside of me. I had seen other counselors before, and although there had been some very helpful "surface changes" in my life, my deep "inside self" was still damaged and untouched.

Questions tormented me. Why try again? What would this therapist do differently from what the others had done? Would she believe me? Would she keep my story confidential? Why do this again? It's so costly.

But I was so very desperate. Everything had blown up in my face. My life was falling apart in every area. So what was my choice? Continue to live this way, believing the intensity of it would cause me to kill myself, or go ahead and once again try therapy as a last-ditch effort. I agreed to go for therapy, but not because I had any sense of hope for change. All I could do was try this once again, knowing inside that if it didn't work, the next decision would be clear—I would take my life—for what would be left? Nothing. Just pain and turmoil that reached to the deepest depths of my soul, and I could not live with that any longer.

Within a couple of months I had the distinct sense that this was going to be a very difficult road to follow. In fact, the only way I felt I could describe it was that it was going to be hellish. Would I be able to persevere and follow through? Did I have the energy to hang in there no matter what took place?

I asked the counselor lots of questions: What will happen? How long will this take? What will it be like? There were no real definitive answers.

Could I go on? Again I had to ask myself what my options were. As I considered them, one little piece seemed different. Something was different with the therapy, and I thought that maybe, just maybe, I might find some answers here. So from week to week and month to month I slowly dragged my heavy feet, distressed heart, and heavy soul into the office for the next round.

Time after time I came into the counselor's office and sat in the corner as far away from her as I could. Fortunately her chair was in an inside corner of the office, and I would sit between her and the door. I needed to know that I was not "locked in" this office but that if I needed to, I could quickly get out. (By the way, her office was very small, and she was very tall, so this "positioning" in the office was critical!) I could not look her in the eye. Months later— actually years later—the same questions I had had when I walked into her office the very first time were still there. Who was she really? Was she telling anyone else what I was telling her? Did she believe me? Could I trust her? The intensity of the questions lessened somewhat, but they were always there and were always being tested.

What about her words? Were they really true? I had experienced too much betrayal and too many broken promises in my life to trust her readily. Over time I began to believe that what she said was true. Although even now, with therapy pretty much completed, I still struggle—Will it still be true?

When children get hurt, when something goes wrong, or when they have a question, most children go to one or both parents for comfort, care, love, answers, attention. I found early on that I would go to a corner in the barn where I could be all alone. For a long, long time, that was the only safe place where I could go to cry and talk (to myself). My therapist would talk about her office being a safe place. Inside I'd say, *Fat chance. No place is ever safe. Things always change.* Even my "secret place" in the barn was found out and became a place of torment. I was convinced that at some point things would always get to be too much and whoever was in my life at that moment would give up, pull away, act as if nothing had ever happened, or even worse, turn and use it as an opportunity to abuse and destroy me. Always in my mind was the question, *Why would this situation and relationship be any different?*

In time, I saw that when the counselor told me that what I said in her office would not leave the room, her actions told me her words were true. I experienced it firsthand. When my pastor asked for information and updates, she always cleared with me *first* what she was free to say. If I said no to something, she honored my decision and would not tell him. I also saw her respecting and honoring confidentiality by arranging and rearranging schedules to avoid any possible overlap of appointments by people who knew each other. If she would go through those kinds of gymnastics to protect confidentiality when scheduling those who see her, I was even more convinced that she would safeguard the contents of the hour. With each proof of her trustworthiness, I could take a small step forward and give her a little more information.

But often with each additional piece of information or memory of the awful details of what I was really like, I would take three hundred steps back, and we would have to work through the whole issue of trust again. As often as we needed to come back to that for my sense of safety with her, we did so. And it was always done without a judgmental, "Can't you just get beyond this and move on?" She never communicated that.

My attitude going into therapy was to get this done quickly and move on. But I found it was one of the slowest and most difficult processes I have ever gone through (yet I'm told I seemed to be on "fast forward" and things moved along rapidly). Often what helped me to hang in there was that the pace or quickness of the process was never an issue. How slowly things went or how often we went over the same thing didn't seem to matter. Whatever was churning in my insides at a particular moment was the most important item in front of us, even if this was the thousandth time she had to tell me the same thing. Through this I began to experience her respect for me and her belief that whatever I had to say was important. Whatever I was feeling was important. It told me that *I* was important. As a result, little by little, and over time, I'd let her in more and more on what *was* happening to me and what *had* happened to me. And always she responded with care, tenderness, acceptance, and hope for me.

Often I would ask her why she didn't walk away. Why didn't she run? She would respond that she had made a commitment to God to see it through—no matter what we found, no matter how long, no matter how dark, no matter how awful. She would be there to the end. She said that for her to walk away from me would be to walk away from God. And that she would not do. Could I believe this? I struggled so often with this. Again and again it was tested. With absolutely every new piece of information I gave her, she had to go through the same test. Again and again I found her to be faithful and truthful.

She told me early on that she would never lie to me. If I asked her a question, she would answer it with the truth. She would not fudge the answer or give a half-truth. She would answer honestly even if the answer would be difficult for me. I did not believe her. I would not trust her on this, for I knew very few, if any (including myself), who didn't take words and twist them or leave something out or say it in a slightly different way to convey a particular message or to hide the truth. Over time I tested this again and again, and with every test I found her words to be true, and her actions supported her words.

When everything first exploded for me, I really thought that things couldn't get any worse than they were at that moment. I found that to be far from the truth. As time passed, I found the pain and torment of the past to be ever present in my life. Certain smells would trigger and set me off into a memory. For example, the smell of a skunk threw me into a memory of something that had happened on the farm. It had happened on an evening when there was a strong skunk scent behind our barn. That smell today sent me back there, and everything else in the present faded away.

Memories that came back like this needed to be looked at full in the face and walked through, or I would end up stuck in them and often unable to function on even very basic levels of life such as getting out of bed, getting dressed, driving a car, figuring out a schedule. Much of this I could not do alone. Part of the therapy process for me was taking these memories and walking through them in the office setting. What was so tormenting and gruesome was that in the midst of these memories I could literally smell the smells, taste the tastes, and feel the physical effects on my body as we walked through them.

As we had to look at the memories that surfaced, I found that being able to listen to and hear the voice of the therapist was extremely important for me. As we wrestled in earlier days with issues of truth and trust, I found that I could believe what she said. She would not and had not ever lied to me. Again and again she would repeat many truths to me as we processed things. That became critical later as this memory work took place. When a memory hit, I would get totally lost in it. It was as if the present faded into a haze and whatever memory was there would return as if it were actually happening at that moment. Because we had repeatedly worked through issues of truth and trust, I found that the voice of the therapist during a memory could help to keep me focused and in the present. Throughout the memory she would talk to me, calling me to listen to her, to believe what is true, to know that I was no longer little—that I was not back at the farm, that he was not here—and for me to stay here, to stay in the present, to listen for her voice, to stay with her voice. She would tell me what was true. She would challenge me to believe what was true, asking me if she had ever lied or if he had lied and so on. It often was the only thing that would help me pull out of a memory that otherwise would often stay with me for hours or days and consume and disorient me so that I could not function in my daily life.

Outside of the therapist's office, memories presented me with other difficulties. I could not control the timing of memories or flashbacks. They would just happen. It could be in the middle of a worship service. It could be when I was driving or even in the middle of a conversation with someone. Things fell apart around me.

I was afraid to be around people because I feared what might happen in that context. I found it almost impossible to focus on one thing for any length of time. My work began to suffer. I made mistakes, forgot things, moved much more slowly, and did not complete some things. Just getting up and getting to work were extremely hard to do.

Nightmares constantly plagued my sleep. I would wake up feeling more exhausted than I had felt when I had gone to sleep. I dreaded even putting my head on the pillow, knowing the torment that soon would take over and consume me. My life from the past seemed to be all that I lived. These nightmares did not just go away as I wished they would. These also had to be worked through in the office. Once I faced them, they would either decrease in their intensity or go away for a period of time. No longer did they control my life.

The reality of the abuse in my life left me in despair, totally exhausted emotionally and physically. I despaired even of life. My relationship with God fell apart. Numerous times I had a suicide plan in place, the needed items purchased and laid out before me. My bills were paid, files straightened, notes written. There was nothing left. I really believed that only death would bring me relief. I felt it was absolutely the only option that assured me that the pain and torment would go away.

It also was clear that I hated and detested myself, believing what I had been told repeatedly as a youngster—that no one would ever want me for anything other than sex, that I was garbage, that no good would ever come out of me, that nobody would ever really love me. As the nightmares, memories, and despair increased, so did my attempts to injure myself and destroy anything that may have been a positive aspect in my life.

Somehow, in the midst of all this, my therapist understood what was taking place inside of me. She did not condemn me for how I felt or yell at me for thinking about taking my life or trying to injure myself in some way. Instead she reminded me again and again that I *do* matter—to her and to others—and that what I had been told as a child was not true, that I am *not* garbage, that others *do* love me, very much, and that they love me for who I am, not what I can or can't do. Again and again she repeated this. Numerous times she demonstrated by her life that she believed it. Although some growth in this area has taken place, this is a battle that goes on, sometimes seemingly minute by minute, other times day by day. Changing all the thought patterns and beliefs is difficult. The roots are very deep, and the process is long and hard. "Change takes time," she says, and patiently she waits for me as little by little I climb up this steep mountain. Patiently she waits, and tenderly she encourages, hopes, and prays with and for me.

Very early in my life I lost all hope for anything that is good or lasting. So many times I had a thought or a hope that maybe this time it would be different, but those hopes were always dashed. I found that this loss of hope stayed with me long after the actual abuse had ended. Later, I longed for many things, such as a lasting positive change in my life. But many of those hopes and longings were totally lost, and some of them gave me only slight glimmers of change that later died out altogether.

As therapy began, I had no hope for significant change, little hope for minor changes that might hold on for a time, and in many ways I believed that all I could ever expect were major failures and total defeat. As I hit many of the hard, bumpy roads in counseling, it was obvious to my therapist that I didn't have any hope. At those points, it was totally impossible for me to have any hope in God. I still did not understand his role in my life as a child or the fact that my prayers for help and for the abuse to stop were left unanswered. In this totally helpless spot, my therapist would often say to me that she knew I had no hope. She knew I could not generate any. But she knew that Christ would bring light to the darkness, that he would redeem my life and bring me hope. She told me that she had enough hope for both of us at that point and I could hang on to hers.

Little by little, I noticed that once again I was beginning to hope, to anticipate that maybe somehow out of all this junk I would find release and freedom. She knew God to be faithful. She believed in him for her life and believed in him for me. She gave words to her belief, but even more important than that, she lived it out in action. She gave me hope. Even though I didn't matter to myself, I mattered to her because she understood Christ's love for me.

I watched her; I listened to her; I saw her life, her actions, her words. As a result, she led me (as if by the hand) and helped me to walk so that eventually I could begin to look at situations and have hope that God's redemptive work would take place no matter what my circumstances were. I began to look back and see God's work. I saw changes taking place. I saw rays of light destroying the darkness in which I lived. Now my hope is not the childish hope that bad things will not happen. My hope today believes that God can take any situation of mine—even if the circumstances do not change one bit—and redeem that moment. That is hope: Christ's work on the cross affecting every aspect and corner of my life.

Coming to understand Jesus and his love for me has not been an easy road. Growing up in a "Christian" home and being abused while my abuser told me, "God told me to do this," did not leave a very sweet picture of God in my mind. On top of that, my own desperate prayers for the abuse to stop or for Daddy to die just left me full of despair and anger, and I walked away from God. Yet beyond what I am able to understand today, and certainly beyond what I understood then, is the fact that even as I pulled away from God, I sensed that I was pulling aside for a season, not dumping or throwing God away forever. I needed to work it out inside of me. I needed to go back to the basics. My very spiritual foundation was shattered, and I needed to rebuild it, but I knew that right then I simply could not do it. My therapist honored that and let me "shelve" it for a time. It was important for me at that time that my therapist didn't attempt to ride herd over me or push me ahead of time on these issues. Yet while that was happening, she gave me many scriptural nuggets. I don't begin to understand all that happened. Much of it I see only as I look back over the years. But as I do, it is so clear to me that even though she did not specifically quote Scripture, she lived out the redemptive work of Christ and his character in front of me all the time. And without a doubt, it was this very loud "quietness" that drew me to want to explore and find Jesus.

Initially I wanted a to-do list—do this and things will change. The therapist would not give me anything of that sort. I was frustrated with her. Yet as I look back, for me that was wise, for if I had

had lots of to-dos, I would have attempted once again to "do it," when ultimately it is the work of God both to will and to do. It also would just have enabled me once again to try by changing outward actions. But the change needed to come from inside, from Christ working in and through me. By pointing me to Christ by the life she lived, and later by her words as well, my counselor taught me about Christ. She urged me to go to Christ and ask him for the truth, to plead with him to show himself to me. These were the only to-do's she would give me: Just read and pray to know Christ. Somehow the work began; God moved inside, and my heart and life began to change. I began to look back and saw my feeble prayers beginning to be answered. I recall the first one that was dramatically answered. It was such an encouragement. As time went on, my thirst for the truth and for Christ grew.

At this point, I cannot do anything other than relay to you this story of what happened to me one day in a therapy session. The therapist had asked a question, and it began to send me into another memory of when I was ten years old. It was important to tell it to the therapist, and as I began to recount what had happened that day many years ago, God vividly intervened and gave me a passage of Scripture and an understanding that has assured me without question of his amazing tender love for me. I will just write it here as I did later for her.

> It seemed that out of nowhere the passage where the disciples were trying to send away the children who were coming to see Jesus came to mind. The passage became "real." I was one of those little children. Someone was holding my hand and leading/pulling/pushing me to him. But there were people in my way—my daddy, the other men—even many others that stood in the way and offered me no help. They were all pushing me away, telling me I didn't belong, that Christ didn't want me. They shouted at me to get away, that I wasn't fit to come near to him. But the one holding my hand continued to lead me and urge me on. She kept

telling me that Christ was safe, that he loved me, that he knew everything about me, and that he wanted me to come to him. She told me that he knew my shame, that he knew me inside and out, and that he still loved me and would love me forever. Then it was as if Jesus turned and saw me. He looked straight into my eyes, and tears came into his eyes. He opened his arms and began to come toward me. As he came toward me, all the people in the way began to back away. They couldn't stand there. The one holding my hand let it go, telling me to go ahead. Jesus and I met, and he took me in his arms and held me tight. There I rested. There I was quiet. There I was loved. And I can keep going back there. He won't ever let me out of his care, out of his arms.

It's as if I've gone full circle. The child I was so many years ago had a daddy who was a liar, a cheat, a perpetrator, an abuser, a deceiver, and many more things not fit to mention. Today in unfathomable ways I was hugged and loved by my real Daddy— one who is always there, trustworthy, honest, faithful, compassionate, and tender. Much more needs to be mentioned, but there isn't enough space or time to do it justice. Today I tasted of something that I believe will affect me every moment of every day.

PART TWO

Treatment: Phase One

10

Helping Clients Feel Safe

The treatment of adult survivors of sexual abuse involves many factors. It is crucial that therapists have a clear picture of what that treatment includes; otherwise it is very easy to shortchange a client. We will consider the phases of treatment and specific techniques in detail. However, it seems important before proceeding to remind ourselves again of the foundation for all that we do as Christians.

We said earlier that all that we do as those who name the name of Christ is to be both incarnational and redemptive. Our words are to communicate *his* truth. Our person is to reflect *his* person. Our lives are to be a living, breathing explanation of *his* character. Those who sit with us hour after hour in the privacy of our offices should leave with a better understanding of who God is because we have, through our obedience to him and love for him, touched them with the flavor of his presence.

Therapy, when done by an obedient servant who is filled with God's Spirit, will be redemptive in the lives of others. To bring the truth and love of God to bear on the life of another, whether by word or by deed, is to bring light and life. The presence of Christ in a life is always redemptive, both in the person in which he dwells and in those who are influenced by that person. His presence always results in a buying back, a restoring of that which was lost. Since we are to live focused on what is unseen and eternal, we know that treatment is far more than simply symptom relief (though such relief is certainly compassionate) or greater productivity (though that may be satisfying). Ultimately, therapy means *being* the truths that we teach. In that context, the therapist is called to demonstrate the character of God in relationship to another so that God's work of redemption can be made manifest.

One of the reasons I emphasize this point so strongly is that I believe that in Christian circles, counseling has often been reduced to a mere *speaking* of the truth to another. Speaking the truth is a vital component of therapy. Words are, after all, one of our main tools. God himself has spoken to us in words. However, God also *became* what he taught (the word became the Word). He lived out in relationship what he said was true. If we follow his example, therapy will be not simply about telling others what is true but also about living out what is true in our relationship with them. Many of our clients have had some measure of the truth spoken by parents whose lives were a screaming contradiction to that very truth. How will our words be any different unless our lives, both within and without our offices, are a living demonstration of that truth?

When clients come to us full of despair and lies about themselves, we will tell them what is true. We will tell them about hope; we will call abuse evil; we will point to the way of redemption. However, when our words seem to fall on deaf ears, we will, like our God, remember that a frail, finite creature sits before us, one who has been repeatedly shaped and scarred by the sins of others. We will remember that God waits while we learn. He remembers that we learn in time, not instantaneously. He recalls that experience and repetition are necessary in order for us to grasp things. He is repetitive without condemnation. We will remind ourselves that he stepped into a relationship with us and allowed us to experience who he is. These truths call us to repeatedly demonstrate over time and with patience that what we hold out to our clients as truth is indeed truth. If we as therapists are to function in this way, then obviously one of the greatest demands placed on us will be an ever-growing relationship with the Father. What this means and how to maintain such a relationship will be considered in greater detail in a later chapter.

The initial phase of therapy involves three components: *safety, symptom relief,* and *memory work.* A client's motivation for entering therapy is usually related to presenting symptoms rather than the sexual abuse. Sometimes a crisis has developed due to delayed aftereffects of the original trauma, a reexperiencing of the trauma in some form, or exposure to events that trigger symptoms. Usually the client is struggling with something such as depression, anxiety, nightmares, or eating problems, and comes seeking treatment for them.

SAFETY

The client's first need when she enters therapy is to establish a climate of safety. This is vital for two reasons. First, change is difficult and often frightening for many of us. Even good change throws us off balance and requires adapting on our part. We gravitate toward the familiar, often even when it is destructive. Change throws us into the unknown. We feel disoriented; we don't know how to read the signs. If we are to undergo change and somehow manage the accompanying anxiety, a sense of safety somewhere is crucial.

Second, those who have experienced chronic sexual abuse have lived with perpetual danger and unpredictability. Frequently, the idea of disclosing the abuse or facing its impact is also felt to be very dangerous. To do so often throws the person right into a storm, an upheaval. Many clients had severe threats handed out to them whenever the subject of disclosure was mentioned. Others firmly believe that they were the cause of the abuse, and thus to reveal it is to let yet another person see how despicable they are. It is very common in therapy sessions for any reference to abuse, especially with memory work, to result in an elevation in heart rate and adrenaline levels. The body senses danger and is poised to flee or do battle. Safety becomes paramount.

God recognizes our need for safety when life is turned upside down. Psalm 46 tells us that "God is our refuge and strength, an ever-present help in trouble. Therefore we will not fear, though the earth give way and the mountains fall into the heart of the sea, though its waters roar and foam and the mountains quake with their surging." In these verses, the Hebrew word for "refuge" means a place of hope, shelter, and trust. Even though everything familiar and seemingly stable gives way, fear is held at bay because God, our dwelling place, is safe.

Part of establishing initial safety may also involve crisis intervention. Many survivors are either still involved with the perpetrator in some way, are allowing their children to be with the perpetrator, or are themselves in other relationships that are unsafe due to battering or some other kind of abuse. Depending on the circumstances, crisis intervention may require assistance in finding a shelter. An assessment of current danger from others and/or self requires a careful response. Often in doing such an assessment and making recommendations, therapists will meet with great resistance from their clients as they attempt to get them to safety. Except when the law requires otherwise, the decision is ultimately the survivor's. Keep in mind that the concept of safety is foreign to many survivors, and their resistance is due not so much to a disregard for your advice or concern for them as it is to an inability even to grasp the concept of safety as relevant to their lives or as something in which they have any say.

With the onset of therapy, it is not unusual for a survivor's life to become chaotic, with everything familiar giving way as she works to deal with the truth of her history. Memories intrude and frighten; nightmares make sleep a place of torment; and old, familiar coping mechanisms cease to bring comfort. Fear will overwhelm and potentially destroy if she cannot find a safe dwelling place. Certainly God is ultimately that place. He is called by the psalmist "a refuge for the oppressed" (Ps. 9:9). However, we are called to be like him in this world, and so we too must be a refuge, a safe place. What better way to teach about the safety of God himself than by ongoing demonstrations of that safety in our relationship with the survivor in front of us?

What does it mean to establish safety for a survivor? Before we consider the ways in which a survivor needs safety, an important point needs to be made. Most of us have ways in which we help ourselves feel safe. For those who have grown up with chronic abuse, those ways are often destructive and are usually found in isolation. When you first bring up the idea of being a safe place for someone who has only found danger in the presence of others, the internal, if not external, response is likely to be, "Yeah, right!" For many survivors, the words *safe person* are an oxymoron. People are not safe. People hurt, abuse, lie, and abandon. You, as the therapist, are a person; therefore, you too will hurt, abuse, lie, and abandon. Even as trust begins to develop, this issue will be raised again and again. It may show up each time a new secret is revealed or a new emotion is expressed. The sentiment is, "Well, you were safe when I told you such-and-such, but once I let you in on this, things will change." Expect to go back and rework this ground again and again and again. Always remember that this is not simply a question about you personally, though that is certainly one component. To respond with, "I have been safe for you for two years. *When* are you going to trust me?" is to miss the point. The point from the perspective of the client is, "I am still not sure; I am still afraid. Can we do this one more time?" The answer must always be yes.

Given the understanding that safety is an issue that will be woven throughout the course of treatment, the question we must answer is this: What does it mean to be a safe place for someone? In order for therapists to provide safety for their clients, I believe they must demonstrate two things: they must *be* a safe person, and they must *do* safe things.

What does it mean for a therapist to *be* a safe person? A safe person is someone in whose integrity we can have confidence. Our word *integrity* comes from the Latin word *integer,* which means whole. For therapists to truly be safe persons, they must be as safe in their private lives as they are in their offices. If that is not so, then what is demonstrated in the office is nothing more than pretense, something our clients are quite familiar with and something that will inevitably break down under the stress of therapy and/or life. We need to be safe not only in the presence of our clients but in their absence as well. As a client of mine once stated, "I need to know that you are the same safe all the way through."

It is important to differentiate between being a safe person who does safe things and guaranteeing that the client will always feel safe in the presence of the therapist. We can never promise that a client will feel safe. Some survivors have never known what it is to feel safe, and every safe place they tried to establish for themselves as children was destroyed. Not only that, but often memories surface and bring with them a blast of terror and a sense of danger.

Do not attempt to provide assurances that are unrealistic, such as that the client will never be hurt again or that you can somehow protect her from harm. You become unreliable and, in essence, unsafe when you attempt to guarantee what you cannot control. What you *can* offer is the promise to work continually at being a safe person in your relationship with that client and invite her questions or discussion whenever anything in the relationship makes her feel unsafe.

An example of this might be when a client communicates verbally or nonverbally that any sudden movement is frightening to her and that makes her feel unsafe with you. You cannot realistically guarantee that in the course of treatment you will never again move suddenly. However, you can discuss with her what frightened her and why, help her see that sudden movement does not always result in abuse, and let her know by word and by continued effort that you will commit yourself to remembering to move slowly and carefully in her presence (not a bad policy with all survivors!).

If we go back to our original discussion about personhood, we will recall that one aspect of the image of God in mankind is that we are relational. The two components to relationship are reciprocal knowledge and reciprocal love. With that as a basis, I think we can say that a safe person is someone who always speaks the truth and who is governed by love. The knowledge that is exchanged in the course of therapy is of value only as long as it is based in truth. The relationship that is established in the course of therapy is healing only as long as it is governed by love. Anything less will not be safe or healing for the client, and it will not bring honor to the name of Christ.

Therapists who are safe will always speak the truth. They will call things by their right names. They will name abuse as evil and as a manifestation of the heart of the perpetrator, not the heart of the victim. They will not pretend that healing from the repeated sins of others will be easy. They will be bold in facing the evils of others when they would just as soon not have such things in their heads. They will faithfully uphold the truths of Scripture in the face of great evil and great fear. They will hold out the promise of redemption again and again to their clients, knowing it is a redemption that can touch both the scars of the past and the responses of the present. They will not promise what they cannot deliver, and they will deliver what they have promised. They will admit to errors without self-justification. They will correctly label their own feelings when asked, without pretense. They will look reality full in the face and not flinch, pretend, justify, blame, or mislabel. To do any less is to compromise their integrity and thus to fail to be safe.

Therapists who are safe will be governed by love. Their clients will know that they can rely on them to be patient. They will be ready to do the work when the summons comes, yet they will not be in a hurry. They will bear all things, believe all things, and hope all things. Because they understand, they can wait. Their words and actions will be laced with kindness. They will count it a privilege to demonstrate kindness to those of God's children who come to them seeking aid. They will work without arrogance. They will present themselves not as people who have all the answers but as creatures utterly dependent on a faithful God. Whatever God has gifted them with will be offered humbly in service to others. They will treat those who come to them courteously and gently. Every word and action will be for the good of the client, not motivated by seeking things for themselves. They will not be easily provoked, even when disregarded, unappreciated, rejected, screamed at, criticized, and hurt. They will provide an atmosphere of encouragement and affirmation. Always rejoicing in truth, they will seek to get at facts, searching for truth with humble and unbiased minds. They will demonstrate a love that ever seeks to protect and preserve. In being thus governed by love, they will not only be a safe place for those who come to them for help but also more accurately reflect the truth that "God is our refuge."

Obviously, if therapists are as we have described, they will *do* safe things. Many of the things they will do have been described above, for they automatically flow out of the spirit of love. Let us add a few more. Any therapists who name the name of Christ will carefully follow ethical guidelines for psychologists and counselors. No sexual touch, comment, or innuendo will ever be allowed to darken the door of the office under *any* circumstances. Even, or perhaps especially, when clients bring sexual feelings for the therapist into the room, it is absolutely necessary that the relationship continue to be utterly safe. Under such circumstances, the clients are bringing that aspect of themselves that they were told was all they were good for, and to respond in kind is simply to confirm the feared assessment. The client is also bringing that most out-of-control aspect of herself. To capitulate in any way is to agree that sexuality is indeed uncontrollable. Boundaries that bring safety have once again become completely meaningless.

Therapists who are safe will carefully adhere to confidentiality. In order for someone to deal with humiliating and frightening material, we must guarantee her safety from prying eyes and curious ears. It is very easy to refer to another's story to illustrate a point or to demonstrate one's knowledge or capabilities to others. Again, we would be using another human being for the purpose of caring for ourselves. Breaking confidentiality is often done and excused in Christian circles. People ask out of genuine concern; we speak under the guise of a prayer request; we tell a concerned pastor more than we have been given permission to tell. People's stories and identities are theirs to reveal. We may disagree with what they choose to tell or withhold, and we can let them know our thinking on the matter, but it is not ours to decide. We are to take care of the client and her story as carefully in her absence as we would in her presence. The words we use to discuss the life of another should always be chosen with *that person* in mind, not ourselves and not the recipient.

Therapy that is safe will always be governed by the needs of the client, not the needs of the therapist. This is certainly not limited to sexual needs but applies to other areas as well. A client recently mentioned guilt feelings over terminating with a former therapist, saying, "He is going through some hard times, and he talks to me about it. If I stop seeing him, then he won't have anyone to talk to."

Clients do not serve the purpose of affirming us, building us up, encouraging us, or helping us sort out our thinking. They are not there to help us feel important or needed. They are in our offices because their struggles have become unmanageable, and we are there for the sole purpose of helping them. A safe therapist will do only those things that contribute to the growth of the client. Therapists must continually ask themselves several questions: Whose needs does this comment or question meet? Whose feelings am I caring for? Whose mind does this line of questioning feed? How am I taking care of my own needs, feelings, exhaustion? Self-deceit is a subtle thing, and it is an easy step from being safe to beginning to use others for the purpose of caring for ourselves.

We must ever keep before us the fact that our clients come to us as vulnerable human beings. To be vulnerable is to be susceptible to injury or attack. The word *vulnerable* comes from the Latin *vulnerare,* which means "to wound." Whoever is in a vulnerable position is capable of being wounded. Those of us who sit in the therapist's chair are in a position of power. We have across from us one who has been wounded and rendered powerless by those who were to have been her protectors. We repeat the dynamic of abuse when we use her to meet our own needs.

The prophet Isaiah sings the praises of God: "You have been a refuge for the poor, a refuge for the needy in his distress, a shelter from the storm and a shade from the heat. For the breath of the ruthless is like a storm driving against a wall and like the heat of the desert" (Isa. 25:4-5). May those who come to us seeking aid for scars from the ruthless and memories that are "like a storm driving against a wall" find us who are God's ambassadors to be like the God whom we represent—a refuge, a shelter, and a shade.

11

Symptom Relief

The second component of the initial phase of treatment focuses on symptom relief. As we noted earlier, survivors often suffer from many difficulties, both cognitive and affective, and it is usually these symptoms that bring them into therapy. One of the reasons it is crucial to address symptoms is that they are often so debilitating that clients are unable to function.

Many clients are very frightened about seeking help because they are not only speaking about something they have been forbidden to mention but also revealing aspects of their lives that they believe are proof that they are "weird," "crazy," or "sick." It is common for survivors to think that when they tell you the truth about themselves, your response will automatically be to lock them up. That requires one of the first steps in the symptom-relief process to be a normalizing of the client's symptoms. Hearing their symptoms reframed as natural responses to trauma often provides almost immediate relief. "You mean, you don't think I'm crazy?" is a common response.

I have often found it helpful to use an example from a different set of circumstances to illustrate the point. I find that survivors often have little ability to be objective about themselves and their experience of abuse. They will respond to themselves with harsh judgment, yet for someone in almost identical circumstances, they will demonstrate compassion and understanding. I have seen this proven over and over in group therapy with survivors. Sometimes an example of "another little girl" will be helpful. Other times I have used examples from Holocaust survivors, such as a woman who became terrified every time she heard heavy boots walking across the floor because they reminded her of the Gestapo coming through the women's barracks looking for someone who had committed some infraction. The immediate response to someone else's struggle with lingering symptoms is one of compassion. It is also easier for survivors to comprehend how symptoms that seem to make no sense, such as a fear of the sound of heavy boots, are indeed comprehensible in context.

Clients repeatedly need us to normalize these feelings: terror whenever they find themselves blocked into a small space, fear when someone is between them and a door, loss of all feeling during sex, inability to tolerate anyone's standing close to them, fear at the sight of a closed fist, and anxiety responses to certain smells, like sweat or semen.

Part of this process is educating the client about the range of responses that survivors might experience. These include depression, memory difficulties, an inability to trust, gastrointestinal problems, substance abuse, dissociation, nightmares, and anxiety disorders. Such symptoms can occur as a result of circumstances other than chronic sexual abuse; however, they are also common responses to a history of incest. To hear for the first time that such symptoms make sense and are experienced by other men and women with similar histories provides great relief. As one client often remarked, "I feel like you just explained me to myself."

Reading the accounts of other survivors or participating in a group of survivors often helps tremendously in this area. Many women have told me of the profound effect of sitting for the first time in a room of women who have in common the experience of sexual abuse. It is a sad yet greatly treasured moment.

It will be important to normalize even the more severe symptoms. You can normalize symptoms such as self-mutilation without condoning the behavior. You are simply explaining how such behavior makes sense in the context of the abuse. An admission of something such as cutting or burning is usually accompanied by great shame, so the normalization of the behavior, along with hope for change, will provide great relief. In this area, as in many others, frequent repetition will be necessary. Your voice and the truths it speaks are a new sound for the survivor. The old messages and lies are strong and well entrenched. You will need to repeat many, many times the truths of normality in the context of abuse and the hope for change.

When the client's depression or anxiety is found to be debilitating, she needs to be referred to a physician for an evaluation regarding the possibility of medication. If she has a history of migraine headaches or gastrointestinal problems, a physical exam is warranted. It is important never to assume that such symptoms are related to the abuse or, even if they are, that medical treatment is not necessary. I had a client who apparently had had thyroid problems for many years, and both she and previous therapists had simply assumed that her symptoms were related to her history of abuse rather than a medical condition. A medical consultation is also crucial when a client presents with an eating disorder. The severity of a client's eating disorder is often kept secret from the therapist for some time. Such disorders can be life threatening, so any indication that they exist warrants a medical consultation.

Many, if not most, survivors are terrified of seeing a physician. Seeing a doctor is related to the body; it often means removing clothes and sometimes includes intrusive procedures. If a client needs to see a physician, you may need to help her plan the visit and suggest that she find a safe friend or relative to accompany her. I have found it extremely helpful to have a relationship with a couple of family-practice physicians who have some understanding of the work that I do and who have graciously allowed me to educate them about survivors so that they are sensitive to the survivors' needs.

Clients who struggle with depression and/or anxiety will need help coping in nondestructive ways. The therapist should question carefully about suicidal ideation or previous suicide attempts. Find out what the client does to cope with the depression or anxiety attacks. She may find helpful some simple education about what a panic attack is and how to walk herself through it. She may need some practical suggestions for how to manage both anxiety and depression. Few clients know that a regular program of exercise can be beneficial for both of these. Exercise can sometimes help lift the depression physiologically and reduce anxiety as well. Entering into an exercise program is often the first experience a client has of assuming control over her own body.

Those clients who have drug and alcohol problems need an assessment and a referral to a twelve-step program or rehabilitation program. The addictive behaviors need to be confronted and stopped because they can be life threatening and also because they tend to be a way clients self-medicate and avoid the emotional pain of the abuse. Substance abuse is not only dangerous but also can interfere with the therapeutic process. If medication is warranted, it is crucial that it be prescribed and monitored by a doctor rather than be self-administered.

12

Memory Retrieval

The third component of the initial phase of treatment concerns memory work. Issues regarding the truth of survivors' memories have become a source of major controversy in recent years. There are questions about whether or not traumatic memories can be forgotten only to surface in later years, whether therapists have the ability to implant memories in their clients, how we determine whether or not a memory is actually true, and whether or not child sexual abuse is as pervasive as it seems.

This aspect of therapy, as any other, must be governed by both a search for truth and a demonstration of love. It is destructive to call what is true a lie. It is equally destructive to speak a lie and name it truth. Our work with any person must be done with great care.

Several factors need to govern our work with the memories of others. We now know that having a vivid memory of an event is no guarantee that the memory is perfectly accurate. Accompanying intense emotion does not prove the truth of a memory. The process of memory storage and retrieval is now understood to be a complex process. Psychologist George Klein has given us a theory suggesting that memory is comprised of four components: (1) registration or perception, (2) storage or retention, (3) categorization within schemata, and (4) retrieval.[1] Some alteration to any given memory can occur within any of the four subfunctions. Obviously, a problem with any of these subfunctions can result in an inaccurate memory being retrieved. In the midst of many differing opinions and high emotion, and given the complexity of the human mind in general and memory in particular, we would do well to proceed with caution.

Current research reveals several conclusions that may provide a backdrop against which we can engage in our endeavors. First, there is some evidence that traumatic memories are stored somewhat differently from ordinary memories.[2] During times of severe stress such as abuse or war, the brain sedates itself with opiate-like chemicals (called endorphins). These chemicals are the body's way of anesthetizing itself in order to cope with pain. It is very likely that these opiates affect how the brain stores a memory.

Second, it appears that trauma "produces not only adverse psychological effects, but also potentially long-term neurobiological changes in the brain."[3]

Dr. Bessel van der Kolk, a research psychiatrist at Harvard Medical School, has developed a biological model for trauma based on his work with animals who face repetitive "inescapable shock."[4] Van der Kolk's findings suggest that the brain's biochemical response to trauma appears to create new pathways for the information.

Finally, one result of creating new pathways can be a disconnectedness of sensory memory from emotional memory and/or bodily memory. So rather than storing all aspects of an event in a cohesive fashion, different parts are stored separately from others. Hence, therapists see clients with what are referred to as "body memories," where the client's body reacts as if the abuse were occurring in the present. Or a client may recount a horrific story of abuse without any affective response to those memories.

There is also evidence of repressed memories from situations other than sexual abuse. One of these was recounted in a story printed in *McCall's* magazine in 1994. Helga Newmark had been forced aboard a cattle car during the Nazi occupation and taken to one of the concentration camps. Like many other survivors of those camps, when release came, she walked out and never spoke of the experience again. Years later, standing at a railroad crossing with her two children, she flashed back to the cattle car. Many other memories came flooding back as well. As time passed, she remembered more and more of the concentration-camp experiences, which had previously been repressed. She referred to the process of dealing with her memories as feeling as if she were peeling back many layers of herself in an effort to find out who she really was.[5]

Many studies done with combat veterans demonstrate not only the phenomenon of repressed memory, or amnesia, for terrifying events but also the correlation of amnesia with greater violence and higher levels of stress. Data from work with Vietnam veterans suggest that combat amnesia is related to such factors as exposure to life-threatening circumstances, the taking of life or inflicting serious injury, participating in or witnessing atrocities, isolation, and the refusal of permission to talk about the trauma with others.[6] The factors listed above are threads running through the stories of many survivors of sexual abuse.

The work of dealing with memories is essentially a search for truth. The fact that a memory has surfaced does not guarantee its truth. The fact that a memory was repressed for years does not mean it is untrue. A client recently expressed to me her great fear that the things she was remembering were the truth about her life. She did not want such things to be true. After a moment's pause she realized that at the same time it was a terrifying thought to assume that the things her mind was throwing at her were, in fact, untrue. There was no easy or certain place for her to stand.

I encourage clients to do two things as they seek to understand the truth about their lives. The first is to realize that God is a God of truth. It is he who knows all things and can reveal what is hidden. I tell them that I go to him again and again as I work with them, asking him to make clear what is true. I also suggest that they do the same. Memory work is not about proving anything; it is about finding the truth.

The second thing I do is suggest ways that a client who is uncertain about her history might investigate the accuracy of her memories. An extremely high percentage of the clients I have seen through the years entered therapy with the knowledge of their abuse intact. Therapy sometimes jostles loose other previously forgotten memories, but the fact of their abuse and specific memories of it are some things clients have never forgotten.

For those who are uncertain regarding the truth of their memories, I suggest that they consider returning to the scene of the memory. Often the best retrieval of any memory occurs at the place where the event happened. The likelihood of recall is greater there because the sights, sounds, and smells all work together to help us remember.

Many women have gone back to the place where their abuse occurred. Even those who have always remembered often feel the need to solidify that remembrance by returning to the place where it happened. An important note is that, as much as possible, I encourage the survivor not to return to the place of the abuse alone. To stand and remember is often an overwhelming and frequently terrifying experience. The company of a safe and loving person is very helpful if that can be arranged. When it cannot, I encourage clients to prearrange a phone call with me following the time of their visit to a particular spot. Journaling is also very helpful during these treks. It is a helpful tool in recording memories, feelings, and questions that can easily be lost due to the intense emotion of the moment if they are not recorded. I have had quite a few survivors through the years who had "lost" large chunks of their lives and have returned to their childhood homes. Through pictures, school records, medical records, and conversations with others, they have pieced together their lives and/or documented newly surfaced memories.

Another suggestion for those who are uncertain about their memories is to have them ask questions of someone who might have knowledge related to the memory. Siblings, relatives, and childhood friends will often have memories that shed light. Some of these people, of course, will not want to talk, for they will be too threatened by the thought of abuse occurring within the family. If such a venture is to succeed, it is vital to assess carefully the safeness of the people being asked and to make a realistic appraisal regarding their responses. If the questions are not handled very carefully, they could easily be heard as accusations or confrontations and end up throwing the survivor into circumstances that are frightening and unexpected.

The use of childhood pictures can also serve as an aid. Simply having the client bring in a photo album and flip through it, giving you a running commentary on the pictures and whatever else comes to mind, will sometimes serve as a trigger for events that have previously remained forgotten. This technique is also often helpful in engaging a client with the affective component of her memories. Many clients are stunned when they realize "how little" they were. Other aids can be medical records, school evaluations, and childhood diaries. Obviously, physical damage and/or scarring serve as confirmation for some.

MEMORY WORK

What does one do with horrific memories, either always remembered or just recently recalled? Such memories often overwhelm to the point of interfering with a person's ability to function. The past intrudes again and again into the present. As one client put it, "What happened to me twenty years ago seems more real than what happened this morning."

The guiding principle in dealing with traumatic memories is the restoration of both voice and power to the sufferer. Typically, the abuse was suffered in silence, was handled in isolation, and occurred with no thought given to the needs or desires of the victim. Healing begins when the truth is spoken in the context of a safe relationship and the pace of recovery is managed by what is good for the client rather than for the therapist. In essence, healing occurs when the client's voice is expressed in a relationship where power is not abused.

The task of facing the truth of abuse, particularly chronic and sadistic abuse, is arduous and demanding for both client and therapist. In her book *Trauma and Recovery,* Judith Herman mentions two major pitfalls to this stage of treatment. On one hand, she suggests that a common therapeutic error is to avoid traumatic material because of its overwhelming and horrific nature. On the other hand, many therapists either precipitate memory work without first establishing safety or attempt to rush clients through because of the pain of the work and end up producing in their clients a sense of being overwhelmed yet again with the abuse.[7]

The purpose of memory work is not simply to retrieve memories. The act of remembering something is not, in and of itself, a healing process. Similarly, the process of abreaction (where the emotions accompanying the original abuse are experienced) is not, in and of itself, healing. Merely remembering and feeling do not lead to redemption. One can remember and feel and simply end up endlessly tormented.

There appears to be something of a debate regarding the importance of memory work. Some people believe that every memory needs to be exposed and abreacted in order for healing to occur. At the other end of the continuum are those who seem to feel that no memory work is necessary and that it is even wrong. Those in the latter camp seem to be a small segment of the Christian counseling community. I have made it clear that I do not think that simply remembering and/or abreacting are, in and of themselves, necessarily healing. I also do not think that every memory needs to be recalled and/or abreacted in order for healing to occur. The important point is that this aspect of the work is not so much about memories as it is about *truth*.

God has called us to truth. He is truth. He reveals truth. And we are to seek truth. The psalmist often asks God to examine his heart and his mind, especially those parts that are hidden. We are complex creatures. That complexity is so great that we are unable to understand ourselves. We all carry within us things that we have been directly taught or have learned inadvertently, things that are laced with lies. We live our lives based on those lies until God uses some means to expose them and teach us his truth instead. When someone has grown up in a home infiltrated with lies and deceit, the impact is profound. Those lies that are embedded in traumatic experiences and accompanied by intense emotion have usually left powerful messages. It is those lies that are exposed during the process of memory work. The memory work has a purpose far greater than that of simply remembering and feeling what occurred.

The purpose of memory work is to afford the survivor a safe place in which to tell the truth about her life so that that truth can be integrated into the whole of her life and its accompanying lies can be exposed. Paul gives us the principle of exposure in Ephesians 5:8-14: "For you were once darkness, but now you are light in the Lord. Live as children of light (for the fruit of the light consists in all goodness, righteousness and truth) and find out what pleases the Lord. Have nothing to do with the fruitless deeds of darkness, *but rather expose them.* For it is shameful even to mention what the disobedient do in secret. *But everything exposed by the light becomes visible, for it is light that makes everything visible.* This is why it is said: 'Wake up, O sleeper, rise from the dead, and Christ will shine on you'" (italics added).

God is light. The result of his light in our lives is goodness, righteousness, and truth. Jesus said that Satan is the father of lies. He deceives, and there is no truth in him (John 8:44). That which has been carried out in darkness needs to be exposed. The lies that the darkness hides need to be revealed for what they are. Those things that are dragged to the light become visible; that is, they are seen for what they truly are. Light makes the truth of something apparent. It is only then that the survivor can call what is evil by its true name, see the lies that have been hidden in the darkness, and find herself free to hear the truth. It is then that the process of redemption becomes evident, for we see one who was marked by the characteristics of death—silence, isolation, and powerlessness—finally awaken from the dead as the life of Christ begins its transforming work.

CHARACTERISTICS OF THE PROCESS OF MEMORY WORK

Elie Wiesel says in his book *A Jew Today* that "memory is not only a kingdom, it is also a graveyard."[8] In his commentary on Wiesel, Robert McAfee Brown speaks of memory as "a kingdom of night, a kingdom of darkness where no light was found, where death, rather than being the daily exception, became the daily expectation."[9] Such a memory serves as a perpetual destructive force in a person's life. Brown refers to the time when Wiesel visited Kiev, site of a massive slaughter of Jews in 1943. Wiesel said to the mayor at that time, "Mr. Mayor, the problem for all of us—for you as for us—is: what do we do with our memories? We must deal with them or they will crush us." Brown says that "confronting memories not only involves acknowledging their reality and honoring those victimized, but determining to appropriate the memories in the present for the sake of the future."[10]

What should characterize the process of accompanying survivors of sexual abuse on their journey to the kingdom of darkness, where no light is found—only death? Such a kingdom is characterized by the death of voice, the death of relationship, and the death of power—indeed, the death of personhood as God intended it to be. What needs to be present during such a journey in order for it to result in a redemption so great that those things meant to produce death are instead transformed into that which produces life?

Before we can understand what should characterize such a journey, we must first be clear about what we are facing. To look evil full in the face is to confront hell brought up from below the earth to its surface. Lest you think I exaggerate, look at what John 8:44 teaches us about hell and its master. "You belong to your father, the devil, and you want to carry out your father's desire [lusts]. He was a murderer from the beginning, not holding to the truth, for there is no truth in him. When he lies, he speaks his native language, for he is a liar and the father of lies." The characteristics of our enemy as described here are that he is ruled by his lusts, he brings death wherever he goes, and his mouth is full of lies and deceit. Are not these the core components of abuse? Is not a father who repeatedly rapes his little girl ruled by his lusts, producing death in her person, and filling her mind with hideous lies? To proceed on such a journey is to face the outworkings of hell itself. The work encompasses far more than listening to memories, and we delude ourselves if we think otherwise. Amy Carmichael sums up what confronts us in a statement she made about facing the ancient and strong philosophy of Hinduism: "These deep-rooted...[problems] are formidable enough, when rightly understood, to make us feel how little we can do to overturn them; but they are just as 'Dust' in comparison with the force of the 'Actual' entrenched behind them. Only superficial Dust; and yet...nothing but the Breath of God can blow this Dust away."[11]

If this is so, and I have found it to be true, then the first thing that is required for this journey is a therapist whose very roots go down deep into the life of God. Yes, this is a work about very painful and terrifying memories. Yes, this is a work that exposes lies and seeks truth. Certainly this is a work that requires an understanding of people and the nature of therapy. It requires a knowledge of abuse, what abuse does to those who have endured it, and what they need in order to change. However, we must never forget that this is also a work about principalities and powers. It is work that often seems literally to skirt the abyss.

Again, from the Amy Carmichael quotation we mentioned earlier: "Those who know nothing of the facts will be sure to criticize. It is not an unknown thing for persons to act as critics, even though supremely ignorant of the subject criticized. But those who know the truth of these things will know that we have understated it, carefully toned it down perforce, because it cannot be written in full. It could neither be published nor read. It cannot be written or published or read, but oh, it had to be lived! *And what you may not even hear, had to be endured by little girls"* (emphasis hers).[12]

Those who would journey into such territory must know the Giver of Life and know him well, or they will find themselves ill prepared for the work they are called to do. The impact of this work on the person of the therapist and on who the therapist needs to be is discussed at length in a later chapter. For now we need to keep in mind the true nature of the work and the perennial call to the therapist to seek after God.

We learned earlier that trauma not only silenced voice but also resulted in isolation and powerlessness. During the process of exposing the truth, everything must be done to try to break through that isolation and impotence.

Relationship was destroyed by the abuse. When we considered the developmental stages of childhood, we saw how much of that work is in the area of relationship or connection. The bonding with the mother, the leaving and returning of the toddler, and the developing identity of the teen all happen within the context of relationship. Chronic abuse in the life of a child cuts through all of that, destroying connection and creating unhealthy disconnection.

Therapy is an opportunity to redeem that. Obviously we cannot go back and make it as if the abuse never happened. We also cannot pretend it was not so bad and will not affect the victim in the future. What we can offer is a safe connection that she can hold on to while she faces the truth of her life. We are offering a strong arm to cling to as she lowers herself into the abyss, a refuge to return to after the storm of a memory, a truthful person to talk to as she struggles to sort out the lies from the truth about who she is. It is easy to see why the establishment and maintenance of safety is such a primary concern.

Dealing with the trauma in the context of a safe connection allows the survivor, often for the first time in her life, to be *herself* in relationship to another. The abuse forced her to live with a split identity. She grew up having to pretend she was not abused, for to speak the truth would result in the destruction of even the appearance of relationship. Many were also threatened with the destruction of their very lives. Within the therapeutic relationship, she can speak the whole truth about herself and still find love and acceptance. That, of course, requires a therapist to be able to tolerate the worst possible truth and still extend love.

When basic trust has been shattered in the early life of a child and when she has been molested by those who should have been her protectors, she will feel abandoned by God. The foundation for any kind of faith relationship has been destroyed. Those who are in charge betray and hurt. The idea of trust is ludicrous. A crisis of faith is inevitable.

The abuse also destroyed any sense of choice or power. If the child grew up with any sense of power, it was more than likely believed to be a lethal power. In other words, she learned that her power was such that she could destroy any relationship she ever entered into. To know her was to be met with evil and badness. At the same time, she was taught that she had no power to stop evil, her needs and desires were irrelevant in relationship, and she had no power to protect herself. Any initiative she attempted was thwarted. To assert herself, to try to do something different, to offer resistance of any kind, was a meaningless and potentially life-threatening exercise.

Again, therapy offers an opportunity to redeem the possibility of choice. Within the context of a safe connection, the pace for dealing with the painful truth will be determined by what the *client* can tolerate. The work of therapy must be managed with the needs and resiliency of the individual client in mind. Trauma is by definition unbearable. The work of dealing with that trauma needs to be done in a way that is as bearable as possible. I realize, of course, that in some senses that is not even remotely possible. To let yourself down into the unbearable is in some ways unbearable, and yet the unbearable must be borne, or healing will never occur. Therefore, the client must carefully choose the pace at which she faces what she believes is unfaceable. On the one hand, the therapist must communicate, "Yes, you *can* do this and live." On the other hand, the question must continually be asked, "How would *you* like to do this?"

I see two dangers that can cause the therapist to alter the pace without the needs of the client being the determining factor. One danger is that the therapist can become fascinated with watching another's pain or can become addicted to the intensity of work with survivors. The therapist's desire for some sort of psychological voyeurism or need for an "intensity high" can be what regulates the pace of the work. Work with survivors is compelling, and it is not hard to fall into such traps. However, the pace of the work should always be determined by the client's need for progress within the context of safety.

A second danger inherent in the process of listening results from an unwillingness to hear because we are afraid that what we hear about others will tell us things we don't want to hear about ourselves or life in this world. Many people do not want to hear because the consequences of the message are too devastating. Who wants to hear about perpetrators when such tales force us to consider the perpetrator that lies just below the surface of our own hearts? Who wants to hear about the rape of little boys and girls when we have vulnerable children out there in the world? Who wants to confront another's ravaged faith when it causes us to look our own barely hidden doubts squarely in the face?

It is very easy to fall prey to dangers such as these. If we are not watchful of our own responses to what we hear, we will end up setting the pace based on our own needs and remaining deaf to the cries of the one before us. How easy it is to resemble a perpetrator!

When memories that are charged with intense emotion are surfacing, the client will find that she cannot function at her highest level. And in fact, she may function well below her norm for a while. Both she and her support system need to be told about this so that everyone can work together to support her and to help simplify her life. You cannot face trauma and have the rest of life proceed as if nothing is happening. That is true whether the trauma occurred recently or many years ago. The word *trauma* means a shock that results in a wound. When such a thing happens in the physical realm, life does not proceed as usual. The same is true when the trauma occurs in the emotional realm. Sexual abuse is a shock to the body, mind, and spirit. Dealing with such a pervasive wound will cause reverberations throughout all aspects of a life.

TECHNIQUES HELPFUL TO MEMORY WORK

No matter how well we structure the process and no matter how attuned we are to the needs of our client, the work of confronting painful memories of sexual abuse is disturbing and terrifying. Although I know of no way to make this an easy or painless process, I have found several techniques that have helped clients through the years.

1. Grounding: Frequently when a client is faced with a specific memory of the abuse, she will seem to get lost in that memory. It will seem to her that your office has faded away, you have disappeared, and the abuse is actually occurring. It is very important to teach your client how to ground herself in the present during these times. As she learns to do that with your help, she will eventually be able to do that for herself.

One of the ways I help ground a client is by the use of my voice. I have found that most survivors are very attuned to the sound of my voice. As a matter of fact, it is often their only connection with me at first, for they are afraid to look up. Many have told me that for a long time they were able to recognize me outside the office only by my voice and my shoes! They seem to attach to my voice even before they attach to me as a person.

When a client is "lost" in a memory, I speak evenly and slowly to her. I call her by name and remind her who I am and where she is. I tell her again and again that she is *remembering* something; it is *not* happening now. I often repeat the phrase, "Follow my voice out of the memory." Many times clients will say that is the only thing that does not "fit" with the memory, that although my voice is faint, they can hear it, and they keep pushing toward it until they can reattach to the present and my office.

A second way that I help clients to ground themselves is a technique they can learn to do for themselves. In essence, I encourage them to use one of their five senses in order to attach to the present. Most clients will use either sight or touch. I almost always have fresh flowers in my office, and it is often searching for those flowers that will pull a client back into the present. Again, I use my voice to remind them where they are and to look for my flowers. When they can tell me what color the flowers are, then I know they are "back." Some clients relate better to something tactile—the feel of the material on my couch or the pillow that sits there. As time passes, I find that clients internalize this process (voice and all) and are able to ground themselves when they are not in the office.

A third way to help a client feel grounded in the present is through the use of prayer and/or Scripture. This can only be done based on a clear understanding of where a client is in her struggle with spiritual issues. If ill timed, the use of prayer and/or Scripture could end up triggering memories because of how these were used before, during, or after the abuse itself.

2. *Storage:* Many clients fear being consumed by a memory not only while they are in your office but also after they leave. They are afraid they will not be able to leave the office and still function. It is often helpful to suggest that a client imagine "storing" a memory in my office and leaving it there. This involves the client's choosing a place where she would like to leave the memory and then picturing herself putting it there. I become the "keeper" of that memory until she returns for her next session. Clients are often able to remind themselves of that process during the week when the memory

threatens to surface and overtake them once again. This technique also begins to provide the survivor a sense of mastery over her memories.

3. Containment: Another way to help a client gain mastery over her memories whenever they surface is to encourage her to find a way of containing them. It is very similar to the idea behind the storage technique. Many of the survivors I have worked with are very creative people. They paint, compose music, write poetry, and express themselves beautifully in journals. Using these methods in a specific place and within carefully chosen time limits enables a survivor to continue to deal with her memories outside the office but in a very controlled fashion. Many will paint or write in a particular place in their home and at a given time. Whenever memories surface, they are then able to set them aside until that place and time. Again, such a technique gives a sense of control over what has always been overwhelming.

4. Timing: As much as possible I try to encourage the survivor to participate in the process of timing her work with memories. One woman early on in her therapy made note of the fact that I seemed to monitor very carefully the timing of looking at her memories or nightmares. "You approach slowly, hit it full in the face, retreat, and gently pick up the pieces before I have to leave." As we discussed this process, she herself began to assume some responsibility for it, and she learned to protect herself by not beginning such work five minutes before she had to leave. Once again, she began to feel more in charge of that which had run over her life.

Obviously such control is not always possible. Something will trigger a memory, and there it is, full-blown, with ten minutes left. However, each time one of these techniques gives even a taste of being able to manage such memories, the client walks away with a sense of competence and hope.

5. Written notes: Often when clients are working through memories, they are either struggling with intense emotion or are dissociating; after they leave the session, they have little or no idea what you have said to them. I refer to it as "session amnesia." Now, I have the perhaps inflated notion that what I said might be important for them to hear. That is especially the case when a particular memory seems to carry within it powerful lies such as "I am worthless," "I am untouchable," "I will die if I tell." When the client and I wrestle together with that lie, I have found it very helpful toward the end of the session to write out what the client has thought is true about herself and then what is indeed true according to Scripture. Often I will include aspects of her relationship with me that demonstrate that what God says is true. The truth seems more believable when it has been seen, felt, and touched on the human level (which is why God was incarnated). Clients take these notes with them and have said they go back to them again and again during the week. I have been told that those notes, coupled with the fact that *I will not lie* to a client (though I may choose not to answer a question), are often what finally enables the truth to begin to sink in and replace the lie.

6. Relaxation techniques: Many survivors walk around in perpetually knotted-up bodies, with no sense of what it means to feel relaxed. Making a tape or using a prerecorded one and teaching them how to relax can be a great antidote to those moments when anxiety is on the rise due to a memory being triggered. Sometime ago as I was teaching a woman how to relax her muscles, she looked up and said, "You mean this is what people mean when they say they feel relaxed? I had no idea what they were talking about. It feels absolutely delicious!"

7. Nurturing: Survivors often feel unsafe in their own bodies. They also view their bodies as the enemy. If it weren't for their bodies, they would not have been abused. Many survivors are dissociated from their bodies and, hence, treat them very poorly. Others are active in hating their bodies and continue to treat them in a way that reflects or mimics the actions of their perpetrators. The concept of nurturing one's own body is not only foreign but also anxiety producing. To care for the body in any way is to ask for further abuse. Better you should ignore it or trash it, with the hope that no one else will notice you have one.

Many survivors grew up with the biological rhythms of sleeping and eating being either chaotic or overcontrolled by the perpetrator. Bedtime, mealtime, and bath time were frightening and anxiety producing. Many survivors suffer from sleep disorders, eating disorders, or at least poor eating habits. The concept of caring for the body has to be carefully taught. It is best to begin in the least threatening area. I have worked with survivors who won't sleep in beds because beds mean sexual abuse, who won't eat at tables because mealtimes were fraught with violence and the throwing of food and dishes, and who work at frenzied paces and for long hours because to sit still means to be "found." The normal regulation of such events, taken for granted by so many of us, is simply unheard of. The process of learning how to eat well and with some regularity, of engaging in exercise, and of sleeping in the same place every night at about the same time takes time and repetition. Each tiny step of nurturing and of caring for the body is a defiance of what was taught, a step of faith, and a small taste of gentleness toward a body that has been violated and trashed for many years. To learn to nurture a body so abused, in response to memories of that abuse, is to taste redemption.

The role of witness to the memories of chronic sexual abuse can be emotionally overwhelming. To be in many ways a helpless witness to the trauma experienced by one you have come to care for is to open yourself up to pain, rage, grief, and deep sorrow. It means that somehow and in some way as you listen, the survivor's story weaves itself into your story and you are forever changed. You will, if you do not flee, be forced to confront the power of the enemy, your own capacity for evil, terrible grief over the expendability and abuse of children, and the tragedy of lives that will never be what they might have been.

Simultaneously, you will be called on to offer a safe connection, a steady hope, listening ears, a voice of truth, and choice to one you cannot control and who might hurt herself. You will stand as a representative of the God who is our refuge, the God who brings hope, the God who hears, the God who speaks truth, and the God who asks us to choose him. In fact, you will be called on to partake of what was the essence of the Incarnation, bringing God himself down into flesh-and-blood actualities and working his life out through your fingertips. The work of Jesus in this world resulted in redemption. His work in and through you in this world will also result in redemption.

PART THREE

Treatment: Phase Two

13

Facing Truths about the Past

The initial phase of the treatment of an adult survivor of sexual abuse focused on the establishing of a safe relationship with the therapist, symptom relief, and memory work. In the context of safety with the therapist, the bulk of the work done tends to focus largely on those events that occurred in the past and the thoughts and feelings accompanying them. This phase of therapy involves both education and comfort. As the client speaks about her memories, you have the privilege of responding to her in healing ways, giving her something she did not receive at the time of the abuse. Comforting her, reassuring her, affirming her courage in surviving and now in dealing with the trauma will enable her to face the truth about her life, form a strong alliance with you, and then move on.

The question is, of course, where do you as a therapist hope she will move to? Once the client begins to recognize what was done to her by the perpetrator and by nonprotecting family members and once her presenting symptoms begin to abate, the focus will shift to helping her see herself as a responsible adult, not as a traumatized child-victim. I find that many therapists do not seem to know how to help their clients make this shift. Sadly, it prevents some clients from moving on from the so-called "victim stage." We do our clients a grave disservice if we fail not only to enable them to face the truth of their lives but also to learn not to allow it to determine the present and the future.

A lot of writing has been done about what is referred to as a "victim mentality," which many rightly see as prevalent in our society. One has only to look at some of the ridiculous and successful litigation today to see this. However, those who are troubled by this mentality are frequently in danger of forgetting that true victims do exist. Scripture makes it clear not only that humans put other humans in the position of being victimized or oppressed but also that those who know Christ are to reach out and assist such people. Any boy or girl, man or woman who has been sexually abused or raped is a victim. At the same time, part of our assistance to those who are indeed victims is to help them appropriately and in a timely fashion to grow beyond that place. That is not to say that the issues of sexual abuse will cease to be a struggle for them. The grave sins of others against us often reverberate through our lives for years, and we do not want to be naive about this. Yet neither do we want to fail to hold out the hope of redemption, a redemption not limited to the life to come but one that is a real possibility in this world as well.

The middle phase of treatment is a turning point and sometimes a bit of a crisis for therapist and survivor alike. I believe it is that fact that contributes to the reasons that therapy often bogs down at this juncture. The middle phase of treatment requires therapists to assume a more directive and active stance toward a person they are comfortable nurturing and comforting. Certainly these behaviors should not cease, but if they continue without more directive approaches being added, the client will stalemate. Regardless of how much courage is necessary to face the terror of incest and its aftereffects, facing such truths is not sufficient condition for change. The therapist needs to begin to treat the survivor like an adult who has a voice and power, characteristics the abuse crushed.

One of the reasons treatment can get stuck here is that the survivor may put up a great deal of resistance. The major fear in her life up to this point has been facing the abuse. She has done that and lived to tell about it. She would probably like to breathe a sigh of relief and settle in to enjoy that fact. There is nothing wrong with that, for she has crossed a major and difficult hurdle—but it is not the end. We read in John Bunyan's The Pilgrim's Progress how Christian, upon being released from his burden at the cross, must then proceed up the hill Difficulty. He begins the ascent. It is steep and high. Bunyan then tells us, "Now about the midway to the top of the hill was a pleasant arbor, made by the Lord of the hill for the refreshing of weary travelers; thither, therefore, Christian got, where also he sat down to rest him.... Thus pleasing himself awhile, he at last fell into a slumber, and thence into a fast sleep, which detained him in that place until it was almost night."[1]

The hill was difficult, and Christian was tired. The arbor was for rest. However, the arbor was not his destination. It was meant to be only a place of refreshment before he continued on his way. His sleep in that place caused him later difficulty. If the growth and struggles of phase one are allowed to be a destination, the client will in many ways stay crippled, and in some sense her abuser will have won. Yes, part of God's work in our lives is to bring us into truth. One aspect of that truth is facing the realities of our history. But there is more. It is also true that the client is now an adult with both voice and power. She is now in a place of beginning to choose how to use her voice and her power to have an impact. She can choose to continue to let God's work of redemption set her free from the past, and as she does, his work will transform her from one who reflects the lies of the enemy into one who bears a growing likeness to Jesus Christ.

The survivor has learned to speak. She has lived through a time in what Wiesel calls the "kingdom of night" and has chosen to tell the truth about what she saw there. In a discussion of Holocaust art, Wiesel says: "Let us tell tales so as to remember how vulnerable man is when faced with overwhelming evil. Let us tell tales so as not to allow the executioner to have the last word. The last word belongs to the victim. It is up to the witness to capture it, shape it, transmit it."[2]

The survivor has not allowed the perpetrator to have the last word. Her very decision to tell her story opens up new possibilities never before available to her. We need to reiterate the truths she has acknowledged before we move on to help her name those new and life-giving possibilities.

The experience of chronic abuse carries within it the gross mislabeling of things. Perpetrators are really "nice daddies." Victims are "evil and seductive" (at the age of three!). Nonprotecting parents are "tired and busy." The survivor makes a giant leap forward when she can call abuse by its right name and grasp the concept that what was done was a manifestation of the heart of the perpetrator, not the heart of the victim.

We must keep ever before us the fact that childhood sexual abuse occurs in a pathological environment and its recipient is a developing, dependent child. Children need attachment, and yet the survivor's "choices" were adults who were either dangerous and/or negligent. In her book Trauma and Recovery, Judith Herman does an excellent job of describing the impossible task facing a child who is living with chronic sexual abuse:

> In this climate of profoundly disrupted relationships the child faces a formidable developmental task. She must find a way to form primary attachments to caretakers who are either dangerous or, from her perspective, negligent. She must find a way to develop a sense of basic trust and safety with caretakers who are untrustworthy and unsafe. She must develop a sense of self in relation to others who are helpless, uncaring or cruel. She must develop a capacity for bodily self-regulation in an environment in which her body is at the disposal of others' needs as well as a capacity for self-soothing in an environment without solace. She must develop the capacity for initiative in an environment which demands that she bring her will into complete conformity with that of her abuser. And ultimately, she must develop a capacity for intimacy out of an environment where all intimate relationships are corrupt, and an identity out of an environment which defines her as a whore and a slave.
>
> The abused child's existential task is equally formidable. Though she perceives herself as

abandoned to a power without mercy, she must find a way to preserve hope and meaning. The alternative is utter despair, something no child can bear. To preserve her faith in her parents, she must reject the first and most obvious conclusion that something is terribly wrong with them. She will go to any lengths to construct an explanation for her fate that absolves her parents of all blame and responsibility...Unable to escape or alter the unbearable reality in fact, the child alters it in her mind.[3]

Such alterations form the foundation for layer upon layer of lies. These lies and the fragmentation of personhood they require have become the basic principle around which the survivor's life is ordered. As the story is told in the context of a safe relationship, the whole person is gradually able to face the whole story in truth.

"I WAS NOT THE ABUSER"

One of the major steps for the survivor will be the actual naming of the perpetrator. By that I do not mean simply identifying who her abuser was—father, mother, grandfather, grandmother, uncle, stepfather, etc.—though that is a tremendous step for some. The naming of the perpetrator involves far more than that. It means facing the truth that the one who planned and executed the crime was the abuser; it means the victim did not cause the abuse. It means coming to terms with the fact that any abusive actions taken against another are a heart revelation of the one taking the action, not a heart revelation of the victim. It means facing the truth that incest or sexual abuse of a minor is a crime, not a mistake. It is a heinous sin against a child whom God has called us to protect.

Many survivors have grown up believing the lie that something about them made the abuse happen. Many were told, "I wouldn't do this if you weren't so bad."

Christ makes it abundantly clear in Matthew 15:16-20 that what is outside a person is *not* what makes that person unclean. The evil that a person engages in stems from his or her own heart, not from the people by whom he or she is surrounded. No matter what the survivor did, the sexual abuse perpetrated against her is *not* a statement about her heart. The lies, the lust, the deceit, the manipulation, the cruelty—all are manifestations of the heart of the abuser.

Some people, clients and counselors alike, seem very afraid of such statements. One of the reasons for that fear is that such statements are construed as blaming the parent for the difficulties of the present. Naming the perpetrator is not about blame but about truth. The truth is that having sex with a child is evil. The truth is that those who do so have demonstrated the evil in their own hearts. The truth is that whenever any of us commits evil, we influence those around us in profound ways.

As Christians, we are to be bold in calling evil by its right name. We are also to be bold in stating the truths of Scripture, and one of those truths is that evil reflects the heart from which it emanates. If I slander others, the act of slander is a revelation of *my* heart, not *their* character. Abuse is the revelation of the abuser's heart, not the victim's. To name one's own father as evil is terrifying. A child who is dependent on that father cannot tolerate that reality. An adult, in the safety of a relationship with you, finally has the freedom to state and absorb that shattering truth. Helping her to do so will assist her in moving on.

"I WAS NOT PROTECTED"

A second truth that the client must acknowledge is the negligence of the nonprotecting parent. For some clients, that involves one parent; for other clients, that involves two parents. Many women have had to face mothers who denied that their husbands were sexually violating their daughters or who pretended the abuse was not happening. I have also worked with men and women whose fathers have abandoned them to mothers who were sexually abusive. For others, the abuser has been a brother, grandfather, uncle, or neighbor, and both parents have turned a blind eye to the signs or a deaf ear to attempts to tell about the abuse. Sometimes the nonprotector was a teacher or pastor who sent the victim back home because, after all, one does not interfere with the privacy of others' homes.

Just as perpetrators are excused by their victims, so are nonprotecting adults. Again, one reason for this is that the reality of having no adult to protect you from abuse is an unbearable truth when you are small and dependent. To face that truth is to recognize that one is, in fact, an orphan and that no one is coming to help. The terror is unmanageable. So is the rage.

As I mentioned previously, I will never forget the first time I sat across from a mother whose daughter had been molested for many years by the father, and I asked the mother why she did nothing to stop it. The response was: "I had so many important things to worry about.... I couldn't be bothered with her problems." The thought of being a little girl repeatedly abused and then confronted with such massive abandonment is overwhelming.

Many survivors have spoken to me about the devastating effects of such neglect, recognizing that such deprivation and lack of protection greatly exacerbated the effects of the abuse. Survivors grow up believing the lie, "I was not worth protecting." One of the most significant memories for many clients is the moment when they tried to tell and were greeted with denial or blame. That was often the moment when hope died. Other memories, often particularly poignant, are those of little girls sadistically abused and then left to find a way to clean themselves off from the blood, dirt, and semen. Little girls, four, six, and eight years old, are trying to find ways to "look like nothing happened" so Mommy won't know. Under healthy, normal circumstances, parents run to the aid of little girls who skin their knees. The pathology and evil of such neglect is screamingly evident.

The psalmist pleaded, "Do not reject me or forsake me, O God my Savior. Though my father and mother forsake me, the Lord will receive me" (Ps. 27:9-10). Such verses represent both the heart cry of the victim and her struggle to believe. Forsaken by both father and mother, it becomes very difficult to trust that God himself will not, indeed *has not,* also abandoned her. Yet how the client's heart longs to believe that though her parents have abandoned her, God himself will receive her. Facing the truth of that abandonment in the context of a relationship that holds steady is part of what will enable the survivor to trust that God will both receive her and not forsake her.

"I WAS A VICTIM"

A third and extremely difficult and threatening truth for the survivor to face is that she was a victim. We noted earlier that in Latin *victima* is "an animal offered in sacrifice." Webster defines victim as "a living being sacrificed." To sacrifice something means, in part, to surrender or destroy something prized for the sake of something considered to have a more pressing claim. A child who has been sexually abused certainly falls under the category of a sacrifice. A precious child created in the image of God has been destroyed for the sake of the lust of an adult. The child is truly a victim.

One of the reasons a survivor finds it so difficult to see herself as a victim is that she has been blamed repeatedly for the abuse: "If you weren't such a whore, this wouldn't have to happen." Each time she is used and trashed, she becomes further convinced of her innate badness. She sees herself participating in forbidden sexual activity and may often get some sense of gratification from it even if she doesn't want to (it is, after all, a form of touch, and our bodies respond without the consent of our wills). This is seen as further proof that the abuse is her fault and well deserved. In her mind, she has become responsible for the actions of her abusers. She believes she is not a victim; she is a loathsome, despicable, worthless human being—if indeed she even qualifies as human. When the abuse has been sadistic in nature and when a child has been forced into things like bestiality, these beliefs are further entrenched. It is not a very big step from such thinking to the assumption that God himself wants nothing to do with her.

A large part of helping the client understand what it means to be a victim is educating the client about what it means to be a child. I will often have clients go to a church nursery or a school just to observe little boys and girls of the age that they were when the abuse occurred. I ask them to watch and simply record their observations. I tell them to note the size difference between these children and the adults who are responsible for them. The results are often startling. It is through the eyes of other children that they get their first glimpse of their own smallness, dependence, ignorance, and vulnerability: "I had no idea I was so little." Many survivors carry a strong belief that they could have stopped the abuse (at the age of five) or at least that they deserved the abuse. A growing understanding of childhood sheds light on these lies.

In an attempt to help clients further understand their position as children, I often have clients study the meanings of such words as *abuse, violation, oppression, trauma, abandonment,* and *rape.* Then we take those specific meanings and pull out a particular memory. For example, *to violate* means "to break through by force." The client's perspective is typically something like, "Well, he was a little rough sometimes, but that was because he was drunk. He didn't mean it." So I respond, "You don't think that when your father pinned your arms down and forced your legs apart to have intercourse with you at the age of four, while you were crying, 'No, Daddy, please don't,' qualifies as an illustration of the word *violate?"* The answer seems obvious, but it is often hard work to get the light to dawn in a mind that is utterly convinced that somehow that event was her fault. This message has been ingrained in her. For example, one woman's sadistic father often tied her up and forced her to endure ice-cold enemas and told her how dirty she was and how she should get used to what he was doing. He had to do this to her because of what she was. If she were a good little girl like her sister, none of this would have to happen. She, however, was scum and needed "cleansing."

Another avenue that is often helpful is that of giving the client the stories of other survivors. They are quick to see how the six-year-old they are reading about was clearly a victim. They can point out the errors in the thinking of another survivor who blames herself for what occurred. This process will sometimes make it easier for a survivor to see herself more objectively.

The process of seeing oneself as a victim means facing the help-lessness and weakness the survivor has spent a lifetime trying to deny. To be helpless is life threatening. To be weak is to be hurt. It seems better to assume responsibility for the abuse itself than to face the terror of powerlessness. The closer the client comes to facing the reality of her helplessness, the greater her sense of danger. To admit her weakness in your presence is, in her mind, to invite you to abuse her. She will work hard to avoid that moment. Confronting the reality of her powerlessness, however, will set her free. She will find herself weak in the presence of another and discover that she is safe. She will find herself free to then connect and depend in healthy ways. She will no longer have to construct her life so as to avoid ever feeling powerless again. The possibility of trust all of a sudden becomes a reality.

"I AM CAPABLE OF ABUSING OTHERS"

The fourth truth is one that many therapists and clients alike want to avoid. One of the reasons none of us wants to hear about abuse is that to confront the fact of abuse is to face the potential for such atrocity within myself. If I say it is unthinkable, I don't have to deal with the fact that I might violate another human being, given the right circumstances.

Allowing into the room the possibility of a client's abuse of others requires a shift that many therapists are afraid of. They are comfortable seeing their clients as victims but are highly resistant to hearing about any abuse that the client may have done to herself or others. It is also frightening to confront abusive behavior that the client enacts toward the therapist. It is very tempting to communicate by one's own denial, silence, or pretense that such things are not realities. It is vital for therapists to ask themselves whether there are any aspects of their client's life they are unwilling to hear about and discuss. To refuse to hear and discuss these things is to assume the role of the nonprotecting, denying parent.

I believe that therapists cannot adequately deal with these issues if they have not faced the potential for abuse within themselves. Until they have grappled with the fact that abuse is the wrong use of another and that they themselves have used others for their own ends, they are not equipped to face such truths in another or help them look at themselves. The human heart is capable of any evil, and the therapist's heart is no exception. When therapists have faced the potential, or actuality, of such evil in their own hearts (no matter how subtle or cloaked it may be) and have dealt with that evil on their knees before the Cross of Christ, they will not fear facing it in anyone else. Such a confrontation with their own capabilities will also enable them to speak without condemnation or arrogance and will enable them to point with confidence to the forgiveness and freedom that are in Christ.

The confrontation of the perpetrator that lies within the survivor can take many forms. It may mean facing his or her own actual abuse of someone. Others have demonstrated it in abusive behavior toward animals. Many survivors reenact the abuse by becoming their own perpetrator, living with repeated self-mutilation. It is a terrifying thing to confront the fact that the perpetrator *and* the victim are one. Others will grapple with the fantasies and thoughts their rage engenders. Though they may never act on such thoughts, they will find within themselves the capacity or desire to hurt as they have been hurt.

For a survivor to admit that she carries within herself the potential to hurt another as she has been hurt is both humiliating and frightening. A survivor often comforts herself with the lie that she is not, indeed never could be, like her perpetrator. Such a lie leaves her encased in deceit and denial about her own sinful capabilities. It is a damning sentence outside of the Cross of Christ. To face the capacity of her own heart without flinching and to discover that it is met with the infinite grace of God will set her free from deceit and denial about herself. When any of us face such realities within ourselves and meet with grace, we are set free forever from the fear that if the truth were known, we would be destroyed. From that moment on, you can tell me nothing about myself that I will be afraid to hear, for I have faced the worst, and grace was sufficient. To offer a client the opportunity to confront with you the worst about herself and still to greet her with love and grace is an awesome gift indeed.

One of the most important outgrowths of facing the above-listed truths is that the multitude of lies planted and nurtured by the abuse will be exposed. You will find that the lies are strong, for they have been woven into the person through the years under horrific circumstances and powerful emotions.

One client responded to the moment of first telling me about the sadistic abuse in her life by writing in her journal: "I just sat there, wishing someone would hit me. I needed to be punished. I was a horrid, vile thing, and I needed the badness beaten out of me. Why couldn't anyone besides my father understand that?" For a long, long time, a client like this assumes that the therapist is responding differently simply because the client has not been clear in explaining what happened. If she could just tell you "right," then you too would agree that she was "a horrid, vile thing."

The survivor will carry deeply entrenched lies about herself (she is trash; she is worthless; she made it happen). She will be full of lies about people (no one is trustworthy; no one will love me; safety comes only in isolation; if you wait long enough, everyone will abuse you). She will also carry many lies about God (he doesn't love me; I am unforgivable; he has abandoned me; I am unredeemable). Again and again your words will need to teach her the truth. Again and again your person will need to be a demonstration of those truths as you relate to her. She needs those words, for she needs them to replace the lies that reverberate throughout her life. She needs more than those words, for in her experience, words are cheap. Your life and your person must be what you teach. As the client confronts the lies and grapples with the above-listed truths in the context of a safe and enduring relationship with you, you will have the great privilege of bearing witness to previously unspoken atrocities, which, as you move through them together, will bring both of you to the Cross of Christ and the unfolding of redemption.

14

Facing Truths about the Present

After facing the truth about the past, survivors need to move toward facing the truth about the present. One of the important aspects of that truth is how God sees the survivors.

FACING HOW GOD SEES THEM

As the men and women I see move through the process of dealing with their history, their feelings about that history, their questions of why, and their struggles with the lies they are burdened by, I have often suggested two particular exercises that have proven helpful. The timing of these exercises varies from person to person, and I do not suggest them to everyone. However, I often find them powerful tools, and I frequently give them at the juncture between moving away from a focus on the past and moving to a greater focus on the present. I offer them now for your consideration.

EXERCISE 1

The first of these exercises deals with Isaiah 53. Although I can never answer the why question for my clients, I can point them to Christ, who entered fully into their experience. They have by this time come to see that the fact that I have listened and entered into their lives has somehow been a healing experience for them. Although neither I nor the survivor is able to adequately articulate why, the act of having another enter into our suffering with us is an incredible gift with profound results. Having experienced that on a human level and seen the results, it is a marvelous thing to wrestle with the truth that God himself has done the same. To begin to get a glimmer of the fact that the God of the universe entered into the experiences of helplessness, weakness, abuse, oppression, rejection, and abandonment touches something deep inside. To hear that he was stripped, mocked, spit on, and struck without cause helps one who has endured similar experiences to draw close to him.

A survivor grasps the gift of these truths more easily when I have her take the fifty-third chapter of Isaiah and rewrite it so that it speaks personally to her. I often have the survivor read aloud her rewritten passage. When she does, it seems as if God were speaking to her individually and demonstrating for her why he understands what she has endured. It is always a moment of significant worship for both of us. I have included an example from one survivor.

****

Parts of Isaiah 53 (As If Christ Were Speaking)

Others had told their story, but no one believed them. Some had told it to everyone they possibly could, hoping that somewhere one—even one—person would listen. The more they talked about it, the more rejection came. It seemed that out of millions only a small number heard, and of that number only a very few would believe. Why would my report be any different? Why would someone listen to me—or believe me—as I gave the very same report?

There was no reason for them to believe. They expected a person of honor and of respect. Someone such as that they would believe. Why would they believe my report? I was not of such a line.

Initially I was unwanted by my parents since they were not married. In a way, an abortion was considered. As I grew up, my heart was touched by what was around me. I hurt for those that seemed to be hurting—holding their heads down, shoulders drooping—yet my situation was not easy at all either. At times it was unbearable, when I knew that I would be rejected and die. But deep inside of me and in my heart remained a tenderness that not even the toughest situation would be able to break.

There wasn't anything about me or going for me that would make someone want me or want to be with me, much less listen to me. I was not beautiful. My body was of an ugly form. People would turn away from me. I wore remade clothes. I was poor. I was laughed at by my peers and shunned by those older than myself.

I was despised. Kids around me rejected me. I know what it means to be hurt. I know what it means to have the heart so filled with pain that it seems you can endure no more, yet it continues. I know what it is like to have people turn and look the other way. I know what it is to have a life of sorrow and pain. I know what it is like—I know what it means to suffer, and suffer to the point of knowing not only that I am all alone—no one is with me who cares—but also that I will die. There is no one else to go to, and no one will listen. No one heard my cry for help and removed the hurt and pain that tears my insides apart and that makes me not care about my outside self either.

I know. I know because my father allowed such evil to happen in my life that I would understand you better. He said he loved me, but how could he when he allowed such awful things to happen to me? He allowed others to tear me to pieces, to whip my back, and to humiliate me. I was cut till my skin would bleed. I was crushed under the wrongdoing of other men. I was spat upon. I was cursed for who I was and was held responsible for all the things that happened. The punishment that others deserved fell on me. I was the one crushed, bruised, hurt. My heart was broken. My will to live died. My ability to see things clearly disappeared. But I had to live. I had to remain stable. I had to stand firm. I had to be someone. I went through everything—every imaginable thing there was. I suffered everything that you have suffered or will ever have to suffer. I know just what it is all about. I know what it means. I know the hurts in the deepest part of your heart. I know the pain of having nails being pounded into my body.

I know intensely and personally the rejection of those you love. I was hung on a cross, and it was only minutes until I would die. There was no question in my mind that God had turned his back on me. He forgot about me. He left me alone. He could have changed things around. They could have been different. I needed him. I called to him. But instead he left me to die. He forgot about me. He left me alone. At a time when I needed him the most, he turned around and looked the other way.

Now listen to me. I was hurt so that you would be able to come to me with your hurts. I was despised so that you could come to me when someone turns and hates you. I was abused so that I would understand you. I was abused so that I could love you. I was scourged so that I would know what it was like to be beaten. I had stakes pounded into my hands and feet and my side split open. I had a wreath of thorns that tore into my head. I knew you would have to go through what you did. I knew what it would mean. But I was there for you in a very special way. I went that route before you. You unfortunately had to follow in some of the same steps I had to step in. But I was there, and because of the pain and destruction that would be done to you, that is exactly why my life was as it was.

You may have given up, and I can't blame you. I would too. I knew the ultimate end of my situation—you don't. You don't have even the slightest idea of what is ahead of you in your life. You've run from me for almost two years. You're my little sheep. My little child. You've gone your way. I've been distressed for you. I suffered on the cross for you. I did not open my mouth to have it taken away because I knew you were forced to keep silent for so many years, and if I would have pleaded for mercy, I would have no answers to give to you. I was silent for you. God caused this to happen. I didn't understand, and it came to the point where I pleaded with God while I hung on the cross—why, why have you forsaken me? God's answer to me was this: "You must do this for _____."

I was cut off from everyone. It was God's will for me to be

crushed and caused to suffer. It was done for you and many others, but especially for you.

_____, after it is all over, there will be light—a new path for you—and you will be satisfied. By knowing me, you will be able to help many.

****

EXERCISE 2

The second exercise is done in order to help a client grapple with the truth about who she is. She is not who her history says she is. She is not who her abuser said she was. She is not what those who abandoned her suggested she was. She is not who her feelings say she is. All of these have worked together to give her powerfully emotional statements about her identity. Through my words and the relationship we have established, she has begun to hope that she is other than who she has believed herself to be. Although my words and responses to her can have great impact, they are not sufficient. The God who sees all, who knows about the abuse and her response to it, has made clear statements about who she is. She needs desperately to hear from him.

Again we go to the Scriptures. Again I have her work with what she finds there to help make it her own. So often survivors believe that what they read in Scripture is true, but somehow it is not true for them. They need to hear it over and over in ways that fight against the tendency to see themselves as the perpetual exception to all good things.

This time we go to the first chapter of the book of Ephesians. Once more I ask her to rewrite what she finds there. I have her begin with verse 4 and rewrite the passage through verse 14 as if the passage were written specifically to her: "For he chose *me*.... In love he predestined *me* to be adopted...." Again she sits before me and reads aloud those eternal truths, hearing in the presence of another that they are true for her as well. I often respond by reading to her, as if they were from me, verses 15 to 23. I have included one woman's writing as an example. She has incorporated truths from several Scripture passages.

What Is the Truth?
from the ends of the earth
from its farthest corners
Friend of Abraham
calls
strengthens
helps
and
upholds
you
you are His
the aroma of Christ
fragrant to God
you
are chosen
adopted
redeemed
forgiven
lavished with grace
and wisdom
and understanding
you
are purposed
included
sealed with a promise
God's possession
you
a fragrance of life
led
in triumphal procession
to
the praise
of
His Glory

Isaiah 41:8-10 Ephesians 1:4-14 2
Corinthians 2:14-16

Certainly neither of these exercises has instantaneous results, but there is power in them because they involve the eternal Word of God. Speaking the truth aloud in the presence of someone who knows all about their lives and still believes that these words are for them is a moment many men and women return to over and over. Time, repetition, and continued work in the therapeutic relationship are all necessary to the process of having these truths take root. However, as we return to them time after time, the light and life they bring become more apparent. These truths, rather than the lies instilled by survivors' histories, become the words that reverberate in their lives.

SHIFTING FROM PAST TO PRESENT

The process of speaking the unspeakable in relationship to another and watching as the past loses some of its power causes the focus of therapy to shift from the past to the present. Those things that are the characteristics of death—silence, isolation, and power-lessness—begin to fade, and the characteristics of life—voice, rela-tionship, and power—begin to emerge in the survivor's life.

Voice

As the survivor goes through the therapeutic process, she learns that speech is possible and that telling the truth does not destroy her. As one woman said, "When I was a kid, I was taught that nothing should be repeated out of the house. This was drummed into me at an early age, and I had never told anyone anything that happened at home. It was wrong to tell. Something awful would happen if I did. As a small child I learned it, and as an adult I had the constant fear that if anyone found out...even now I don't have the words to express the devastation that my mind imagined. Even as I write, I feel anxious."

Later on, this same woman, after first revealing an incident of sexual abuse (gang rape by her father and four of his friends), wrote the following: "That week I spent a lot of time trying to understand what had gone on in the counselor's office. I couldn't figure it out.

Why had she believed me? I had always been told that no one would believe me, even if I tried to tell. It didn't make sense. Also, my dad had always said he would know just by looking at me if I had told anyone and that he would kill me if I did. I was in the house with him all week, and he never knew I had told Diane. Could Diane be right? Was it possible that it wasn't my fault? If he had lied about the other things, maybe he had lied about that too." Such a moment as this is the rebirth of a long-dead hope. It is the birth of a voice that has been as silent as the dead.

The truth "I can speak" evolves out of such experiences being repeated again and again in the client's relationship to the therapist. To speak is to be a person. To speak means there is the possibility of being heard. To speak even includes the "unlikely" possibility of being believed! One result of this woman's telling her story was that she began to entertain the following prospect: "I had never thought about myself in the same way I thought about people. I began to think, 'She really thinks I am a person, like everyone else.' That probably sounds strange, but up to then I had always thought of myself as something less than a person—like trash, a slut, a whore, or the like—but never as a person! Being a person implied worth, and I had always been told that I was worthless. And I believed it. Now, someone whom I respect was implying that I wasn't worthless. I was a person. I wasn't sure what to do with that. It changed everything."

Having been created in the image of God who speaks, we too are meant to speak. One of the purposes of speaking is to speak truth, for we follow a God who is truth. The survivor enters a world full of new possibilities when she begins to speak and to speak truth. Often that truth is hideous and unimaginably painful. Many will say, "I can't look. Don't make me look!" And yet, with patient support and love, they learn to look. They learn to speak of what they see. They experience the belief of another, the comfort of another, and the hope for new life from another. You see, hideous evil and its consequences cannot be redeemed unless they are spoken about. As long as they lie hidden, they remain untouched by life. As the survivor learns to speak, she learns to say what she feels. She learns to express what she wants. She begins to offer thoughts and give opinions. She learns to voice disagreement with the lies. Carefully and slowly, she finds her way into that world where people interact with respect and grow from that interaction.

Relationship

Another outgrowth of the therapeutic process is that the survivor learns that relationship is possible. Not only is relationship possible, but it can actually be safe. Relationship was previously a vehicle for destruction and death. Now there is the hope that it can be a conveyor of life. Isolation was a core component of the abuse. Connection or relationship is a core component of recovery.

It is during this stage that the therapeutic relationship lessens somewhat in intensity. The crises of the previous stage become less and less likely. Certainly, memories still surface and need to be confronted. The phases of treatment are not discrete stages without overlap; however, the relationship shows signs of becoming more relaxed, spontaneous, and secure. The survivor is able to be more objective about herself, and humorous moments occur more frequently. The client's view of the therapist is less idealized and more realistic, which makes the relationship feel somewhat closer to the ordinary than previously. It is a shift that is enjoyed by therapist and client alike.

Having been created in the image of a God who is relational, the survivor begins to experience and enjoy this aspect of her person. Again, she is entering a world full of new possibilities. It is often at this stage that she begins to seek a deepening of her own relationship to God. She shifts from feeling threatened and afraid of him to wanting to know him and feel a sense of closeness to him. She is more willing to struggle and study on her own rather than simply doing so in the presence of the therapist.

The client's perspective on other relationships also seems to broaden. For some time, those relationships either have been put on hold or have functioned only insofar as others are able to be supportive during the upheaval of dealing with the past. Many people seem to fall by the wayside during the initial phase of treatment. Sometimes this is due to the client's pulling back and feeling unable to be with people. Other times it is because people do not understand what is going on or how to be helpful. Many would just like to see her "put it behind her."

The therapeutic relationship is a place where the survivor has known and been known, has loved and been loved. That relationship now serves as the basis for her to seek the same dynamic in other relationships. Initially this process requires a lot of discussion and interaction with the therapist, for most of her relational skills were learned in the context of abuse and neglect. Speaking up, learning to say no, handling conflict, not assuming everyone thinks about her the way her abuser did, asking questions, and learning how to recognize "safe" people are all skills the survivor will have to learn.

As she moves out into other relationships, the survivor will begin to see that what she assumed was inevitable is, in fact, not so. One woman wrote: "As time went on, I actually started to feel as if I was one of them, a real person. I noticed it one day when someone said something I knew wasn't right and I actually called him on it! I really surprised myself! I began to understand why Diane had wanted me to get away from my family. I realized that while I was in their house, I was constantly being torn down and spent most of my time trying to survive. There was no way I could grow where I was planted. That house would always be a place of death for me, a reminder of how bad or dirty I was. I needed to be somewhere that I wouldn't get pulled apart every time I made a mistake. I found I received acceptance from other people." (This was written by a woman in her twenties who was still being physically and sexually abused when she was at home.)

Slowly but surely, the survivor begins to widen her circle of safe people. When she began therapy, she lived isolated from others entirely or at least she kept her "true" self hidden. Through the relationship with the therapist, she is learning that the whole truth can be spoken and the whole person exposed, and yet she can still find safety and love in relationship. It is a place she was certain would never exist for her.

One of the arenas in which new relationships often begin to develop is within the church community. As far as I am concerned, this is the ideal place if the survivor is involved in a church community that has some grasp of the depth of her struggle and is able to come alongside in helpful ways. When a survivor is in a community that expects instant healing, that believes that if you speak a truth once or twice it should be "gotten," that is naive about the depth of the evil of sexual abuse, then that community fails to reflect the love and grace of God where it is so desperately needed. On the other hand, I have often seen women and men who love Christ and understand people give sacrificially to broken people over the long haul in ways that have greatly eased and probably shortened their struggle. If our God is a refuge for the needy and a shelter from the storm, then we who name his name should reflect his qualities. If our God understood that we needed him to come down to earth and live among us as someone with skin on, then how can we as his people offer less to those who have been robbed as children of that which he intended? The safest place in all the world ought to be the community of believers.

Created in the image of a God who is relational, the survivor is now opened up to the possibility of relationship. Rather than see relationships as simply something to be endured, relationship begins to be a place of hope, love, and joy. As time goes by and the survivor learns what relationship can give, she will then move toward becoming someone who gives those same qualities to others. With the therapist, she has found what she had lost. She has hope of growing in relationship to God and others. She desires to become for others what she did not experience as a child. It is once again a glorious unfolding of the process of redemption.

Power

In this middle phase of treatment, not only has the survivor found her voice and experienced relationship, but she is also coming to grips with the fact that she has power to have an impact. She is created in the image of a God who has left his mark on the world and his creatures. She was not meant to be invisible, ineffective, or helpless. She was meant to leave her mark as well!

One of the results of chronic abuse is a constriction of initiative and planning. The survivor has grown up in an environment that allowed no room for mistakes. In fact, she was often punished for things she did not do. She has learned to scan her surroundings before taking any initiative, looking for any hint of retaliation.

Chronic abuse also results in the abandonment of hope. The survivor has learned that to hope is to increase her pain. The letting go of hope produces a restricted kind of thinking. The ability to envision the future or the possibility of successful impact atrophies. Many survivors have been repeatedly forced to participate in acts that repulse them, so they begin to see themselves as able to have an impact on others only in evil ways. The shutdown of any capacity to affect others seems like the best option.

Many years ago I had a client who became terrified when she realized I cared about her. Before that time, she had in her life three people who had been caring: an uncle who died, a friend who died, and a neighbor who died. She perceived herself as a lethal phenomenon. If she had any impact on others, it was fatal to them. My care for her, desperately needed and longed for, was also terrifying because she was sure that it would result in my death. Impact was not a desirable quality. It was much better to be invisible, absent, and ineffective.

Often the survivor's perception of herself as helpless and insignificant is furthered as she moves through adulthood. It is common for a survivor to end up in relationships with a dynamic similar to that with which she grew up. She may be involved in short-lived, unsatisfying relationships that leave her feeling as if she doesn't matter, as if she is easily tossed aside and forgotten. She may find herself in a marriage with someone who batters her, is abusive in some other way, or seems unable to give her or her needs any significance. Some survivors feel utterly helpless and without power because they live daily with ongoing self-injury, a behavior they find shaming and yet are unable to stop. As one woman put it, "I can't even protect me from myself."

The phenomenon of repeated victimization seems to be a rather common occurrence in the lives of women who have suffered chronic childhood abuse. It is often tolerated passively as something they cannot avoid no matter how much they hate it. Often, they believe that the alternative is no relationship or touch at all. The concept of saying no and having it matter to someone is utterly foreign.

Another loss that makes the concept of impact so difficult to conceive is the death of vision. When hope is lost, so is the possibility of a future. Hope brings an intolerable yearning, so it is better dispensed with. In her book *Trauma and Recovery,* Judith Herman quotes a survivor of the Nazi death camps as saying, "In the month of August, 1944, we who had entered the camp five months before now counted among the old ones.... Our wisdom lay in 'not trying to understand,' not imagining the future, not tormenting ourselves as to how and when it would all be over, not asking others or ourselves any questions.... For living men, the units of time always have a value. For us, history had stopped."[1]

The concept of a vision for the future is very difficult for the survivor to grasp. What is, will always be. She cannot remember a time when she did not suffer. She cannot remember a time when what she thought and felt truly mattered. How can she possibly envision a future where she is significant and can have an impact for good? Hope of that possibility arises out of her relationship to the therapist, who has listened and to whom she has mattered. It also grows out of the therapist's hope for her. Many survivors have said to me that one of the greatest gifts I have given them was a steady hope when they had none. I was full of hope that their suffering would ease in time and that their person and gifts would be helpful to others. Many will ask, "What do you think I can do/offer?" "Do you really think I have that ability/gift?"

Our God is a God of hope and power. He entered into our suffering in order to impart that hope and power to us. As we also enter into the suffering of others—listening, loving, and allowing ourselves to be affected—we become vehicles of the hope and power of God to others. It is a marvelous thing to allow God to use us in the working out of his redemption in the life of another. It is never without awe at the work of God that I hear a survivor say, "I was silent, but now I can speak. I was alone, but now I am known and loved. I was helpless, but now I matter." Not only do I hear her, know and love her, and treat her as significant, but she is coming to believe with confidence that God hears her, knows and loves her, and has given her power to have an impact for his glory. It is a hard-won and wonderful beginning!

15

Major Issues of Phase Two

The main work of the second phase of treatment involves three issues: grief, confrontation of the abuser, and forgiveness. None of these is possible until the work of phase one is well under way. Survivors cannot grieve unless they acknowledge loss. They cannot decide about confrontation unless they can name the perpetrator. They cannot forgive what they do not name as wrong and evil. They cannot enter into these areas until they have discovered that they have a voice, can have impact, and have a safe harbor. With rare exception, it is my experience that these issues arise of their own accord when survivors have done the work of the initial phase. Sometimes they will come up prematurely, and it is crucial that therapists help clients see why time needs to pass. Some will want to "forgive" so they do not have to grieve. Some will want to confront because they want their memories confirmed or because they want to just "put it all behind" them.

GRIEF

As the survivor works with you to face the history she has long tried to avoid, she will find herself repeatedly confronted with loss. Telling her story aloud in the presence of another often makes the reality of the horrors seem greater. It is not unusual for a survivor to stall over relating an incident of abuse because, "If I say it out loud, then it will be real." Many survivors have worked hard to alter reality in their minds so they can pretend the abuse did not happen. Therapy always involves juggling the survivor's need to face what has happened and her need to feel safe. To tell is to feel unsafe. To remain silent is to be stuck and alone.

Facing trauma or abuse in one's life always involves confronting loss. Therapists who work extensively with survivors experience grief and loss. If that is the case for those who listen, what must it be for those who endured? After one experience of rape, life becomes a different color. The world feels unsafe. People are dangerous. Isolation sets in. It seems as if nothing will ever be the same, and in fact, that is so. If one trauma in the life of an adult can have such profound effects, what must it be like for those who were repeatedly abused as children?

The process of grieving is inevitably dreaded. Clients fear they will get lost in their grief and never come out. Many will say, "I am terrified to start crying. I don't think I will ever stop." Many survivors say they do not know how to cry. Crying was severely punished, so they have spent years stifling it. When tears rise up, their anxiety goes off the charts, and out of fear they shut themselves down. When the first tear is finally allowed to trickle down, it is a moment of terror and a moment of triumph.

Grieving is also thwarted by the survivor's adeptness at minimization. She has coped with massive losses by whittling them down to a manageable size. So no one ever touched her with love, so her body was not her own, so she was forced to engage in acts that repulsed her and that she believed were wrong. "No big deal." She managed, didn't she? What is all the fuss about? It is often hard for her to grasp the fact that she managed because her survival depended on it, not because it was a measure of the losses endured.

What are some of the losses that a survivor might have to grieve? She lost the opportunity to be a child, the knowledge that her parents loved her no matter what, a sense of safety in her own body, a sense of competence, a sense of moral integrity. All these losses need to be grieved.

A client recently listed some of her losses for me: "Knowing someone wants to hear your thoughts, being able to go to bed and not shake, having privacy in the bathroom, someone who said 'I love you,' hugs when I cried, being able to learn nursery rhymes before my own children did, having a clean mind while I was a child, not to feel like a slut, a feeling of safety, having a true mommy and daddy (some days I still want one), tenderness, not to have honesty seem like a death sentence, having a sense of hope, knowing what joy felt like, having someone to trust, having someone pick me up gently just once." Her comment at the end of her list was: "A kid like this should have died. It would have been easier and more kind."

Many survivors must do the terrible grieving over the loss of their own children: stillbirths because of no prenatal care, forced abortions (sometimes performed at home), babies taken from them at birth with no knowledge of their whereabouts. Years ago, a woman in her sixties sobbed in my office over the loss of a child she had never spoken about before. She had been raped by her father many times and eventually became pregnant. He flew her out of the country to get her an abortion. She had carried the weight of that knowledge and loss in silence all of her life. For many of these women, the loss of children means that every holiday and everyone else's pregnancy become a sword that goes deep into their heart. Such things remind them of what they had yet really never had. No gravestone, no memorial, no pictures...nothing. One client made the journey back home to ask her stepfather where he had buried his and her stillborn child years ago. She returned to me with a picture of the corner of the inside of their barn. He had silently walked her out there and pointed. That picture was all she had (and yet it is more than many others have).

Such grieving as this is a passing through the valley of the shadow of death. Many clients fear there is no end to this valley. They often ask how long they must endure such pain. The answer is most unhelpful: As long as it takes. The stories will be, indeed must be, repeated over and over. That is how we all grieve. We talk about our loss; we take out our memories and turn them over many times until somehow we find a way to wear the unwearable. We retell the story until we find a way to live with what was but will never be again.

Such grieving as this is a long, painful, dark process. Your steady presence will be necessary. Your hope may be all that she has to hold onto. I often suggest to my clients that they "piggyback" on my hope. They have none; mine will carry us both. It is similar to a small child whose little legs simply cannot carry her any farther. The loving response is to bend down and lift her up so that your legs may carry the both of you for a while.

Suicidal threats that were perhaps prevalent in the early stages and have been absent for some time may return during the grieving process. Hope is a new thing for the survivor. What little has grown up within her during the course of therapy is usually not strong enough to carry the weight of her grief. She feels that the only way she can stop the pain is to die. It is not that she really wants to die. It is simply that, awake or asleep, she is overwhelmed by her grief. The pain she truly could not endure as a child, she can barely weather now. She could not do so at all had she not learned to trust your voice and believe your hope. Remind her again and again, without minimizing the depth of her pain, that there is hope, that the valley does not go on forever, that she will emerge in a new place, free from the specter of her great grief finally catching up with her.

In this place of grief, you are the representative of the God who has come "to bind up the brokenhearted...to comfort all who mourn, and provide for those who grieve...to bestow on them a crown of beauty instead of ashes, the oil of gladness instead of mourning, and a garment of praise instead of a spirit of despair.... [He] will rebuild the ancient ruins and restore the places long devastated; [he] will renew the ruined cities that have been devastated for generations.... Instead of their shame my people will receive a double portion, and instead of disgrace they will rejoice in their inheritance; and so they will inherit a double portion in their land, and everlasting joy will be theirs" (Isa. 61:1-7). Represent him well.

CONFRONTATIONS

Sometime during the course of therapy many clients express

a need or desire to confront their abuser and/or those who did not protect them; clients wish to do this with the help of and sometimes in the presence of the therapist. The desire to confront is both resisted and feared. A great deal of ambivalence surrounds such thoughts, and they require careful consideration.

It is absolutely crucial to note that the desire for such a confrontation comes from the client, not the therapist! Such a confrontation is not to be based on the need or beliefs of the therapist. No therapist should insist that it is a necessary part of healing. I certainly have not made a rule that all survivors need to do this. For some, it seems a necessary part of their growth. They feel that maintaining silence continues the feeling that somehow the incest is unreal or "made up." It feels to them as if they are continuing to support a lie, pretending that something horrific never happened. Some make the decision because of their realistic concern that their abuser is now abusing a sibling or niece or nephew. To choose silence is to be like the nonprotecting parent.

Several years ago I received a phone call from someone in another state. She had been seeing a counselor who was insisting that she confront her mother and grandmother about the abuse she experienced from her grandfather. She had told him she did not want to do so and was terrified to do so; the counselor's response had been that if she did not confront, he would not continue seeing her and she could not progress in her growth. He felt he could do nothing more for her unless she did as he said. It is very clear here that the counselor was repeating one of the dynamics of abuse. He was failing to give his client any choice in the matter and threatening to abandon her should she fail to do as she was told. My question about such an interaction is, Who is really the one with unresolved family issues? It is grossly presumptuous to assume that as therapists we have the right to determine whether or not our clients should confront those who have proved so dangerous to them, and may indeed continue to be.

It is my experience that even survivors whose perpetrators have died will at some point need to wrestle with questions such as "Would I confront him if he were alive?" "Should I tell others in the family?" and "How can I handle the anger I feel because he is not around to confront?" It is crucial to remember that, regardless of circumstances, this is an area almost all survivors will want to wrestle through, and it is equally important to know that ultimately the choice about what to do is theirs. After all, it is they, not the therapist, who will have to live with the consequences of that choice!

Sometimes after working hard and long to express the truth *about* her life, a survivor will choose to then speak the truth *into* the family and/or situation in which the abuse took place. If this confrontation is to take place, there is much work to be done. It should *never* be handled impulsively or superficially. The client's choices should be respected at all times. If at some point she chooses to change her course, honor that choice. Certainly be honest regarding your thinking about what she is doing, but never forget that this is *her* life, not yours, and therefore *her* choice, not yours.

Four Principles Governing Any Confrontation

If the awesome task of confrontation is to take place wisely and well, what are the principles that need to guide such work to ensure that it is handled in the best way possible? I would like to suggest four principles that I believe ought to govern any confrontation, and then consider three practical matters necessary in assisting your client through this process in a constructive way.

1. Every confrontation should be governed by a purpose. It is vital for you and your client to be clear together about what the purpose of such a meeting is. It would be very destructive if you entered into the confrontation at cross-purposes. God's parameters are to mold our purpose. One of those parameters is given to us in 1 Peter 3:9: "Do not repay evil with evil or insult with insult, but with blessing, because to this you were called so that you may inherit a blessing." It is human nature to return in kind what we have received from others. We can return evil with evil in two ways. One is simply to seek revenge or find some way to hurt those who have hurt us. A second way is to fail to speak the truth about what was done. To minimize evil and abuse, to pretend or enter into deceit, is to do evil to another. So on the one hand, a confrontation is not about getting even, and on the other hand, a confrontation is not about denial and pretense.

The purpose of a confrontation is not to destroy a family or verbally beat up on a perpetrator. At all times both you and your client are responsible for how you treat those involved in the confrontation. God's standard for all communication is that we speak the truth in love, and this kind of confrontation is no exception to that. It is extremely difficult to speak the truth of incest. No one wants to hear it, least of all the family in which it occurred. To name it is to crash through an almost impenetrable barrier that family members have colluded to erect. However, to confront evil and abuse in a manner that does not taste of revenge is no less difficult.

Peter says that when we are the victims of another's evil we are to respond in a way that blesses them. *Anything* that fails to reflect the character of God in Christ is not a blessing. Revenge, hateful words, attacks, and insults will not bless. Denial, pretense, excuses, and a failure to call evil by its right name will also fail to bless. Either of these extremes, so common to us all, means that we are reflecting the abuser and/or the nonprotector rather than the person of Christ. Either of these responses also means that evil will have triumphed, for we will have been in some fashion molded into its image. Either of these reactions will mean that we have been shaped into the image of the evil one, who hates and lies, rather than the image of the Redeemer, who speaks truth without revenge and brings blessing as a result.

2. Every confrontation should be done with care. That would seem obvious, given the great difficulty of maintaining the above stance. The care that should undergird any confrontation of evil is made clear in Deuteronomy 13:12-15: "If you hear it said...that wicked men have arisen among you and have led the people of their town astray, saying, 'Let us go and worship other gods,'...then you must inquire, probe and investigate it thoroughly. And if it is true and it has been proved that this detestable thing has been done...you must certainly put to the sword all who live in that town." Truly, in the case of chronic sexual abuse of children, wicked men have led them away from the worship of God. When we learn of such a thing, we are to "inquire, probe and investigate." An accusation of sexual abuse is incredibly serious. To confront anyone about evil in their lives is never something we should do lightly. Confronting someone regarding something so heinous as the sexual abuse of a child must be done with great care.

In saying that confrontation must be governed by care, I am not suggesting that it is the job of the therapist to prove the truth of a client's memories. Although I find that such memories can frequently be validated by the testimony of others or by other records, the therapist is not to play detective. You are not investigating a crime, although indeed one has been committed. The therapist's job is in part to help the client face and respond to the evil done to her in such a way as to always hold her to the highest standard. Just as we must never minimize the evil of sexual abuse, so we must never minimize the seriousness of an accusation of same. Some survivors have been led away from the truth of God by those who were to teach them truth. Jesus said those who do such a thing are better off dead. Wisdom dictates that the laying of such a charge at the feet of another be done with great care.

I have seen disastrous results from emotionally charged, premature confrontations. Once an accusation is spoken, it can never be retrieved. It is my policy to discourage such confrontations unless truth has been credibly demonstrated and the client's recovery is in its final stages.

This carefulness is as much for the sake of your client as it is for anyone else. To speak the truth of sexual abuse into a family is to blow it up. What was can never be again. Either the family will be thrown into utter chaos as they strive to face such a detestable truth, or your client will be immediately orphaned because family members simply refuse to hear such a truth. The purpose, timing, and manner in which such a confrontation is handled deserve a great deal of searching out and care. To fail to be careful as a therapist or to fail to encourage carefulness in your client is a failure of both safety and truth. By your lack of care, you will have failed in assisting your client to protect herself from a potentially damaging or even violent situation, and you will have failed to speak the truth regarding the seriousness of the matter and its possible outcomes.

3. Every confrontation requires maturity. The writer to the Hebrews says, "But solid food is for the mature, who by constant use [or because of practice] have trained themselves to distinguish good from evil" (Heb. 5:14). According to this verse, one of the distinguishing marks of maturity is the ability to discern good and evil. One of the most profound consequences of chronic sexual abuse is the confusion of good and evil. Fathers say that what they are doing is "good for their little girls." Children are told that the evil within them has caused the abuse. They are told that they "made" the perpetrator do it. Many are told that God sanctions the abuse. Not only do such lies run deep, but the place where they are the most difficult to discern as lies is in the presence of the perpetrator. Many survivors who have learned to speak clearly the truth about their abuse revert quickly to confusion and uncertainty when faced with the perpetrator. It is a relationship in which they have experienced profound powerlessness, and to reenter that relationship with a strong voice that names evil by its right name requires much hard work.

One of the tasks that parents perform for their children is helping them name the things in their world. Children point to a flower, a door, or a dog, and the parent tells them the right label for it. Parents also label things that are far less tangible, such as truth, lies, love, hate, good, and evil. Suppose a child grew up relatively isolated and in a home where the parents persistently taught her that the sky was green. Entrance into the larger world and hearing others say that the sky was blue would throw the child into utter confusion. Not only would she have to relearn what is blue and what is green, constantly testing the testimony of others in the process, but her entire relationship with her parents would have to be redefined once she discovered she had actually been taught a lie. How much greater the difficulty of discerning good and evil when one has been taught lies about oneself!

One of the things the verse in Hebrews tells us is that the maturity that enables us to discern is arrived at by practice. We are trained to distinguish good from evil through repetition and constant use that occurs over time. What a grave injustice we do to our clients if we think that we can simply speak the truth to them and then expect them to "get it." They have been trained all during their developmental years to call evil good. A few words from us or even from God himself will not turn that around. The mature discernment will come over time and with many, many tellings. To encourage a client to confront her perpetrator prematurely is to set her among wolves. One of the ways we care for our client and strengthen her in the truth is by understanding her great need for maturity before she seeks to confront the lies that surrounded her and by patiently nurturing her newfound ability to discern good and evil.

4. Every confrontation must be governed by truth. The apostle Paul talks about the confrontation of those who are immoral. He says not to let such people "deceive you with empty words.... Do not be partners with them" (Eph. 5:6-7). Again, the need for the discernment that comes with maturity is made clear. Otherwise, how easy it is to be deceived and partner with the perpetrator by allowing his definitions to determine truth. Paul goes on to say, "For you were once darkness, but now you are light in the Lord. Live as children of light (for the fruit of the light consists in all goodness, righteousness and truth) and find out what pleases the Lord. Have nothing to do with the fruitless deeds of darkness, but rather expose them.... Everything exposed by the light becomes visible, for it is light that makes everything visible" (Eph. 5:8-14).

Our God is a God of truth. Jesus himself is the embodiment of that truth. The enemy of our souls is the deceiver, the father of lies, and Jesus said that "there is no truth in him" (John 8:44). To lie, pretend, fudge, minimize, or deny the truth is to live as children of darkness. We are not only to have nothing to do with anything that is of the darkness, but we are also called to expose it.

When we looked at the verses in Deuteronomy 13 that called us to probe and investigate thoroughly when we hear about a detestable thing leading others away from the worship of God, we also read that when such a thing is shown to be true, all those in the town are to be "put to the sword" (Deut. 13:15). In the situation of abuse, we are talking about a family rather than a town. We are also, I think, called to wield a different sword—that of the Word of God. It is a living and active sword. "Sharper than any double-edged sword, it penetrates even to dividing soul and spirit, joints and marrow; it judges the thoughts and attitudes of the heart" (Heb. 4:12). Such a sword, wielded wisely and carefully, goes into a family long practiced in the art of deceit, a family that has dressed wounds lightly, as if they were not serious, saying "_'Peace, peace'...when there is no peace" (Jer. 6:14), and illuminates what has been hidden, speaking the truth of God into the darkness. Many people say that family confrontations are not good because they are simply about blame. The purpose of the confrontation I have described is not blame but exposure. If I cheat you out of some money and try to pretend it isn't so, for you to speak the truth about my wrongdoing is to expose what is of the darkness and call it by its right name. The God of truth would have us call evil, evil. When we fail to do so, we fail to reflect his character accurately.

Proverbs 12:17 says, "A truthful witness gives honest testimony, but a false witness tells lies." We can tell a lie by saying someone did something when in fact they did not. We can tell a lie by exaggerating the wrongdoing of another. We can also tell a lie by saying something did not occur when in fact it did. We can do that in words, and we can do that by our silence. We can also tell a lie by saying something was little when in fact it was big. In any of the above situations, we are a false witness.

One of the greatest gifts of truth telling is that it offers someone the opportunity to move into the light and out of the darkness. By offering others such an opportunity, we are blessing them. It is only as we walk in the light that we find freedom. It is only as we step into truth that we have hope of redemption. Freedom from the lies and darkness can never happen unless we call such things by their right name. There is no hope of redemption until we see and name the evil in need of redemption. Extending to others the invitation to join us in the light does not in any way ensure that they will choose to do so. However, having given such an invitation, we have not returned evil for evil, but we have given blessing instead. Although our grief and sadness over their lack of response may be great indeed, we will at least know with certainty that we have pleased our Redeemer. It is a privilege to assist a client through such steps, for in doing so, we have truly loved her and held her to that which is highest—the standard of God himself.

Practical Ways to Prepare for a Confrontation

Having wrestled through the principles that should govern any confrontation, several practical areas need to be considered if you are to prepare your client for this very difficult part of her therapy. You will need to help her establish realistic goals, confront her fairy-tale endings and expectations, and then assist her in deciding how to contact the family and how to conduct the sessions.

1. Establish realistic goals. In working to establish goals for such a meeting, I often find it helpful to start with the ideal. With what would you walk away from this meeting if all your hopes were realized? One reason I find this helpful is that I have learned through hard experience that many clients try to articulate realistic goals because they sound more reasonable or because it is an attempt to control their hope. However, they end up not being honest with themselves, and the goals about which they have been silent are still very much alive and well on the inside; the result is that they have actually gone into the meeting with unnamed idealistic goals and no opportunity to adjust them in light of what they know to be true about their family.

Usually when clients truly put their hope into words, they express a desire for a full disclosure of the truth, an awareness by the family about the aftereffects of the incest, an acknowledgment of guilt with a true apology, and reconciliation. In essence, they long as adults for what they lost hope for as a child—a family that lives out truth and loves them unconditionally. Such goals may indeed be possible in some circumstances. Certainly our God is able to bring them about. However, God's ability is not in question. What will influence the degree to which such goals can be achieved is an assessment of a particular client's family and what is known about their previous responses to difficult issues, how they typically handle conflict, the status of the client's current relationship with the family, the strength of various members, whether or not other siblings are also speaking up, the degree of spiritual blindness in the family, and the extent of their general denial about other issues.

2. Confront fairy-tale expectations. As your client works to articulate her goals for the confrontation, part of your job will be to find the balance between crushing her hope for change and helping her to be realistic, given the dynamics of her particular family. Clients will tend to err on the side of hope (i.e., we will all live happily ever after) or on the side of despair (i.e., doing this will have no impact on anybody, including me, so what's the use?). On the one hand, you will best prepare her by reminding her of the truths you both know about her family and what is likely to happen based on that knowledge. On the other hand, you will need to remind her that even if her family walks away deaf, dumb, and blind, she herself will not. Such a confrontation, rightly done, will strengthen her and mature her and therefore will never be wasted, even if she is left saddened and grieved by their response.

Part of the process of helping your client articulate her idealistic goals and then setting realistic ones involves assessing the level of danger or the probability that the family members will react strongly. Ongoing substance abuse, a history of violence, or a history of suicidal or homicidal threats are all serious contraindications to a family confrontation. Particularly when violence is a threat, the usual outcome is to break off contact with the family because of the level of danger.

3. Plan the confrontation session. Many questions must be answered before proceeding to the actual meeting. Who will call the family and ask them to come? Which members will be asked? Where will the meeting be held? Assuming it is at the therapist's office, at what time will your client and her family arrive? Does the client want to arrive early and/or stay late to debrief with you? Usually she does. Does she need to come in by a different door? What should the seating arrangement look like? Often she will want to make certain you are in her view. Who will begin the meeting? Who will decide when it should end if things get out of hand? How will such a problem be handled? Role-playing is often very helpful at this juncture. Throughout all such decision making, the client's wishes need to be honored as much as possible.

Case Study

Many years ago I worked with a woman whose grandfather had repeatedly abused her over the course of about twelve years. He had since died. She knew that her grandmother, who was also dead, was aware of the abuse because she had walked in on them on several occasions. The grandmother's basic response had been, "Now so-and-so, you know you shouldn't do that." She would then turn and walk out. My client believed that both her parents were ignorant of the abuse and that her grandmother had never told them what she had seen. Her grandmother had also never made mention of it to her. Very close to the end of my client's therapy with me, she decided that she wanted to tell her parents about what had happened and how her life had been impacted.

One of the issues we had worked on together was my client's growing awareness that her parents were good at responding to crises but were not nurturing or responsive for the long haul. She had recalled many times in which something critical had happened when she was growing up, and her parents had responded quickly. However, when a problem continued or when my client's emotional response to it lingered, she was often greeted with impatience and condemnation. As we talked about the possibility of telling her parents about her grandfather, I pointed out to her that she was likely to get a good response initially but that over time the old pattern would be likely to set in. My client decided she wanted to tell her parents for two reasons: first, she felt that a major piece of her life was hidden from them, and she wanted them to know her more fully; and second, she felt she had grown enough that should their response alter after the initial telling, she was strong enough to be open about that with them.

We spent many weeks preparing for her parents to come to my office. She decided what she wanted to say and how she would explain why she wanted them to know after so many years of silence. She felt it wise to write out what she needed to communicate. She called her parents and asked them if they would meet with her at my office. She asked them to honor her request to wait until they got to the office to hear why. They came willingly.

My client chose to arrive early and meet with me for about fifteen minutes first. She then chose to escort her parents into the office. She arranged the chairs so that she could see both of her parents and yet still have eye contact with me. She basically asked me to sit quietly while she read to her parents what she had written and then interacted with them. She wanted me to intervene only if they hit a "stuck" place or had questions she could not answer. I had encouraged her to express clearly to her parents why she was telling them about the abuse and what she hoped would happen in their relationship together as a result.

Her father was furious with his father (the abuser). He had a sister whose life had been full of problems, and he wondered aloud if his father had abused his sister as well. My client's mother was shocked and teary. She was very upset that she had not known ("I didn't know. I didn't know.") and required some help from me in understanding why her daughter had not told her while it was going on. My client was very clear with her parents about what she needed from them. She was also very compassionate toward them and verbalized concern over their need to process such upsetting and surprising information. At her initiative, we agreed to meet together again in a couple of weeks.

Several things resulted from this confrontation. My client gained a sense of strength and boldness in speaking out about difficult things. This enabled her to pursue her mother when she found her beginning to withdraw. She was able to express her desire for her mother to stay open to her. After several meetings together, my client's father decided to ask his sister whether or not their father had abused her. The answer was yes, and he found himself able to encourage her to get the help she needed. Doing so seemed to ease his terrible pain that he had not known about his own daughter.

****

Let me give you a more common scenario regarding a family confrontation. These are a client's comments about her own family situation:

> I chose to disclose the abuse to my abuser and my family. I felt very strongly that I needed to do this, though I would not have done it without a strong support group of women and my counselor. The

impact on my family was traumatic. They went through various stages of shock, denial, anger, and blaming me. It was a difficult process. My brother, who was my abuser, totally denies everything, claiming he does not remember. Fortunately for me, I have another brother who remembers the events. This brother walked through the trauma and splintering of my family unit with me. He gave me sanity and dignity many times. The brother who abused me does not speak to any of us. This silence has been going on for four years. Today my family is still split down the middle. My sister is close to my brother, the abuser, and still struggles with me. I have been blamed for much of our family problems now. But I have communicated with my parents in a way I never thought I could. I have realized that they were not capable of supporting me in the way I longed for. I am coming to accept them where they are and love them anyway. It can still be very painful at times and seems to be a lifelong grieving process I will go through. There is, however, much healing inside me, and I am far more realistic about what my family can give to me.

Few situations have a clear-cut beginning and end. Many families find themselves engaged in a long and painful process, as individuals struggle with what has been disclosed and make choices about how they will respond to that disclosure. Many clients find themselves grieving deeply over the fact that their family is far less able to love and support them than they had hoped. The struggle to accept that reality without bitterness is a difficult one.

The Therapist's Role in a Confrontation

In addition to directing the meeting, the therapist's role throughout this process is to support the client and to model to both the client and her family how to confront and interact. Sessions such as these require confidence and assertiveness. They may require saying such things as, "Stop negating your daughter like that," "You need to listen to what your daughter is saying rather than simply focusing on your own feelings," "I will not allow you to demean your daughter that way as long as you are in my office." Responses such as these greatly assist your client in her own growth whether or not the family responds positively. For many survivors it is the first time they have heard themselves valued in front of their family members. Many have never heard another person work to keep them feeling protected in a frightening situation with their family. Such responses also model for your client ways of asserting herself with her family without curling up, slinking away, letting go of truth, or belittling in return.

One technique that is quite simple but often very effective with clients as they walk through a family confrontation is to suggest that they write on a piece of paper something that would encourage them in their task or help keep them on course or remind them of what is true. If at any point during the meeting they feel frightened or overwhelmed or as if they are losing perspective, they can put their hand into their pocket and remember what is there. Many clients will use a Scripture verse, some a statement that reminds them that I am there with them, or a simple statement of a hard-won truth. It is not unusual during such a meeting to watch a client's hand disappear momentarily into a pocket, followed by a straightening of the shoulders and a deep breath.

A final matter in conducting such sessions involves drawing up a definite plan for how the family should proceed if indeed the meeting results in some glimmer of hope regarding an acknowledgment of the truth and possible reconciliation. As wrong as it would be to fail to nurture such a possibility, it would be equally wrong to let the words *I'm sorry* immediately eradicate years of suffering, lies, and abuse. Reparative work needs to follow an apology. Repentance is verbal, certainly, but it is far more than that. Repentance is a transformation from the inside out, demonstrated over time. Scripture takes sin seriously, not lightly. Repentance from sin is seen as a change in words, yes, but also in attitude and behavior, indeed in the whole person. For us to do less is to cheapen what God has named radically expensive, for it cost the death of his Son. If either the perpetrator or the silent parent says "I'm sorry," your response might be, "I am so glad to hear you say that to your daughter. Now let's begin to talk about how you might demonstrate that to her." At least to some degree, your client should have a very active part in articulating what needs to be done to demonstrate the reality of a professed apology. Again and again, through varied writers and in many ways, Scripture expresses the truth, "Dear children, let us not love with words or tongue but with actions and in truth" (1 John 3:18). Those who would suggest that the words *I'm sorry* should be sufficient and who then put the burden of making the relationship good on the survivor deny the truth of these words. If I have stolen money from you repeatedly and then come and apologize, the truth of my words will be tested over time as I demonstrate to you that I will no longer steal your money and that I will make every effort to restore what I have destroyed. God says words are not enough. We dare not say otherwise.

FORGIVENESS

Sometime during the course of treatment, the issue of forgiveness inevitably arises for the survivor. Forgiveness is an incredibly difficult issue for two reasons. Many people have all sorts of strange notions about what forgiveness is or is not, and most of those notions seem to have nothing to do with the truths of Scripture. On top of that, humanly speaking, your client will probably find that the thought of forgiving her abuser for repeated, often sadistic, sexual abuse seems impossible, if not actually outrageous. It is a crucial area requiring very careful handling.

What I have to say about forgiveness arises out of personal study, personal experience, and many years of work alongside those who have had much to forgive. The following thoughts are by no means the last word on the subject (or even my last words, for that matter). Perhaps we could see them as thoughts in process, presented by one who is very willing to have them altered and clarified by the one who has forgiven us at unimaginable cost.

dangerous thing to deal with, for it alone has the capacity to separate us from God. It then follows that there is no such thing as a "little" sin, for no attack on God can be defined as "little." However, it also means that to put a child in the position of repeatedly experiencing that which attacks God himself is to hammer her with those things characteristic of Satan himself. That the impact of such an experience should be so devastating is far from surprising when you consider that a developing, vulnerable child is repeatedly suffering the lust, death, and deceit characteristic of the father of lies. It is an astounding testimony to the redemptive power of Christ that a life so battered by evil could be restored to where it reflects the beauty of Christ himself!

What is to be our response to such a heinous attack against the person of God himself? First, if we truly understand the serious nature of sin, we will never take any sin, our own or another's, lightly. We have already stated that this means we will not mislabel sin, excuse sin, pretend about sin, or deny sin wherever we find it. I think that also means we will not be naive about the impact of sin on the life of the one sinned against. When we push others to "just forgive," as if somehow it was something that could be done quickly or easily, without a consideration of the consequences of that sin, we have adopted a superficial view of sin. If sin is truly as serious as we have said, then we will not only be eager to confess our own but we will also be very tender and loving toward those who have been hammered by the sins of another.

Second, if we acknowledge that sin is fundamentally an offense against God and that our primary purpose is to bring glory to him, then we will long to have our response to sin protect his name, not our feelings. On the one hand, that means that we will not allow our desire for comfort to lead us to pretend about sin, deny sin, excuse sin, or take sin lightly. It also means that we will be on guard regarding our own hearts, for we will not want our own responses to the sins of others to in turn mar God's name. Inward attitudes such as malice, hate, or revenge result in spreading more of the same poison that was spilled out by the perpetrator. Any role we have in the restoration process will be governed at all points by the desire to bring glory to God. Our heart attitudes will honor his name. We will buy truth and not sell it at any price. Our words and actions toward others—both sinner and sinned against—will glorify him. Our definitions of sin, repentance, and forgiveness will be governed by his Word and his character so that neither his holiness nor his great love are ever compromised by our handling of the matter. To forgive another or to engage in the process of helping someone wrestle with his or her need to forgive is indeed a sobering task with consequences far beyond what we can see.

Recognizing that forgiveness is about sin and keeping before us what sin actually is, we need, then, to consider three questions: What do we mean when we speak of forgiveness? What does forgiveness look like practically? What is the purpose of forgiveness?

What Do We Mean When We Speak of Forgiveness?

To forgive means to lay aside, let go, put away, yield up, pardon. Inherent in its meaning is the realization that something awful has been done; otherwise, there would be nothing to lay aside or pardon. Forgiveness is founded not on denial or minimization but on truth. Forgiving a debt first requires accounting what is owed. The process of forgiveness begins with the truth about the sin and its consequences. God's forgiveness began with an accounting of what we owed—we owed our lives. The Cross is certainly the place of forgiveness; it is also the place of accounting.

To speak of forgiveness is also to enter the realm of the supernatural. Forgiveness is the work of God. No therapist can bring about forgiveness in the heart of a client. It is God alone who begets in us a forgiving disposition. Simply to tell people that they need to forgive and then somehow expect them to say, "Oh, all right," is to fail to recognize the source of forgiveness. That God has wrought in us the ability to forgive another is one of the evidences that we have come to understand God's forgiveness of us. I often find this entire concept to be utterly foreign to survivors, for to forgive is to release, to refuse to demand payment. That is very difficult to comprehend when they have grown up having to pay even when they owed nothing and when they were cruelly punished for the most minor offenses or for no offense at all.

It has been my experience in my work with survivors that rather than simply telling them they need to forgive—a statement that often overwhelms them with despair—it is much more helpful to teach them, as they are ready, about the work of God in Christ on the cross. It was on the cross that God took what was intended to dishonor him and caused it instead to bring honor to his name. Over time, clients see evidence of that work in their own lives and recognize that God has taken those things in their lives that were intended to dishonor him, whether their own sins or those committed against them, and instead caused them to bring honor to himself. The recognition of that wonderful redemption almost always results in a hunger to be like the one who has loved them so faithfully. It is that hunger, born of the work of God in their lives, that leads them to ask me, "How can I forgive my abuser?"

I continue to take the client who asks such a question to the Cross, for it is there that we see forgiveness perfectly demonstrated. I ask them what they see as they study. They see that forgiveness does not compromise the holiness of God. It does not deny truth. It is costly beyond words. It is offered and waits for a response. When forgiveness is received, it brings forth life in place of death. They begin to understand that the purpose of offering forgiveness to another is to invite a sinner to repentance. The truth is spoken about the sin, and repentance is called for. Forgiveness is offered in the hope of awakening one who is dead in sin. The awakening and repentance of such a one is what brings glory to God, and so we desire to offer forgiveness for his great name's sake.

I recently worked with a woman who was both enraged at her abuser and tormented by guilt regarding her own actions toward others. She mistakenly assumed that forgiving her abuser meant saying that what he had done was no problem. I took her to Isaiah 53 and pointed out to her the words used to describe some of what happened to Jesus. He was "pierced," "crushed," "punished," "wounded," "judged," and offered as "a guilt offering." As she began to comprehend the meaning of such words to the person of Jesus, she began to see how costly God's forgiveness was. The Son of God had truly received the blows meant for sinners. It was indeed "finished."

Another example I find powerful in working with survivors is to help them focus on the hands of Jesus. Hands are very powerful in a survivor's life. Hands have been used to violate, molest, and do violence to. Often their own hands have also, under duress or by choice, done many things they find abhorrent. I worked with a woman who constantly clawed at her hands because she thought they were evil. My hands terrified her as well. Over the years, she learned to trust my hands. It was with great joy that I was then able to introduce her to the hands of Jesus. Healing hands, safe hands, yes. But also hands wounded so she could be forgiven. After many gentle repetitions, she learned to let her hands rest because another had paid her debt.

What Does Forgiveness Look Like Practically?

As a client begins to wrestle with these eternal truths, we then move on to the practical outworking of those truths. For those whose abuser is alive, such struggles often lead to a confrontation with the perpetrator, as I described earlier. The struggle is a little bit different for those whose abusers are not alive. However, the hope is that the survivor's heart will want to exhibit those attitudes found in one who is free to offer forgiveness, whether or not it is or can be received.

The work of forgiveness also means wrestling with repentance and what it looks like. This is particularly crucial because perpetrators can often be dangerous, and a hasty reconciliation can have fatal consequences. Scripture is very clear that light and darkness can have no fellowship. It also teaches us that we lie when we *say* that we have fellowship with God but continue to walk in darkness (1 John 1:6). Fellowship with one another comes only when both parties are *walking* (living, dwelling) in the light. We are reminded again that words alone are not sufficient evidence of repentance. Repentance is significant and sustained change, evident over time. Forgiveness can be extended by the survivor to the perpetrator. Whether or not actual reconciliation occurs depends on many things, such as repentance and safety. Still using the example of stolen money, reconciliation occurs when one has accounted what is owed, lets go of the need for payment, and chooses to lend or give to that person because they have admitted to the debt (truth) and have agreed to change how they "borrow" (by making restitution and demonstrating prompt payment in the future). It is possible to forgive the old debt and still make the decision not to lend again.

What Is the Purpose of Forgiveness?

Again, the purpose of forgiveness is a right relationship with God, not a nice family. What forgiveness looks like in any situation is not to be governed by what would make the family feel better but rather by what would call each and every member to a restored relationship to God himself. Anything less will not honor him.

Finally, as we attempt to come alongside our clients in this difficult and often highly emotional area, let us keep two things in mind. As humans, we are creatures who live in time. That means everything we do is in time. Forgiveness is no exception to that. Apart from the miraculous (which does occasionally occur), God works with us as he made us. We will struggle and learn to forgive over time. Forgiveness is not some spiritual "just add water" quality. Those who tell their clients, "You need to forgive, and if you can't do that, I can't help you anymore," are seriously misrepresenting God and clearly misunderstanding his creatures of dust. Fortunately, God himself does not treat us in such a fashion. He remembers that we are dust, that we are finite, and that we live in time. He himself has entered our time and experienced our finiteness, and so he understands our struggle.

Christ also entered our world to demonstrate forgiveness for us and lovingly and patiently to call us to look like him. Not only do we as therapists need to remember the frailty of humans (ourselves included) as we work with our clients, but as his representatives to those whose view of him has been twisted and marred, we also need to demonstrate who he is. As we demonstrate those attitudes that reflect a forgiving spirit to our clients, and as we lovingly and patiently call them to look like him as they have ears to hear, we will find that we have by God's grace made them homesick for what we have. What better way to teach forgiveness than to live before others a life that carries the aroma of the Redeemer! And here again we are reminded of the awesomeness of our task as therapists; what we say and who we are will be redemptive in the lives of others only as we demonstrate in the flesh the character of the one we follow.

PART FOUR

Treatment: Phase Three

16

Relationships

Entrance into the final phase of treatment for an adult survivor of sexual abuse is in many ways a time of both joy and hope. Therapist and client have formed and tested a strong alliance. The client has faced again and again the feelings and memories that she felt with certainty were so threatening and overwhelming that they were sure to destroy her. She has exchanged many of her destructive coping skills for healthy ones. She has established relationships that are supportive and safe. The family-of-origin issues have been handled in whatever ways the client has decided are both safe and wise. The work of therapy is far more present and future oriented than in previous stages.

However, hard work still needs to be done. Several areas require undergirding and nurturing if the client's growth is to continue. It also does not mean that memory work, the client-therapist relationship, or family-of-origin issues will not need further work. You will probably find that various events still trigger memories, that the question of trust still surfaces, and that survivors will need to rethink choices about their families. Growth is a fluid thing, and we said earlier that it certainly does not occur in discrete stages without overlap. There are growth spurts in the therapeutic process, but there are also relapses, plateaus, and surprises. As you and your client rejoice over her growth and work on her present life together, do not be discouraged by what may feel like throwbacks to previous stages. Any issue that resurfaces with persistence needs particular attention, and its persistence is often indicative of unfinished work. If that occurs, then stop whatever you are presently focused on and direct your attention to the area that continues to make noise (for example, grieving over losses may still need some work).

Four major areas need attention in this final phase of treatment. The first two are continuations of previous stages: ongoing work in the area of relationships and the reclaiming of the body. The third area is that of re-creating life. One almost inevitable outcome of your client's growth will be a strong desire to serve or comfort others in some way. It is a beautiful outworking of the redemptive process. The final area of phase three is termination. As the client feels stronger and more individuated, the stage is set for separation from the therapist. How this is managed is of crucial importance.

RELATIONSHIPS

The area of relationships is one that requires ongoing work for all of us. It is a lifelong task. This is an important truth to communicate to survivors, for they often idealize relationships. It is common for survivors to divide relationships into two categories: abusive or wonderful. The assumption has been that they can expect only abusive relationships because there is something wrong with them. Those who are fortunate enough to avoid abusive relationships live in a world full of hope for idealistic and wonderful connections with others. Most survivors do not know how to love, trust, speak the truth, and handle conflict through the normal ups and downs of human relationships. Normalizing both the wonder and the disappointment of relating to others is an ongoing therapeutic task.

It is important to keep in mind that the effects of abuse are silence, isolation, and helplessness. Whenever difficulties arise in a current relationship, survivors may be tempted to fall back into those three characteristics. The more upsetting the situation and the more anxiety the survivor feels, the more likely this is to be so. Continued repetition of the truths of voice, connection, and choice will be necessary. This is often done in the form of questions: What do you want to say? What are you feeling? What would you like to see happen? How do you believe God has called you to speak or act? What do you fear? What are the options? What things do you need to help you do what you believe is right?

The writer to the Hebrews speaks of those who are mature (5:14). He speaks of the mature as those "who by constant use have trained themselves to distinguish good from evil." The therapeutic relationship provides an arena for that training "by constant use" to take place. Part of distinguishing between good and evil is helping clients differentiate between what their personal history taught them and what God says. History said, "You are worthless." God says, "You are my loved one." History said, "Be silent." God says, "Speak truth." History said, "Manipulate." God says, "Love." The abuse trained the survivor to deny evil, to pretend, to assume she had no value, and to believe that relationships were to be feared. Within the therapeutic relationship, you have treated the survivor with dignity, provided safety in relationship, and called her to speak the truth and call evil by its right name. In this end phase of treatment, you will continue to do those things, encouraging and teaching your client to extend these truths and skills into her other relationships.

Three relational areas need attention during this phase if termination is to occur successfully. The first is ongoing development of a strong support network for the survivor. The second area, if the survivor is married, is often intensive marital counseling. The third area is the further nurturing and strengthening of the survivor's relationship with God.

Development of a Strong Support Network

First, during this phase of treatment, I will work hard to assist my client in developing a strong and healthy support network. If she stays isolated and hidden from others, she will relapse and cease to grow or stay in an unhealthy dependence on the therapist. Many therapists are worried about excessive or misplaced dependence in the therapeutic relationship. Certainly there is a place for such concern.

We must be careful, however, not to allow such concern to result in our missing the point of what we have called incarnational therapy. Jesus became flesh and lived among us for the purpose of explaining the Father to us. One of the conclusions I think we can draw from this is that in order for us to understand who God is, we need him demonstrated under our noses, in the flesh. I suspect that sometimes we want to ignore the awesome responsibility of being that demonstration because of the demands it would place on us. If all humans, created in God's image, needed a physical demonstration of who he was in order to know him, then surely those who have grown up without any human representation of love, security, and truth will need to lean hard on us for a while. So although we should be very careful in the dependency we allow (for we never want to take the place of God in the life of another), at the same time we must not flee the responsibility of becoming for our clients a clear demonstration of the nature of the Father. As therapy proceeds, the weight of that dependency will shift from therapist to God himself and from therapist to outside support network.

Ideally, a good portion of the support system should come from within the church. This enables a survivor to connect with couples and families as well as individuals. Since many survivors have never seen healthy male-female relationships or family interactions, these connections have inestimable value. It is wonderful for them to observe men and women treating each other with love and care, handling conflict with respect, asking forgiveness and seeking restoration, nurturing children in loving and safe ways, using touch appropriately in relationships, and, above all, actually living out in relationship what God has called us to. The church community, if it will heed the call, has the privilege of providing the survivor with the family and friendships she never had.

Marital Counseling

If the client is married, the end phase is also the time for concentrated marriage counseling. Obviously, some attention to the marriage has probably been given throughout treatment. This is important if the spouse is to be appropriately supportive. I find that the more a spouse understands about treatment and is able to be supportive of the process, the more likely the marriage is to grow and change with the survivor. When a spouse actively fights therapy or is abusive in some way, both the growth of the survivor and the marriage are injured.

It is important to note that the appearance of significant relationship difficulties during the treatment process is not necessarily proof that marital therapy should begin at that moment. The needs of the survivor, the needs of the spouse, and the needs of the couple are separate yet interwoven issues that must be very carefully assessed.

I find it very important to continually educate the spouse as to what might be expected. That education is part of what will enable him not to take things personally and also help him respond to problems in the sexual relationship, nightmares, flashbacks, and withdrawal in helpful rather than destructive ways. Spouses will function better within the marriage if they understand the emotional roller coaster they may be riding for a while. It is often helpful and sometimes necessary for spouses to seek individual treatment for themselves. When a survivor is married to a batterer or someone addicted to pornography, individual treatment is a necessary precursor to marital therapy.

Expertise in marriage counseling does not always accompany expertise in treating sexual abuse. It is important for counselors to know their limits and refer the client to a skilled marriage counselor if such skills are not part of their repertoire. Obviously, one of the areas included in marital counseling is the sexual relationship. It can be a fragile area, and careful handling is vital. Incest is sexual, and so it often has sexual repercussions. Problems can include lack of arousal, lack of orgasm, flashbacks during sex, aversion to certain touches or smells, dissociation during sex, or an inability to say no to sex.

Part of what needs to happen here is that both survivor and spouse need to understand the other's perspective. The survivor needs to see that the incest has had a profound impact on her spouse and express appreciation for his support, concern, and patience. She needs to understand that her spouse sees sex from a very different perspective and likely views sexual intimacy as something to be desired and something that results in many good feelings.

The spouse, on the other hand, needs to validate the experience of incest and its capability to bleed into the marital relationship, acknowledging that the bleed-through is not simply the survivor's rejection of him. It is absolutely vital that a spouse understand that attempting to force a sexual encounter, overtly or covertly, will be extremely destructive to the marriage. Helping a spouse see that this is not about winning and that recovery comes in stages is necessary if he is to understand and honor the survivor. At the same time, the spouse can gently remind the survivor that he is safe, that he is not the perpetrator, and that sexual touch and abuse are not the same thing. It is very important that the spouse understand that incest means not having a choice and that the marriage relationship needs to be secure enough and elastic enough to allow for the survivor to say no without punishment or threat of termination.

It is often helpful to give a couple some specific guidelines for how to deal with flashbacks during sex, since that is a common occurrence. As soon as a flashback begins, the survivor needs to open her eyes (if they are closed) and focus on where she is. What room is she in? With whom is the sex occurring? What things are different now from when the abuse occurred? Some survivors can do this silently. Others will need to stop what is happening and have their spouse walk them through it. It is crucial that a survivor stop trying to respond in a sexual way until the flashback is over. The fact that she is stopping needs to be verbalized so the couple can work together to help the survivor refocus. The couple needs to decide ahead of time what words might be comforting at such a time. One client's husband always stops and gently reminds her that "I am _____, your husband. Your father is not here. You are in a safe place." Both people need to know and agree ahead of time that choosing to stop sex is a viable option. Proceeding under duress when a flashback cannot be overcome feels abusive and is damaging to the marriage.

Often I assist a couple in working through a book about sex in marriage, much as I might discuss sexual concerns in premarital counseling. Many survivors have a lot of distorted information about male and female sexuality, and many have little knowledge about their own bodies and how they work. They may have felt that sex has been something to endure from an emotional distance. The idea of being present during sex is terrifying, and the possibility that sex would be pleasurable and safe for both partners is incomprehensible. Teaching both partners how to be safe for each other, how to communicate clearly about sexual intimacy, and how to give and receive pleasure is an important task in the end phase of treatment.

Strengthening the Survivor's Relationship to God

The third relational area that needs to be supported and nurtured during this phase is the survivor's relationship to God. Incest frequently has devastating consequences in the spiritual life of the survivor. Even if the survivor's relationship with God seemed strong before treatment, facing the truth of her life will often rock her faith in profound ways. As we saw in Meeka's story, survivors will have to go back and rebuild their faith from the beginning, for previously their relationship with God was built on a reality that denied the incest.

In his book *Night,* Elie Wiesel says the following: "Have we ever thought about the consequence of a horror that, although less apparent, less striking than the other outrages, is yet the worst of all to those of us who have faith: the death of God in the soul of a child who suddenly discovers absolute evil?"[1] Although we say otherwise, we often base our faith not on belief in the truth of who God says he is but rather on the goodness of our circumstances. When confronted with evil or terrible suffering, we find our faith in the goodness, love, and power of God to be profoundly shaken. As the survivor confronts her life without pretending, she will have to rework her faith so that her relationship to God is not predicated on denying the truth. Is God good, loving, and powerful even though the evidence in her life appears to scream to the contrary? In part, the crisis of faith is whether or not truth will be derived from life's circumstances or from God's Word.

This crisis requires wisdom and carefulness from the therapist. So often when we are confronted with a faith crisis, we are tempted to simply provide answers to questions or attempt to explain God ("Here's what's true; now just believe it"). It is not that we should not give answers, but we must do so carefully. Our goal is not simply to provide answers or even to resolve a crisis of faith but to help our client develop a living, growing relationship with God, a relationship in which she seeks answers from him for herself. I had a client who was being harshly criticized for her faith struggles and told by many people that she knew what the truth was and she needed to "just believe it." With great anguish she said to me, "I don't know *how* to believe in God if these things are true [meaning her history of sadistic abuse]! Why can't they give me time to learn?"

I would hope that throughout treatment, the therapist has lived before the client in a way that demonstrates the character of Christ. It is often true that a whiff of the fragrance of Christ in the life of another is what awakens in us a hunger to know him for ourselves. It is also true that seeing Christ's life incarnated in the life of a believer is what enables us to see him more clearly. I recently had a client say to me that she had discovered that God shared a particular quality with me. I gently suggested to her that I thought (and hoped) it was the other way around. If I demonstrated qualities that were good, then their origin was in the person of Christ. She laughed and said she knew that was really how it went but that I needed to understand that it looked quite different "on the way up." She had encountered me first on her way to understanding and knowing God. It is a sobering and humbling thought to realize that our clients encounter us "on their way up" and that who we are speaks to them about who God is. May we, like Jesus, continually "explain" the Father to them by word and deed.

One of the issues that will probably surface during this time is the concept of God as father. Struggles in this area are very intense for female survivors who grew up abused by their natural fathers. At the same time, I find that many survivors, male and female, whose abusers were extrafamilial, also struggle to think of God as father. The point of difficulty seems to be around the thought that if God is a father who truly cares about his children, then why did he let the abuse happen? How can I believe that he is the compassionate father he says he is? Obviously, when the abuser was one's own father, the struggle becomes even more fierce.

Think back to Meeka's story. What did her life experience teach her about fathers? She learned that they are untrustworthy. They have a great deal of power. They are unpredictable. They inflict pain on those they are supposed to care for. Such pain is inflicted because the child is "bad" and "makes" the father do it. That makes it very dangerous to do anything wrong in front of one called father. That means the safest way to be in relationship with a father is to be very distant, very guarded, and to pretend to be very good, whether or not you are. In essence, anyone called father is not safe.

And what does Scripture say about God our Father? The psalmist tells us that just "as a father has compassion on his children, so the Lord has compassion on those who fear [revere] him" (Ps. 103:13). Jesus says, "If you sinful people know how to give good gifts to your children, how much more will your heavenly Father give good gifts to those who ask him" (Matt. 7:11, NLT).

How does a child like Meeka put these two realities together? How does an adult with a history like Meeka's put these two realities together? Anyone who has even a small grasp of the magnitude of such a task will understand why Jesus said that though stumbling blocks were inevitable in this dark world, "Woe to that man through whom the stumbling block comes" (Matt. 18:7, NASB). He says later on, in Matthew 19:14, that no one is to hinder or get in the way of children coming to him. Meeka's father spent years creating hindrances, blocks, to her ability to know and love God as her father.

People's struggle with the massive hindrance that has been put in their way may go on for years or for a lifetime. Yes, God tells us who he is and calls us to believe in his Word no matter what circumstances seem to say. However, we must not be guilty of glibness regarding someone's ability to do that. An honest wrestling before God with this issue over the span of a lifetime is hardly worthy of condemnation. It is a fine balance to honor the difficulty of the struggle while simultaneously holding forth the truth that our Father-God is indeed who he says he is. I believe that as a therapist bears witness to this struggle in the life of another, the call to that therapist is to respond so as to not introduce any more stumbling blocks and thus add to the burden. Rather, as those who know and love God as Abba, may we demonstrate his compassion, gentleness, and security so that those who struggle may find him easier to comprehend.

When a client is ready and interested, I take time during this final phase to help her learn about how to nurture and strengthen her walk with God. Many survivors find steady routine very difficult. Their lives were controlled by the unpredictable, so daily disciplines of body, mind, and soul are hard to develop. Many also find the idea of intimacy with God as frightening as intimacy with people. One client talked about how difficult it was to get close to God and trust his great love for her. Every time she attempted to imagine closeness, she was flooded with images of physical abuse, and her immediate response was toughness and distance. Keeping these two things in mind, I encourage clients to begin to develop a devotional life in ways that they are comfortable with and yet that challenge them.

Help the client understand herself. Is she a "night" or a "morning" person? What is her usual attention span? What, then, are realistic expectations? Many survivors spent half their academic years in a dissociative state, so reading and study skills are lacking. All of these areas need to be assessed. Having done so, we will set up a goal that takes everything into account. Some women may begin with daily goals, others with goals twice a week for fifteen minutes. Persistent failures mean reassessment, not condemnation.

I very often suggest particular psalms as a place to begin. Many survivors have found it helpful to learn to rewrite some of the psalms from the standpoint of one who has been abused. David's experiences of violence, oppression, and fear of his enemies can provide the survivor with a vehicle for expressing herself to God. David's continued trust and hope in God will challenge the survivor as well.

Another aspect of spiritual development is found in connection with the life of the church. If a survivor's faith is to continue to grow, then she must involve herself in a community of believers who will nurture that growth. Slowly and carefully, help the survivor put into place the supports that will enable her to continue growth in all areas of her life, long after therapy is terminated.

17

Reclaiming the Body

꿈꿈꿈

One of the challenges of therapy with a survivor of sexual abuse is helping her find positive ways of thinking and feeling about her body. The body is one of the central arenas in which the abuse was played out, and it is often very difficult, especially for a survivor of chronic and/or sadistic abuse, to connect with and assume some control over her body. Many have worked hard to avoid any sense of connection with their bodies, so they may express powerful resistance initially. Elie Wiesel captures for us the need to get rid of one's body when trauma is ongoing: "I was putting one foot in front of the other mechanically. I was dragging with me this skeletal body which weighed so much. If only I could have got rid of it. In spite of my efforts not to think about it, I could feel myself as two entities—my body and me. I hated it."[1] Obviously, work in this area will confront the client's use of dissociation as a coping mechanism. It can involve work with eating disorders, compulsive sexuality, and self-mutilation. Many of these issues will have been handled somewhat in phases one and two; however, such work will continue here and, as with relational issues, will need support mechanisms if growth is to be ongoing.

The regulation of both bodily and emotional states has often been severely disrupted for the survivor.[2] Many clients are profoundly disconnected from their bodies and are thus unable to monitor physical and emotional states. Self-mutilation or binge eating carried out while in a dissociative state cannot be monitored until the client is able to connect enough with her body to recognize what she is feeling and manage such feelings in nonpathological ways.

It is often helpful to focus on bodily sensations in nonthreatening ways. Encourage clients to notice the feeling of warmth from the sun, of soft material against the body, of cold water running through the fingers, of the vibrancy that often follows strenuous exercise. This will help them connect with their body and enjoy the use of their God-given senses. These are simple delights, meant by God for our pleasure. I recently had a survivor come in filled with wonder over her discovery that her children's skin was soft to the touch. She had typically either not touched them or not allowed herself to "feel" them when they did touch.

Once clients are able to connect with their bodies and discover pleasant sensations that bring joy, they can then begin to assume some regulation of their physical lives. The good feelings we have when our bodies are well cared for by a healthy diet and consistent exercise are foreign to many survivors. The rhythm of regular sleep is also something many survivors have not had since early childhood, if they had it even then. Little by little, clients learn safe ways to quiet themselves and feel good about their bodies.

As work in this area proceeds, feelings of fear and self-loathing may often resurface. Many women have used excess weight or a certain style of clothing to hide their bodies and help them feel less vulnerable. As their weight drops or as they choose to change the way they dress, people will often compliment them. This can easily generate a sense of being threatened, and panic will set in. It will be important to help your client discover new ways of feeling safe. Some women will find that self-loathing resurfaces at this point. "My body is not good. I don't deserve to feel good. I hate my body because it makes bad things happen." When such feelings arise, it is time to stop momentarily the work of change and to refocus on truth about the body (the body did not cause the sexual abuse; God gave us our bodies and said they were good) and to help your client find nondestructive ways of feeling safe.

As the survivor connects more and more to her body, she will be able to increase her ability to monitor her emotional responses and, therefore, decrease her dissociative responses. When she can learn to recognize anxiety, agitation, fear, or other emotional pain before such feelings become unbearable, she will be able to find a way to quiet herself without self-injury. During molestation, incest victims are subject to high degrees of stress—physical and emotional. Their child bodies are undeveloped and unprepared for sexual activity. They are flooded with feelings of fear, panic, confusion, and anxiety. Coping is necessary to both survival and sanity. Many cope through dissociation, disconnecting or divorcing themselves from the experience. Later on in life, whenever similar feelings of stress occur, the survivor continues to rely on the mechanism of dissociation. This disconnection from oneself prevents the survivor from being able to recognize negative emotions in their early stages. Many survivors talk about not noticing anything going on inside themselves until they are "jacked up" or "wound up." It is important to educate survivors about typical bodily responses, such as "butterflies" in the stomach, a knot in the stomach, rapid breathing, a racing heart, and clammy hands. As they learn to read the signals their bodies give them, they can then learn safe ways of coping. Learning to name their feelings correctly, to express them in writing or in relationship, and to dispel them through physical activity will provide new ways of managing emotions.

I find it very important to educate those clients who self-mutilate about the biochemical changes that accompany post-traumatic stress disorder and what role those biochemical changes play in the survivor's vulnerability to self-abuse.[3] The endorphins (endogenous morphines) released into the bloodstream at the moment of trauma have a tranquilizing and antidepressant property. The self-mutilation occurs in order to relieve the survivor from unbearably painful internal states, not because the client is "sick" or "weird" or "likes pain." As clients come to understand this mechanism, they can begin to see the benefit of regular aerobic exercise of some kind because such activity is also known to release endorphins. The gradual release of endorphins during aerobic activity contributes to a longer lasting sense of well-being and a reduction in stress, eliminating the urge to self-abuse.

One woman I worked with would say "I don't know" every time I asked her what she was feeling. We took a few steps back, and I began instead to ask her if she felt any change in her body. She was able to report rapid heart rate, shallow breathing, or a "weird feeling" in her stomach. I had her note in her journal any time these sensations occurred. Several sessions later, she noted a high correlation between such physical sensations and self-mutilation. We began to label what feelings these sensations might represent: fear, anxiety, nervousness. As she learned to name the feelings, she then learned to ask herself questions: *Why am I anxious? What has frightened me? How am I feeling helpless?* Such questions led to answers that resulted in finding help or a solution of some kind. Slowly but surely, albeit with many setbacks, she learned to name her feelings and find ways to ease them without self-mutilating. Such growth is a long, hard battle with many relapses, but it is wonderful to hear the words, "I haven't hurt myself in a week [a month or a year]."

Connecting with good bodily sensations, recognizing and naming feelings early on, and managing emotions partially through exercise combine to enable the survivor to begin to feel good about her body and have some sense of control over her physical and emotional self.

18

Re-Creating Life

⚜

The third area of work in this final phase of treatment is a natural outgrowth of all that has gone before. Within the context of a safe relationship, the survivor has found her voice and her ability to have an impact on her world. Out of that safe place she has begun to widen her circle and develop a network of healthy relationships with others and a growing relationship with God. She has moved from a focus on the task of recovery to a focus on the more ordinary tasks of life. She finds joy in life and in relationship. What naturally flows from that is the increasing desire to give to others what has been given to her.

I would hope that she who has desperately needed both comfort and a companion in her suffering has found them in different ways in the therapist and in the church community. Ideally, both arenas will have served as incarnations of the "God of all comfort," comforting her steadily in her afflictions (2 Cor. 1:3). Having served faithfully as such demonstrations, both therapist and fellow believers will have taken the survivor by the hand and led her to the Redeemer, who bore her griefs and carried her sorrows and who now has not left her comfortless. She will discover with relative ease that not only was the purpose of the process to redeem her life from the pit (Isa. 38:17) but also "so that [she] may be able to comfort those who are in any affliction with the comfort with which [she herself was] comforted by God" (2 Cor. 1:4, NASB). She will discover with great joy that just as the evil of abuse reverberates throughout a life and through the generations, so does the wonder of redemption.

Two practical concerns occur repeatedly in this area. *First, many survivors have experienced a loss of awareness about where their gifts and abilities lie.* All of us have been gifted by God for the good of his kingdom. Many survivors will need your assistance in discovering what their gifts are. The survivor will be most effective and satisfied in her service to others if that arena is chosen according to how God has gifted her. Once again, the church community can be a wonderful place for such discoveries to take place. Is she gifted with children or adults? Is she better with groups or individuals? Do her abilities fit her for "frontline" work or "behind the scenes" work?

As an awareness of her gifts and abilities grows, a survivor may decide to return to school or to change careers. Vocational counseling may be necessary at this juncture. Single mothers may need the assistance of a church community in order to make such changes. Once again, the church has the great privilege here of providing the support the survivor never received from her family of origin.

Second, many survivors almost impulsively assume that they are called to counsel other survivors. This conclusion is neither surprising nor necessarily wrong. It does, however, need to be handled with care. The fact that one is a survivor does not mean that one would therefore make a good counselor. It also does not mean that one would be effective with other survivors. Having lived through sexual abuse is not the sole qualification for being able to help others with their abuse history.

The possibility of training in order to work with survivors needs to be assessed in the same way that any such decision would be. Is the choice supported by the gifts and abilities necessary for that particular work? If so, one possible avenue to test that choice is through volunteer organizations that work with survivors. Many organizations will train survivors to assist as coleaders in groups, and such experience can serve as an excellent testing ground.

Whenever a survivor goes on to function in a therapeutic role with other survivors, I strongly recommend ongoing supervision. I believe therapy of any kind, and most certainly therapy concerned with trauma, requires ongoing supervision. An added history of abuse only underscores the need for supervision. Such therapy can easily trigger memories for a survivor or be controlled by areas where work is still unfinished. If the survivor becomes a counselor, she will need help separating her own experience from her clients' experiences. She will, like all of us, need a place to debrief. She will also have the extraordinary capacity to offer hope, based on personal experience.

I have known survivors to reach out in many ways. Some have cared for the terminally ill; others work with children. Some have involved themselves with shelters for battered women; others have gotten involved in women's ministries in their churches. Both male and female survivors have chosen to come alongside adolescents from troubled families. The work they choose is as varied as the survivors themselves. The joy such work brings is a delight to behold. To see someone who came to you focused on simply surviving now begin to minister to others is truly to witness the work of the Redeemer!

19

Treatment Termination

As the survivor feels less and less encumbered by her past and as her life skills and relational network grow and are solidified, the thought that the therapist is not so necessary anymore begins to surface. It is initially a frightening thought and requires a response of reassurance, accompanied by a statement that termination is the client's choice, not something that will be forced by the therapist. The therapeutic relationship must continue to be a safe place where the client can give voice to her thoughts and discuss the choices available to her.

My initial response to a client's mention of termination is simply to give her room to consider the idea. How long has she had the thought? Why does she think she is ready? What are her hesitations or fears? What things are important in order for termination to occur safely? As the survivor's thoughts and feelings are considered, we begin to move toward actual termination.

I think it is important to proceed toward termination at a careful pace. Sessions will first be reduced to every two weeks, then once a month, once every three months, once every six months, and finally, an appointment is scheduled for a year later. Each step is held until the client signals readiness to move on. Keep in mind that if you have been working with a survivor of chronic childhood abuse, you have probably been seeing her for several years, sometimes more than once a week. To make a sudden move to terminate a relationship of that nature would result in feelings of abandonment and insecurity. Support the move toward separation, but do so in a gentle way that tests readiness as you proceed. Some clients will push to proceed too quickly because they fear saying good-bye. I suggest being firm in maintaining a more cautious approach and explaining why. Some clients will get stuck at a particular point and fear moving on. In that case, it is crucial to back up and deal with the underlying anxieties.

I always make certain that as long as life circumstances allow, I am available to my client down the road should she feel the need to touch base. A former client will sometimes call because of a major life change or because major stress in her life has triggered some old memories or symptoms. It is important to let a survivor know before she leaves you that such a return is in no way a failure on her part. It is, in fact, the better part of wisdom.

SUMMARY

We have considered the three phases of treatment of an adult survivor of chronic sexual abuse. Obviously, we will work with clients whose abuse has not been chronic and with whom we may use only parts of what is included here. It is also certain that not all survivors of chronic sexual abuse will choose to proceed through all three phases. For various reasons, some will terminate therapy prematurely. Others will leave at a particular juncture, take a "break," and return later to finish the process. Whatever a specific client chooses, these stages give the therapeutic process some structure. A picture of what therapy might optimally look like enables us not to sell our clients short. I find that untrained or young therapists often fail to encourage growth in the therapeutic process with survivors simply because they have no idea of what it might look like.

Therapy with survivors can be long and hard. I have found it to be inexpressibly rewarding. There is great joy in helping human beings find their voice for the first time. It continues to be a marvel to me to watch a crushed and broken human being who has faced darkness and evil while yet a child pursue truth and light. It is a bittersweet moment to say good-bye to someone who came stuck in a destructive past and who leaves growing and with hope for the future.

Recovery can seem long and difficult, but it is possible. It will require courage and stamina from your client, and from you as well. It is vital to remember that your joint efforts will result in change not only in the survivor's life but also in the lives of many others. It is a beautiful unfolding of God's promise that "he who began a good work in you will carry it on to completion" (Phil. 1:6). What a marvelous privilege it is as a therapist to be a vehicle for the redemptive work of God in another's life!

PART FIVE

Special Considerations

20

Dissociative Disorders

Three areas need special attention in our consideration of the treatment of adult survivors of sexual abuse. The first two are complex issues, and a thorough discussion of them would be quite beyond the scope of this book. However, they are important and in some respects "hot" topics. The first area is dissociative disorders, more specifically, dissociative identity disorder (DID). The second is false memory syndrome. The third subject, male survivors, is an area that I think deserves a few specific comments.

ETIOLOGY

Dr. Richard Kluft, director of the Dissociative Disorders Program at The Institute of Pennsylvania Hospital, has developed a four-factor theory regarding the etiology of DID. In essence, a client with DID is skilled at dissociation; the client used that ability to cope with severe childhood trauma; the form of a particular client's DID depends on temperament and other factors; and finally, the abuse was relentless, without the relief of comfort or restorative experiences.[1] According to the *Diagnostic and Statistical Manual of Mental Disorders IV*, the following are the criteria in diagnosing dissociative identity disorder: (1) the existence within the person of two or

more distinct identities or personality states (each with its own relatively enduring pattern of perceiving, relating to, and thinking about
the environment and self); (2) at least two of these personalities or
personality states recurrently take control of the person's behavior;
(3) inability to recall important personal information that is too
extensive to be explained by ordinary forgetfulness; and (4) the
disturbance is not due to the direct physiological effects of a
substance.[2]

It is currently thought that the creation of dissociative identity
disorder arises out of severe physical and sexual trauma, accompanied by psychological trauma. Studies have shown that DID clients
report the highest rates of childhood physical, sexual, and other
forms of abuse and trauma among those suffering from any known
psychiatric disorder. Most DID clients describe repeated forms of
multiple types of trauma and abuse that usually began before they
were five years old. The abuse was usually profound, relentless, and
intolerable, occurring in an environment lacking in nurturance.[3]

It is important to note that the occurrence of traumatic events
alone is not sufficient for the creation of a dissociative disorder.[4]
Also of importance is the person's experience of the self and of
others within the context of the traumatic events. Trauma occurs to
a specific individual within a particular context, familial and otherwise, and a consideration of that individual and that context is as
important as the traumatic event itself. To fail to grasp this
complexity can easily lead to a diagnostic error or an oversimplifi-
cation of the treatment process.

Historically, we have been told that DID is extremely rare, and
graduate school programs have typically given little to no training
in either the detection or treatment of the disorder. It is common for
clients with DID to be in the mental health system for several years
before being correctly diagnosed. In recent years, many clinicians
who treat people with DID have stated that the incidence of the
disorder is much higher than originally thought. Many have made
strong and, unfortunately, unsubstantiated statements about the
incidence of DID. Some speak derogatorily of their colleagues for
failing to diagnose and treat a disorder they claim is flooding the
offices of unsuspecting clinicians. Alternatively, other people are

highly skeptical, adamantly stating that DID exists only in the mind of deluded therapists and their highly suggestible clients.

I, frankly, have no idea what the rate of incidence is. I have worked with DID in my practice and have found that clients with DID respond very well to treatment. I probably fall somewhere in the middle of the continuum in that I do not believe the mental health system is flooded with undiagnosed DID clients, and I do not think the disorder to be as rare as was originally thought. Diagnosis of any kind must be done very carefully, and DID is no exception. DID can certainly present in a covert fashion and escape detection by those well trained in the field. One thing that contributes to this is the fact that many clients work hard to keep their dissociative experience a secret because they are certain that if it is known, they will be "locked up." At the other extreme are clients who were diagnosed as having a dissociative identity disorder about twenty minutes into an interview with a therapist who could "just tell." As with any aspect of treatment, diagnosis should be done with care and consultation, if necessary.

TREATMENT

I believe that the treatment of dissociative identity disorder falls along the same lines as the treatment for sexual abuse in general. That means that anything we say here should be seen against the backdrop of all that has already been stated. Frank Putnam, chief of the Unit on Dissociative Disorders at the National Institute of Mental Health (NIMH), divides treatment into three phases that are very similar to the three treatment phases we have just discussed. He says the first stage involves diagnosis, stabilization, communication, and cooperation. Phase two involves working through the trauma, and phase three is the resolution and integration of the traumatic material as well as the development of postintegration coping skills.[5]

Phase One: Safety, Stabilization, and Temporary Relief of Symptoms

The first stage of treatment is concerned with safety, stabilization, and temporary relief of trauma symptoms. During this time the client often feels tossed about by unpredictable emotions, flashbacks, and uncontrolled dissociative phenomena, such as switching and amnesia.

It is usually during this stage that the diagnosis of DID is introduced to the client. As the client slowly reveals what she believes are symptoms that prove she should be "locked up," I suggest DID as a possible framework for understanding her life. It is a diagnosis I offer tentatively and carefully. It is also a diagnosis I offer only after I have either witnessed clear signs that DID is a viable option (blank years, the presentation of a different identity) or my client steadily reports a symptom like "losing time" ("I have no memory of Wednesday afternoon." "I have in my closet clothes I did not buy"). I have found that the possibility of DID is greeted with feelings of relief, humiliation, and fear. Clients are usually amazed and surprised that I do not think they are "crazy." It is often the first time they have ever had a framework that made sense out of the way they experience life.

As with all survivors, the focus of this stage is the formation of a strong working alliance between therapist and client. It is a stage that will cycle through stabilization, crises, restabilization. I find many times that therapists mistakenly think the primary objective of treatment is the evoking of traumatic memories. Many seem to assume that the more rapidly they uncover the history, the more rapid and effective treatment will be. We must be very careful here because such an approach can very easily destroy a client's quality of life and even jeopardize her safety. I believe that the essence of trauma lies not in the pain experienced, though that is great, but in the fear generated by the trauma. If that is so, the client's history needs to be uncovered very carefully and within the context of an established, safe relationship, or destabilization will result. Therapy is to be a safe place, not a place where more fear is generated.

DID is a complex disorder with affective, cognitive, behavioral, and interpersonal aspects. Each of these domains requires specific attention. Affectively, clients will struggle with fear, anxiety, shame, guilt, rage, and self-loathing. Cognitively, clients will experience memory and identity disturbances as well as specific cognitive distortions (thoughts such as *I am evil. No one can ever love me*). Behavioral disturbances are evidenced in self-mutilation, suicide attempts, drug and alcohol abuse, and destruction of property. Relational difficulties can range from instability in relationships and impulsivity to a strong need to perform or achieve perfectly.

Another component of the first stage of treatment for DID is for both therapist and client to come to an understanding of the individual's particular system. This will be especially helpful in managing crises as they occur. The more cooperation that exists between the various personality states, the better the chance of establishing and maintaining safety guidelines with the client. Since self-destructive and suicidal tendencies are common, this becomes very important. It is my experience that the more typical therapeutic contracts between client and therapist are less helpful or reliable than are internal agreements among the identities.

It is important to note that while clients come to understand their particular system, from the initial stages of treatment they must be encouraged to accept the fundamental unity of their personhood. Many will reject this as impossible to grasp, given their experience. However, DID is *not* many individuals in one body. It is rather many discrete self-identities in one body, all sharing one DNA and *one* life history. Contrary to previous thinking, NIMH's Frank Putnam suggests that rather than there being a "birth" or "core" personality from which others are split off, there are identities that develop out of repeated severe trauma prior to a child's ability to maintain a stable sense of self across extreme shifts.[6]

I find that as my clients come to understand DID from the standpoint of their life histories, they begin to see it as simply a method they used for coping with intolerable circumstances and unbearable fear. This helps them to avoid feeling that they have no say over the functioning of their minds, as if somehow they have to coexist with something alien to themselves. They can also begin to see that this mind that creatively and courageously coped with the impossible is now being set free from that history so that it can be used as a whole mind, fully present, with access to all parts, and growing toward greater harmony with the mind of Christ.

Phase Two: Establishing a Strong Therapeutic Alliance

Entry into the second stage of treatment is characterized by the establishment of a strong therapeutic alliance. It is important that by this point therapist and client have found a way to collaborate on the timing and working through of the therapeutic issues. Phase two consists of working to resolve dissociative symptoms and to integrate dissociated aspects of the self. We also give attention to switching and its resulting amnesia, to dissociated memories, and to dissociated identity states. Although such work has probably occurred somewhat in the first phase, systematic efforts begin after a strong and safe alliance has been well established.

The process of facing the traumatic memories needs to be entered into collaboratively. I have found it vital to schedule more frequent appointments during this stage. We often set aside an allotted time and agree to deal with a specific group of memories. Collaborating various identities becomes important as other people may need to assume responsibility for day-to-day activities while the client deals with the memories. It is also frequently helpful (and necessary) during this juncture to arrange some extended sessions. One way of titrating the memory work so the client is not overwhelmed is to deal with a particular segment, take some time off from looking at traumatic memories to restabilize, and then agree to return to another segment. Slowly but surely, with safety needs always being considered, the work of integrating the trauma into the client's life occurs.

This method is extremely important because at the core of all traumatic memory is sheer terror. As we said in our previous discussion regarding memory work, when the client is facing memories, she is often unable to differentiate between past and present, and any thought of the future is seen as ludicrous. The terror is diminished only as the therapist's voice repeatedly reminds the client that what occurred is past, that she is in a safe place, and that there is no one present to hurt her. She also needs to hear repeatedly that her worst fears were not realized. She believed she would not survive. The fact that she is present and is finally able to articulate the trauma is proof that she did.

This retelling of the trauma is not just about the memory of the events that occurred but also includes the emotional responses to those events. Very often the events and the affect they elicited are stored separately. It is vital to the process of integration that all aspects become unified in the telling.

Following Kluft's model, I differentiate between fusion and integration of identities.[7] In fusion, the various parts come together and lose their experience of separateness. It is a step where dissociative barriers collapse. Often it occurs when a specific group of identities becomes very similar or communication and collaboration among them is ongoing. Kluft refers to it as an initial compacting process that lays the groundwork for integration.[8] Integration, which occurs over a period of weeks to months, is characterized by clients' ability to live congruently and presently with all the facts of their lives. Integration can occur both spontaneously and purposefully. It is not something that occurs in a moment of time but rather is a process of learning how to live with memories, feelings, impulses, and thoughts that initially seem foreign but ultimately are "owned" and managed appropriately.

Phase Three: Postintegration Work

Phase three of therapy with DID clients is the necessary work of postintegration. The work of grieving is prominent in this stage for two reasons. The first is because the client finally comprehends for the first time the often massive losses that her traumatic history caused. The impact of that without the use of dissociative defenses can be overwhelming. It is often the first time that a client fully realizes that her life was indeed as bad as she thought it was. Not only are all memories present, but the ability to stand back and look at her life more objectively is present in a new way. Sometimes this will require a reworking of some experiences she had previously dealt with in therapy. Such work is not indicative of an inadequacy in the previous stages but rather indicates an absorbing of the material in its unity.

Grieving also can occur because the client, who is used to being a "we," is now an "I." Loneliness for the "others" may be experienced because they often provided a sense of companionship. A very familiar, albeit internal, world is now gone. The survivor requires a time of transition before she is comfortable with life and relationships being lived out on the outside of herself rather than the inside. She also has fears about how she will manage difficult situations that were previously handled by other identities.

Postintegrative therapy is in many ways simply individual therapy, so it varies according to the person being treated. The issues of therapy are basically those discussed in previous chapters, largely focused on a strengthening of voice and the ability to choose, while nurturing external relational connection.

I believe very strongly that therapists who encounter what they believe to be dissociative disorders and who have received no training in these disorders need to seek supervision from a therapist who has expertise in this area. There are also quite a few good texts written about the subject (see Suggested Reading), although they are no substitute for supervision.

It goes without saying that dissociative memory has become a controversial subject in recent years. It is crucial that clinicians not ignore the basic findings regarding memory and its reconstruction and the power of suggestion, context, and expectancy to affect memory recall. Such factors also underscore the need for supervision, for it is crucial not to lead a client or assume the ability to verify memories.

Treatment of those with DID is intensive and compelling work. It is immeasurably rewarding. I have found my DID clients to be courageous, creative people who have survived against all odds. They are for me a living illustration of the fact that we are "fearfully and wonderfully made" (Ps. 139:14). I stand in awe of the Creator of such marvelous complexity and the Redeemer of such horror. Both counts are cause for worship!

21

False Memory Syndrome

ᭇᭇᭇᭇᭇ

The nature and reliability of traumatic memories is a controversial issue. Such memories are very difficult to study since they cannot actually be approximated in a laboratory setting. Trauma can be defined as an inescapably stressful event that overwhelms an individual's ability to cope. Obviously, however upsetting a videotape of a rape may be, it is not the same as being repeatedly raped as a small child by one's own father. To assume that a person's response and ability to remember such a video are the same as a little girl's response and memory of her father's raping her is poor reasoning. We can certainly learn much about memory from laboratory studies, but they are hardly equivalent to actual childhood trauma.

At the same time, working with delayed-memory and traumatic-amnesia cases is extremely challenging because for the most part, few or no standards have been developed. The American Psychological Association Working Group on the Investigation of Memories of Childhood Abuse published a report in February 1996. That report basically stated that yes, survivors of childhood abuse can forget memories and later remember them, and yes, a therapist can suggest a "memory" that the survivor later recalls as true. Both the researchers and the clinicians said that the majority of people who have been sexually abused as children recall what occurred at least to some degree. The psychology practitioners often fail to acknowledge the limits of experiential or anecdotal data, while the psychology researchers often fail to acknowledge anything that is not obtained through an experimental study.

I am obviously not going to resolve the debate here. I do think it is important to consider some of the latest research on trauma and memory. It also seems crucial to respond on some level to those in the False Memory Syndrome Foundation. Finally, I would like to suggest some guidelines for those of us who work with the sexually abused and their memories.

According to the *Diagnostic and Statistical Manual of Mental Disorders IV* definition of post-traumatic stress disorder (PTSD), trauma can result in extremes of both retention and forgetting. Terrifying experiences can be vividly recalled, highly resistant to integration, or some combination thereof. A survivor may vividly recall terrifying experiences, or those terrifying experiences may be highly resistant to integration into conscious memory. Sometimes these two dynamics happen simultaneously. Bessel A. van der Kolk, who has done extensive research on the nature of traumatic memory, found that subjects with post-traumatic nightmares said they saw identical scenes repeatedly over a fifteen-year period.[1] Unlike more easily assimilated ordinary memories, some aspects of traumatic events seem to become fixed in the mind.

Many of those who have studied trauma have observed that the mind seems to handle memories of traumatic events differently from the way it handles memories of ordinary events. Clients repeatedly state that the emotional and perceptual components of trauma are more prominent than the narrative ones.[2] These observations have led to the thought that the mind may encode traumatic memories differently from ordinary ones. It is postulated that this difference may be because attention has a different focus when trauma occurs and/or perhaps because extreme emotional arousal interferes with hippocampal memory functions.[3]

When dealing with memories of childhood trauma, it is important to keep several things in mind. First of all, children have fewer mental capacities than adults do for constructing a coherent narrative out of traumatic events. Second, the use of dissociation at the moment of trauma makes it very difficult to relate a precise account of the traumatic events, for dissociation has the effect of fragmenting the memories. Third, memories of trauma often have no verbal component whatever. This is often because children had little to no verbal ability when the trauma occurred. Instead, survivors tend to experience such memories as fragments of the sensory components of the event, and when these fragments are retrieved, they have little or no linguistic component. Piaget said that a failure of semantic memory leads to memory's being formed on somatosensory levels.[4] Fourth, memory appears to consist of networks of related information. If one aspect of a particular network is activated, the retrieval of associated memories often results. Emotions and sensations often serve as the cues for such retrieval. Hence, generalized physiological arousal can set off trauma-related memories, and vice versa.

Van der Kolk points out that while trauma may leave an indelible imprint in the form of sensations or feeling states, once people begin to talk about the trauma, their accounts are subject to interpretation, condensation, and embellishment. Relating the trauma narrative subjects it to distortion. So even if traumatic memory is encoded with a vividness and accuracy unlike ordinary memory, as soon as a client begins to tell the story, the story is altered somewhat.[5] Ultimately, whether or not images and sensations can be etched in the mind and remain there unaltered is a question that remains unanswered.

Against the backdrop of increasing numbers of people telling their stories of childhood sexual abuse, The False Memory Syndrome Foundation was formed in 1992 in Philadelphia, Pennsylvania. Executive director Pamela Freyd says that the FMS Foundation was formed to aid victims of what is being called false memory syndrome. This syndrome is based on the idea that clients who claim to have recovered memories of childhood sexual abuse are often the hapless victims of irresponsible therapists. According to the foundation, many adults (primarily women) have had memories implanted by their therapists and then, on the basis of these false memories, have been urged to confront and sue their parents.

Unfortunately, many engaged in the debate that has arisen have become vitriolic and highly emotional. Those on one side suggest that the FMS Foundation is nothing more than a safe harbor for perpetrators. Others suggest that most to all therapists are bad, motivated by money, overzealous, and even unethical. Although there may be a grain of truth in both extremes, for the most part neither is an accurate representation of the situation.

First of all, any parent can call the FMS Foundation, say they have been falsely accused by an adult child with "implanted" memories, and become a member of that foundation. They do not undergo any rigorous questioning or any form of testing, and they are not required to "prove" that *their* memories are accurate. At the same time, any adult can walk into a therapist's office and relate a narrative of horrendous abuse, and the therapist will probably not doubt her, test her, or require her to prove the accuracy of those memories.

Second, for the most part the debate is not between those who care about victims and those who care about truth. That is a false dichotomy and tends to result in each side's seeing the other as the enemy. I believe that both sides care about both victims and the truth. I suppose I am stating the obvious if I say that neither side has a monopoly on the truth, and neither side has only victims and no perpetrators involved.

Part of what feeds the above dichotomy is that advocates of false memory paint a picture of an ideal family victimized by an unethical therapist and a deluded or lying client. They fail to discuss things like sociopathy, lying, amnesia, dissociation, alcohol blackout, and the fact that perpetrators are known for their denial of the truth. I suspect that some proportion of the membership of the FMS Foundation has truly been unjustly accused. At the same time, a key characteristic of a perpetrator is denial, so I suspect that some proportion of those crying false memory have been rightly accused.

Advocates of repressed memory present the single possibility of an adult who was sexually victimized as a child and who was previously fearful or unable to speak the truth of her life. They often fail to mention manipulation, ignorance, the search for personal aggrandizement, and lack of ethics among therapists. However rare such therapists may be (and I *do* believe they are rare), we are foolish to assume they do not exist. Not only have some therapists acted unethically by insisting that a client with no memories was sexually abused, but others have contributed to the mess by insisting on a family confrontation that was not adequately prepared for or not truly chosen by the client.

If the polarization between these two groups is not curtailed, it will impede progress in learning about memory and it will "create" victims on both sides. It is absolutely vital for both sides to maintain dialogue and to exercise caution in applying their theories, beliefs, and research to individual cases.

Those of us who are psychologists and counselors to the sexually abused need to monitor the field and ourselves wisely and carefully. To fail to do so is to act unethically toward those we say we are trying to help. The effective practice of counseling requires close attention to ethical principles. Of all groups, this should be characteristic of Christians in the field. Dr. Sam Knapp, professional affairs officer of the Pennsylvania Psychological Association, noted that techniques commonly associated with implanted-memory complaints include age regression, "body work," trance writing, high-pressure "support" groups, "reparenting," or the inappropriate use of hypnosis and bibliotherapy.[6] We need to be very careful about the kinds of treatment techniques we use and the promises of help we offer based on those techniques.

In an effort to suggest some guidelines for working with traumatic memories, we must keep in mind the characteristics that are typical of clients who have been sexually abused. Many survivors are more likely *not* to reveal their secret and to minimize what happened to them. Abusers often intimidate their victims into silence. Survivors usually carry great shame and humiliation about the abuse and hesitate to tell anyone about it. Survivors also fear that no one will believe them. It is most unusual to find someone who has fabricated a story of abuse parading it in hopes of some return. Many years ago I encountered one young woman who did just that in an effort to punish her politically prominent father. Needless to say, such a client presents in a vastly different way from someone who has always known or just discovered that she was sexually abused.

If in the midst of this debate we as counselors are to take

informed and ethical care of the hurting people who come to us, what guidelines might we follow? To the best of our ability we need to ensure that we do not further injure someone whose suffering is great enough to propel her into the office of a stranger to ask for help.

1. A degree in counseling does not automatically qualify some-one to work with trauma survivors. Effective treatment of any specific difficulty requires study, training, and supervision. This area is no exception.

2. As much as possible, all questions should be asked from an unbiased standpoint. It is not possible for any human being to be completely neutral or even to avoid asking questions that appear to lead in a particular direction. However, questions based on the presumption that a therapist "knows" about a client's life something that the client does not know are arrogant and unethical. No matter how much therapy we have done or how much knowledge we have, we *cannot* read other people's minds for them. Frankly, I believe that more experience results in a greater awareness of the complexity of the mind and how little we know. A healthy dose of humility is in order when "tromping" around in other people's heads.

3. No single set of symptoms automatically indicates that a person is a victim of childhood sexual abuse. Some of the checklists are so general that it would appear likely that no human being has escaped molestation in childhood. There is no scientific evidence that supports the conclusion that people with a certain set of symptoms have unequivocally been victims of sexual abuse as children. Any competent scholar knows the difference between correlation and cause and effect. Two people can exhibit an almost identical constellation of symptoms and yet have very different causes for those symptoms.

4. Ethical therapists will neither offer an instant child-abuse explanation for a group of symptoms nor dismiss reports of sexual abuse without serious exploration in therapy. Ethical therapists will ask a client whether she thinks childhood sexual abuse is possibly an underlying issue. They will ask, not tell. Even with a known survivor, insistence on facing the truth of the abuse when the client has slipped back into denial or is not ready to proceed is a reenactment of two of the major factors of abuse: coercion and

denial of what she is feeling.

5. An understanding of human beings will include a keen awareness that there are some very dependent people capable of suggestibility and grave distortions. As a therapist, you are in a position of power and influence. Your words and suggestions have great impact. Choose them wisely and well. Therapists need to have a deep respect for the trust placed in them, particularly with regard to a suffering person's need to make sense out of an internal world that is often confused and frightening.

6. We have already established the fact that memory is either stored and/or narrated with the perceiver's interpretations of that memory. Anyone who has returned to a childhood home as an adult knows this, for it is amazing to discover how small things have gotten in twenty years' time! Keep in mind that the point of therapy is not to get every detail absolutely correct but to tell the story in the context of a relationship that will enable the client to grow in her ability to live free of the aftereffects of the trauma.

7. An accurate understanding of the human heart, clearly given to us in Scripture, states that every heart, no matter how nice or wounded a person it dwells in, is capable of deceit, hate, and slander. If the human heart is capable of the atrocity of the sexual abuse of little boys and girls, it is certainly capable of lying about such abuse.

8. Bibliotherapeutic and/or group therapy should not be suggested unless the client is reasonably certain that she was sexually abused. I do not think that group therapy with known survivors or reading the stories of other survivors is a profitable method for uncovering possible hidden trauma. Part of the reason is that clients usually enter therapy motivated by the pain they are experiencing, and many are desperate to find a reason for that pain. That is understandable, for most of us long to know why we are suffering. To take someone who is unclear about the cause of her suffering and place her in a room full of people who know they have been abused and who may even exhibit similar symptoms is suggestive and leading.

9. If hidden trauma is strongly suspected on the basis of objective criteria (amnesia, dissociative tendencies, nightmares) and the client's suffering is severe, exploratory methods may be justifiable.

These are aimed not at proving sexual abuse but rather at attempting to understand what is underlying the client's symptoms. The contextual clues can be relatively neutral. For example, the therapist may ask the client to look through old photograph albums, visit a childhood neighborhood, review school or medical records, or talk to siblings or former schoolmates. Rather than requiring the client to "produce" a trauma of any kind, the therapist is simply encouraging her to learn more about herself than she currently remembers.

SUMMARY

Over the past twenty years, public and professional awareness of sexual victimization has dramatically increased. As recently as the 1970s, rape was considered a rare occurrence and incest a universal taboo. The character of victims was disparaged, and the credibility of women alleging assault was routinely questioned. The social climate has changed tremendously in the last two decades.

In the midst of that change has arisen a debate regarding whether or not many who say they were sexually abused as children are remembering true events or reciting stories based on memories implanted by unethical therapists. It is extremely crucial that clinicians and researchers not allow the current polarization to compromise either research about traumatic memory or clinical discussion surrounding memory work with adult survivors. We owe it to those who have suffered much at the hands of others to work collaboratively and ethically as we seek to increase our understanding of these issues. Those of us who counsel and call ourselves Christians should most certainly be characterized by an adherence to ethical standards, humility, wisdom, and an ever growing dependence on the Holy Spirit. If such characteristics are present, then our contribution to the discussion and to our clients will be both worthy and beneficial.

22

Male Survivors

Research on male victims of childhood sexual abuse has not been as extensive as the research on female victims. Research results have been mixed. In 1979, David Finkelhor found that 5 to 9 percent of college males surveyed reported childhood sexual victimization.[1] More recently, in a study of 595 male college students in the Boston area, 29 percent reported childhood sexual abuse.[2] Nielsen noted that male victims make up 25 to 35 percent of the caseloads of clinicians working in the area of childhood sexual abuse.[3]

Based on recent data and clinical experience, John Briere, well known for his research on interpersonal violence, states that "much of post-sexual-abuse trauma manifests equally in males and females, and that treatment approaches appropriate for one sex are usually applicable to the other."[4] Although it is thought that males report sexual abuse less often than females, they are evidently no more immune to its negative effects.

Finkelhor and others have shown that most boys, unlike girls, are sexually abused outside the family.[5] Many male clients seem to have difficulty acknowledging that such encounters are abuse, however. Often the perpetrator was a camp counselor, male teacher, clergy, or youth leader. Male survivors often see such encounters as "no big deal." There is also great ambivalence about the experience when the boy's father was distant and uncaring or absent. The boy treasured the attention from a respected male figure, even while that attention was abusive. Another cause for ambivalence is that our culture views victimization as a feminine or weak position. It socializes men to be sexually aggressive, not passive and easily victimized. Acknowledging such weakness does not come easily, and great self-loathing and humiliation often accompany its recognition.

Victimization often has the effect of being very destructive to a growing boy's sense of masculinity. To be a victim means something was "done" to you, a concept abhorrent to many men in regard to anything sexual. In addition, many male survivors struggle with and are confused by the fact that they were molested by another male. The combination of perceived weakness and sexual contact with another male often leads to confusion regarding sexual identity. Many men talk about the terrible anxiety over their sexual identity that resulted from the abuse.

Studies show that a large majority of male sexual offenders are also victims of sexual abuse. It is postulated that this is because males will cope with the abuse by identifying with the aggressor. It is perhaps a way of rejecting the position of victim and assuming a position of power. It is important to note, however, that although many sexual offenders have histories of childhood sexual abuse, the majority of male survivors do *not* go on to become perpetrators.[6]

However, because of the increased potential for sexual aggression, it is important to inform male survivors of the therapist's duty to warn. This should be done at the time of screening and at the point of any disclosure during therapy. I also think that therapists who are not trained to work with perpetrators ought to refer such clients to an individual or program that not only can deal with the client's own abuse history but also has expertise in working with perpetrators. Expertise with survivors is not sufficient.

Like female survivors, many male survivors have great difficulty admitting to the painful and frightening feeling engendered by the sexual abuse. This seems to be complicated further for men because the culture deems men more masculine when they can control or do not even experience feelings of weakness, fear, and submissiveness. Many male victims have worked so hard to manage these "unacceptable" feelings that they are almost devoid of any emotional expression at all. Others manage these emotions by acting out in aggressive ways or by abusing substances.

A therapist working with male survivors may find that the need to normalize such feelings as sadness and fear is greater with males than with females. On the other hand, therapists who treat male survivors also need to be able to handle strong expressions of rage. Many therapists are more comfortable responding to the expressions of sadness and fear in male and female victims alike than they are responding to expressions of anger.

Whether the therapist is male or female, power dynamics also play an important part in work with male survivors. Briere notes that male clients seen by male therapists will often try to be either "one up" (verbally aggressive, challenging) or "one down" (passive, eager to please) with the therapist.[7] When the therapist is female, the client may attempt to place her in the subordinate position of sex object or elevate her to idealized mother.

In my practice, I have probably seen male survivors in a one-to-ten ratio to female survivors. Most of the men I have worked with were molested by extrafamilial members, although some were abused by older male siblings and others by their mothers. Several of these men were abused by men who were extremely violent and whose violence had resulted in the death of other boys. When mothers have been the perpetrators, they have usually been the single parent or they have dominated the home. In my experience, a high proportion of male survivors struggle with pornography addictions, voyeurism, transvestic fetishism (cross-dressing), exhibitionism, and fetishism. Whether that is generally so or has simply been the case within my practice, I do not know.

SUMMARY

It is my experience that childhood sexual abuse generally affects males and females in similar ways. Therefore, treatment is similar for both populations. However, because sexual abuse occurs within a cultural context, some specific clinical issues are more prevalent in male survivors: denial about the abuse, difficulty expressing sadness and fear, potential identification with the perpetrator, identity confusion regarding sexual preference, and incidence of acting-out behaviors and expressions of rage.

PART SIX

The Person of the Therapist

23

The Impact of Trauma Work on the Therapist

To enter into a therapeutic alliance with a survivor of trauma such as incest is to be touched by that trauma. We do not have to be the direct recipient of a traumatic event in order to be traumatized. The concept of secondary traumatization is included in the Diagnostic and Statistical Manual of Mental Disorders IV's description of post-traumatic stress disorder. We are told that the characteristic symptoms following exposure to a traumatic stressor can occur as a result of "learning about unexpected or violent death, serious harm, or threat of death or injury experienced by a family member or other close associates" (italics added).[1]

The process of sitting hour after hour, often for months or years, with people who matter to us and attending to their traumatic experiences has a profound impact on us as listeners. The dynamic of being affected by another's suffering is prevalent even in less intense relationships, where we often hear someone say, "She will just have to stop talking about that because I can't handle it anymore." Such a statement is made when the receiver cannot tolerate any further exposure to the distressing event that is being recounted.

I have noted throughout the years that many of my colleagues have abandoned their work with traumatized clients. Perhaps that is because they did not learn how to endure for the long haul. Many have started out eager to help and have fallen by the wayside after five or seven years. If you and I hope to run this race with perseverance, then we must give careful thought to what it involves.

Before we consider specific ideas about what enables a therapist to endure, I first want to look at the broader picture. You and I call ourselves Christians, and we have chosen to work in what we refer to as the "helping professions." Saying that we are *Christians* means a wealth of things. At least in part it means that we know and love Jesus Christ and are called to live in obedience to him. Saying that we are in the *helping professions* means not only that we are to know and love people but also that knowledge and love are to be evident in the work we do with them. Saying that we are Christians *in* the helping professions should mean that the love and obedience we give Jesus Christ are clearly demonstrated in the knowledge and love we have for people.

There is another significant factor at work because we are Christians living in "this present evil world" (Gal. 1:4, KJV). So often we believers seem prone to dwell on "the bright side" of things. No one can question that life in Christ has a bright side. Yes, we worship a God who loves us infinitely and brings joy, peace, and hope into every soul he indwells. However, it is also true that we live in a dark world and that our lives are lived out in the context of the battle of the ages.

As Christians, we live in the midst of the conflict between our great Redeemer and principalities, powers, rulers of darkness, and potentialities unknown and unimagined. Not only do we live in the midst of that great conflict, but we are also players whose every word and deed matters in the battle. Every day we come in contact with evil and suffering, seen and unseen. As Christian therapists, we encounter such things in an intense manner as we work to minister to the brokenness of other human beings. We cannot help but be profoundly affected. To fail to acknowledge and understand the impact of that is foolish.

Recent writing in the field of trauma therapy has pointed out that over time, therapists who work with trauma survivors can begin to display what has been called secondary traumatic stress disorder. Charles Figley defines secondary traumatic stress disorder (STSD) as "the natural consequent behaviors and emotions resulting from knowing about a traumatizing event experienced by a significant other."[2] The symptoms for STSD are nearly the same as for PTSD. The difference resides in the exposure to the trauma. In STSD the person is exposed to the *knowledge* of the trauma, whereas in PTSD the sufferer *experienced* the primary traumatic stress.

Laurie Pearlman and Karen Saakvitne, in their excellent book *Trauma and the Therapist,* refer to a phenomenon they call "vicarious traumatization." The construct of vicarious traumatization is defined as "the transformation in the inner experience of the therapist that comes about as a result of empathic engagement with clients' trauma material."[3] The authors discuss the impact of graphic descriptions of violence and cruelty on the therapist who listens empathically from the position of helpless witness to historical events and oftentimes present reenactments. These authors also make the important distinction that it is not the *person* of the client who is traumatizing but rather the material the client brings.

In essence, trauma is contagious. Jung spoke about the danger of contagion when working with psychotics. Such contagion seems to be even greater in trauma work. This phenomenon is certainly not limited to therapy. We see similar symptoms in emergency-room personnel, among staff members of rape crisis centers, and among workers responding to those affected by natural disasters. Being a witness to an atrocity has a profound impact on a human being. Dr. Judith Herman, in her book *Trauma and Recovery,* says that engagement in the work of trauma "poses some risk to the therapist's own psychological health."[4] Many therapists begin to experience symptoms of a traumatic stress disorder, such as sleeplessness, nightmares, intrusive images, anxiety, numbing, hypervigilance, and irritability.[5] In addition, therapists may experience challenges to their faith, growing cynicism, a burgeoning pessimism, and a heightened feeling of vulnerability to disaster and evil.[6] The conclusion, I think, is that if one is going to work with explosives, one runs the risk of getting burned.

It is common for therapists to experience an overwhelming sense of helplessness when confronted with trauma and not only to react with symptoms of traumatic stress but also to throw themselves into the role of savior or rescuer. Faced with the reality of cruelty and evil, confronted with the inability to have stopped it, and then repeatedly exposed to present-day reenactments in the client's life, many therapists begin to ignore therapeutic boundaries, live a life managed by crisis phone calls, and assume something of an advocacy role by taking on tasks best handled by the client (e.g., finding a place for the client to live). Such attempts to play God are destructive to both the client and the therapist. They teach the client that she is not capable of acting for herself (a message already learned at the hand of her abusers), and they crush the therapist with the burden of filling a pair of infinity-sized shoes.

If we are to know how to avoid the potentially destructive consequences of trauma therapy, we need to be clear about what our clients bring to us. If trauma is contagious and if we are in danger of "catching" it, then we must grasp its nature so that we can find the proper antidote.

We have already stated that as Christians in a helping profession, we daily and intensely come into contact with evil and suffering. I believe that as counselors, we often blind ourselves to the impact of that evil and suffering by referring to what we do only in clinical terms. Now, I am all for the use of clinical terms. I find them helpful for conceptualizing many things. However, I also think they can prevent us from truly seeing what we interact with day after day, hour after hour, in our offices.

I want to list for you some of the things that touch you daily if you are involved in a clinical practice of some kind. You witness or interact with lies and deceit, immorality, hatred, violence, jealousy, outbursts of anger, sorcery, disputes, death and dying, the occult, seduction, dissensions, cruelty, abuse, cursing, fear, rage, bitterness, and oppression. What an overwhelming menu!

If we look honestly at our list, we can see that we are talking about terrible evil and incredible suffering. In order to understand how these might affect us when we sit so close to them, we need to comprehend their nature. I am aware that volumes have been written on the nature of both evil and suffering. If truth be told, it is likely that none of us is satisfied with the explanations and wisdom of the ages regarding these difficult areas. I certainly am not deluded enough to think I am going to solve the riddle of suffering and evil for you. I simply want to highlight a few points so we have some sense of what we are dealing with and how it might affect us.

I am aware that although we are Christians in the field of psychology, we rarely speak about evil. We talk about pathology, dysfunction, abuse, and aberrant behavior. All of these concepts are realities, and we need to talk about them; but so is evil. In fact, evil is the greater and more powerful reality.

When we discussed the process of forgiveness in chapter 15, we mentioned four characteristics of sin, all of which are germane to this discussion. We said that evil is opposed to God, opposite to our good, a poison that spreads, and an offense against God himself.

As therapists, you and I encounter evil every day of our lives, both in and out of our offices. Behind our closed doors we sit with decay and death. In the name of Jesus, for his sake, and for the sake of his people, we choose to connect with the consequences of evil in others' lives.

In addition, we need to face the fact that we encounter evil not only in the lives of others but also in our own hearts. This is considerably worse than the idea of contagion. It is no longer something we can just "catch" from others. Not only must we wrestle with evil personally, but I find that mine often blinds me to yours and yours can feed mine. If we are people who truly love Christ and long for the light, then we live in a dangerous world and we are engaged in a dangerous profession. We live with, sit with, walk among, listen to, and handle those things that seek to destroy the life for which we long and to which we are called.

SUFFERING

It often seems that counselors are more comfortable talking about suffering than about evil. However, although we speak about suffering more readily than others do, I am not certain that we understand how entering into the suffering of others day after day might affect us. None of us likes suffering. Most of us are afraid of it. We do not want it to enter into our personal lives if we can help it. At the same time, suffering can hold a certain fascination for us. It often seems so mysterious, so inexplicable, that we are drawn in by our never-ending attempts to make sense out of things. However, philosophically and practically, for most of us suffering remains an awful problem and essentially an unexplainable mystery.

In spite of its mysteriousness, we can say several things about suffering:

1. Suffering rarely makes sense. We know that suffering is unreasonable; it is irrational. We work very hard to make sense out of it. We write books and give talks that attempt to make suffering reasonable. Although such attempts can be very helpful to us, I often think that the ability to explain suffering is the clearest indicator of never having suffered. Who can give a rational explanation for why two parents are, for the third time, burying one of their adolescent sons? How can we make sense out of the death of a thirty-year-old mother? Who of us can look the Holocaust full in the face and adequately explain it? It does not make sense. It seems incomprehensible.

2. Suffering rarely seems just. How many times have you encountered suffering in your own life or another's and thought it was truly fair? We try hard to balance it out. The disciples did too. When they passed a man blind from birth, they asked Jesus, "Rabbi, who sinned, this man or his parents, that he was born blind?" (John 9:2). Balance it out for us. Tell us it is fair because of something someone did. Jesus was not very helpful in this regard. He said, "No one." You can rarely balance it out. There is no balance for the gang rape of an eleven-year-old girl. There is no justice in the brutal molesting of a child. It is not fair that a boy's trusted youth director should involve him in sexual activity. There is no fairness in the suffering of an AIDS baby. You cannot make suffering fair.

3. Suffering in and of itself is not good. It is wrong. It was not intended to exist. Death is not good; abuse is not good; violence is not good. Sometimes as Christians we sound as if we think it is good. We sit across from indescribable suffering and glibly pronounce that "all things work together for good to them that love God" (Rom. 8:28, KJV). Now do not misunderstand. I believe that verse with all of my heart. But it is not a glib verse, and it does not say that suffering is good. It does not say, "Don't worry about what you are enduring; it will all turn out nice in the end." It *does* say that the God we worship is capable of redeeming the deepest agony, the most hideous suffering, the pain beyond words, into something that gives life to others and brings glory to him. But make no mistake, the transfiguring of agony into redemption cost Jesus inestimably. Death does not normally transform into life in this dark world. God's redemption worked out in the life of one of his children always costs. The beauty of redemption in a life *never* comes easily. Whenever it does come, we can be certain we have stepped into the realm of the supernatural.

In summary, you and I, sinners ourselves, sit daily with those things that are a direct attack on God. We witness those things that are opposite to him and our good. Because we also are sinners, the danger of contagion increases exponentially. We enter into irrational and unjust circumstances that torment and twist people whom we have come to know and love. We cannot control it, stop it, manage it, or fix it. What will happen to us if we stay in such a place?

RESULTS OF EXPOSURE TO TRAUMA

Obviously, many things can result from allowing ourselves to be vulnerable to evil and suffering in the lives of others. In essence, we can easily end up in the image of our clients rather than in the image of our God. What we are exposed to as creatures will shape us. Part of being human is the ability to be affected by the people and circumstances of our lives. If being human means being malleable, capable of being affected, then what we allow to shape us becomes a central point of concern.

1. We are vulnerable to secondary stress. We have already noted that the literature suggests that trauma therapists often manifest symptoms similar to their clients. The research says if you sit with trauma long enough, it will traumatize you too. Certainly the trauma we experience as therapists differs from the trauma experienced by the survivor. However, in their particular ways, both therapist and survivor can be profoundly affected by the brutality and violence they encounter.

2. We are vulnerable to spiritual struggles. Not only can therapists demonstrate symptoms of secondary stress disorder, they can also reflect their clients' struggle to hold simultaneously the reality of evil and suffering with the eternal truth of a loving and sovereign God. Many of us, client and therapist alike, respond to this tension by attempting to deny the reality of suffering in some fashion ("It couldn't have been that bad. If you just do these three things, you'll be better"), or we face the depth of the evil and lose sight of God.

We are all aware of those who work hard trying to minimize evil and suffering and who expend great energy to get their theology to assist them. I have always found that surprising, given that our faith is centered on the one we call the Suffering Servant. However, I know it is done, for I see the casualties of such thinking in my office often enough.

Many of us err on the other side and lose sight of who God is in truth. To look on suffering and not dilute it, especially in the life of one we love, is to wrestle with the temptation to slander God. We cannot be confronted with a crack baby, the rape of a little girl, the senseless death of a high school senior, the ravages of cancer, and a thousand other things and not ask questions. If you do not ask questions, then I doubt you have truly entered into the other's suffering. However, such questions easily lead to wondering whether or not God is good, whether or not he is love. And how easy it becomes to suggest he is not! God is shrouded; he seems callous and indifferent. Jesus told us who he was, yet everything around us seems to scream to the contrary. To sit with suffering is to be a companion to those things that will wage war on the core of your faith.

3. We may find our voice silenced. Earlier we spoke about three aspects of the image of God in human beings: voice, relationship, and power. As we considered voice, we noted that we are created in the image of God, who speaks. Those things that distort the voice of

God (confuse or hide truth) result in destruction to person. Oppression, cruelty, sexual abuse, and trauma can silence voice not only in the client but in the therapist as well.

Our voice can be silenced when feelings become numb and we make an effort to avoid certain thoughts and activities. Voice can be silenced when we must carry intense, difficult material alone because of the need for confidentiality and the absence of anyone with which to debrief. Voice can be stilled by thoughts such as, *No one would believe this anyway.* We can be shut up by others' stating that the extreme nature of the information therefore renders it unlikely to be true or something they do not want to hear about. Voice is silenced because we often can find no words to communicate the feelings and questions the trauma material generates in us. How like our clients!

4. We may feel isolated. Trauma work, like trauma, isolates. We said that a second aspect of the image of God is relationship. Relationship as God intended it is to include reciprocal knowing and loving. Obviously the experience of sexual abuse shatters relationship. It is also true that bearing witness to trauma can result in isolation.

Isolation occurs when a therapist experiencing STSD shows diminished interest in normal activities or begins detaching from others. Isolation can occur when someone points out a darling four-year-old and you wrestle with whether or not to let yourself be known by revealing that your first thought was, *I wonder who is abusing her?* Isolation occurs when you find you have been crying in your sleep and don't even know how to explain why. Increased pessimism and a heightened sense of vulnerability strain relationships. Isolation becomes profound when, driven to help yet one more person, we become so consumed by our work that we reach a point where we have no life apart from therapy. Spiritual isolation frequently results because of unshared doubts and struggles and the great challenges to our faith. How easy it is for the therapist to be made in the image of the client.

5. We may feel powerless. The third aspect of the image of God in human beings was that God gave us power to have an impact. We were meant to have influence, to create, to govern. We were not intended to be invisible, helpless people who leave no mark. However, trauma therapy can overwhelm us with feelings of helplessness. It is common in supervision to hear about terrible struggles with feelings of inadequacy. The therapist's skills and knowledge seem like spoon-sized tools when facing the prospect of emptying the ocean. The client's sense of impotence is also contagious, and it is easy for the therapist to treat the client as if she is utterly helpless in the face of crises or pain. A therapist's sense of helplessness often skyrockets when repetitive self-abuse is a problem for a client. Like our clients, we see and experience terrible things and feel powerless to stop them.

SUMMARY

I believe that the experiences of vicarious traumatization are inevitable in working with adult survivors of sexual abuse. It is also true that if the therapist's struggles go unnamed and untended, there can be disastrous results in the lives of both the client and the therapist. However, while the impact of such work is unavoidable, experiencing destructive consequences is not.

Oswald Chambers said, "The sheep are many and the shepherds few, for the fatigue is staggering, the heights are giddy and the sights awful."[7] Assuming vicarious traumatization to be inevitable and assuming that Chambers describes our work accurately, how are we to survive such conditions? We cannot sit with suffering and evil in the lives of others without contamination unless we find ways to protect ourselves. We cannot enter such things as depression, sexual abuse, rage, death, despair, grief, and terror without precautions. If we do, not only will we find ourselves shaped by them, but our responses in turn will shape others in twisted ways. We sit surrounded by and carry within us those things that are of the nature of death. Unless we are in fighting trim, we will be swallowed up by that death or end up pretending it does not exist.

What does it mean to be in fighting trim? What are the strategies that will enable us to endure over the long haul? The word *endure* means to hold out against, to sustain without impairment, to bear with patience. If we are to sit with suffering, listen empathically to the trauma our clients have endured, and persevere as people through whom the redemptive life of Christ flows, then we must learn the art of endurance.

24

Strategies that Foster Endurance

In the previous chapter we stated that we cannot eliminate vicarious traumatization or secondary stress symptoms while working with adult survivors of sexual abuse. With this in mind, we will consider four strategic areas or techniques that I believe are crucial to persevering as an effective therapist.

Knowing Ourselves

The first strategy is one that is vital to all therapists, no matter what kind of work they do. It is crucial that we know who we are. We need to be aware of our strengths and weaknesses, our limitations and resources, where change has occurred, and where ongoing work is needed. If we are unaware of our limits, physically or emotionally, we risk damaging ourselves and our clients. If we do not comprehend the strength of our personality, we could easily run over others. If we are unaware of how emotionally needy we feel at a particular juncture, we may fall into the trap of using others to fill us up. If we are afraid of confrontation, we will avoid speaking truth when it is hard to do so. If we fear facing the truth about ourselves, we will be unable to accept feedback from our clients, and we will end up denying our clients' reality in the same way that their abusers denied it (i.e., whatever is a problem between us is your fault). To be unaware of our own interpersonal anxieties, anger, disconnection, confusion, or lack of understanding is potentially to become a lethal weapon.

Setting Limits

A second strategy for managing the trauma our clients bring to us is that of setting limits. We can do this in a variety of ways, and our need for such limitations can vary over time. A primary way to limit our exposure to traumatic material is to set parameters regarding the number of survivors we carry in our caseload. Depending on your personality, experience, personal circumstances, and coping skills, this might range from being able to manage one or two cases to having trauma victims make up over 50 percent of your caseload. Just as our clients can deal with traumatic material only in doses, so it is with us. We may be able to tolerate sizable doses for many years and then find we need to decrease the amount for a significant time. Obviously the ability to make such decisions is closely tied to our level of self-awareness.

Other specific ways we can limit our exposure to traumatic material include screening what we read, monitoring the types of movies we see, keeping a tight rein on conversations so that talk of our work does not bleed into every other arena, and limiting the amount of supervision we do for other trauma therapists. I recently had a supervisee of mine say of her own accord that she would bring me graphic details of her cases only when doing so was necessary for the supervision. I greatly appreciated her sensitivity.

Maintaining Strong Professional Connections

A third strategy is to maintain strong professional connections with other therapists. I find this helpful in four ways. First of all, there are times when it is simply necessary to debrief. The process of debriefing involves telling another therapist something of what we just heard because it is too big for us to handle alone. Debriefing can reduce the size of what feels like overwhelming tragedy and keep us from feeling lost in it.

A second aspect of professional connection is the benefit of ongoing supervision. Supervision provides the therapist with a place to process feelings about the content of sessions, to get feedback regarding work, and to bring a sense of connection in what can be very isolating work. Supervision can occur in a one-on-one relationship and/or a peer supervisory group.

Third, it is also wise to find ways of reminding oneself that there are other aspects to one's professional self besides trauma work. This is partly achieved by doing therapeutic work other than trauma therapy. It is also good to attend conferences and lectures that discuss aspects of therapy that are not focused on traumatic material.

The fourth aspect of professional connection involves broadening one's work base. Many therapists find it helpful and healthful to balance their therapy work by teaching, doing seminar presentations, writing, or doing research. This can give us a sense of greater effectiveness because we find ourselves able to reach a larger audience with our knowledge and skills. It also balances the isolation we often feel working with one person at a time behind closed doors. Work that involves interaction with the public also results in more immediate feedback than is likely in individual therapy. All of these things work together to keep us grounded and to remind us that we are more than trauma therapists and that the field in which we work is rich in its diversity and contributions.

Maintaining a Healthy Personal Life

The final strategy that has been both helpful and necessary to me involves finding ways to maintain a healthy personal life. In their book *Trauma and the Therapist,* Laurie Pearlman and Karen Saakvitne state, "Probably the most important recommendation we make to our colleagues about their personal lives is to have one."[1] They go on to emphasize the importance of play and rest in the therapist's life.

It is interesting to note that a common problem area for many trauma therapists is caring for their bodies. Lack of physical care for our bodies is a very basic way in which we can become made in the image of our clients. Often therapists' lives get reduced to *doing* trauma therapy, *reading about* trauma therapy, and *thinking about* trauma therapy. Proper diet, rest, and exercise are not attended to, and it is easy to become physically depleted.

Lack of attention to one's body is a very short step away from lack of attention to one's feelings. The experience of numbing and being depleted can easily lead to an abuse of drugs, alcohol, and/or food. We cease to listen to our bodies and our emotions. We drive ourselves yet one more day and end up living on a survival level. When this happens, we mirror our clients rather than model for them the fact that one can choose to be fit and healthy and connected with life.

As I have worked with trauma material over the years, I have found it necessary to actively pursue those things that for me are antidotes to the evil and suffering I hear every day. Like my clients, I need ways to keep myself grounded so I do not get lost in the traumatic material. I do this in various ways, from hobbies to my involvement in the lives of my husband and sons. I have found three specific and easily doable activities to be consistently nurturing. When I have listened to evil and trauma for hours, a hike through the mountains or by a running stream is wonderfully beneficial. The quiet and beauty are direct pointers to the beauty of God my Savior. When clients have spilled out chaos, past and present, in my office, listening to music by Bach and Mozart reminds me of order and harmony. When feelings of disconnection and isolation set in, the laughter and prayers of friends and colleagues often surround and comfort me. These are things that nurture me and enable me both to persevere and to maintain my enjoyment of life.

It is not enough to make a professional commitment to the work of trauma therapy. If our commitment does not extend to our own persons as well, then our effectiveness will be short-lived, our potential to harm those who seek our help will be increased, and our ability to endure will wane. I cannot emphasize enough the riches

I have gleaned from my work with survivors. I have been challenged by their courage and their endurance. To walk with them requires the same from me. I dishonor them if I fail to maintain my person so that together we might continue to the end.

25

The Spiritual Life of the Therapist

I have found the strategies listed in the previous chapter vital to my work as a trauma therapist. However, they alone are not sufficient. Such strategies are life giving, yes, but ultimately they are only auxiliary life givers. They would dry up quickly were it not for the Life Giver himself.

To be a Christian in this world is to live with death and darkness. To work with traumatized clients is to encounter death and darkness intensely. We have said that such work will have an impact on us. I can personally say that I am forever changed. I can also say that I have begun to grasp some wonderful truths. Jesus said in Matthew 10:27, "What I tell you in the dark, speak in the daylight; what is whispered in your ear, proclaim from the roofs." Over the years I have begun to learn some things from the one who brought light and life into this world. I would like to pass on to you what God has whispered in my ear throughout the course of my work.

In Isaiah 45:3 God says, "I will give you the treasures of darkness, riches stored in secret places, so that you may know that I am the Lord, the God of Israel, who summons you by name." This book would not be complete if I did not to try to articulate for you some of the treasures and hidden wealth I have found in the darkness.

We said earlier that ultimately therapy needs to be incarnational and redemptive. Through the Incarnation, Jesus came into this world to explain the Father to us. Like Jesus, we are called to demonstrate in flesh-and-blood actualities the character of God himself. Our lives are to be living epistles that explain who God is to those who read us. Those who sit across from us in our offices or live with us in our homes should be able to say, "Now I better understand who God is because of the way you have lived before me."

We have also said that Jesus became incarnate for the purpose of accomplishing redemption. He came to buy back what was lost, to make all things new, to set free the captives. Only a life that manifests the character of God can be redemptive. If we want the work that we do to restore and make new, then we ourselves must incarnate who God is.

Finally, we stated that since the beginning, life begets after its own likeness. As human beings, we are capable of shaping and being shaped. We produce after our own kind, genetically and in many other ways. We noted in chapter 23 that it is very easy for a trauma therapist to be made in the image of his or her clients. If you and I sit with criticism long enough, we can easily become critical as well. If we sit with trauma long enough, we also begin to look traumatized.

If you and I desire to explain the Father to others and serve as a vehicle for redemption in their lives, then clearly we must find a way to look like Jesus rather than be shaped by the many other forces that surround us. I certainly do not have the final answer on what it means to look like Jesus in this world. What I can do is lay before you the treasures I have gleaned—treasures I hope are beginning to shape me.

First and foremost, there is a foundational principle from which all else flows. If we look at the life of Jesus, we see that the Incarnation led to redemption by way of the Cross. If the perfect Son of God had to go that way, it is unlikely that you and I will be excused. The way of the Cross involves many things: The Cross shows us the truth about what God thinks. The Cross teaches us that this world and we who inhabit it are so hideously dark and wrong that only the death of Christ himself could remedy it. The Cross also demonstrates for the unlovable a depth of love that is utterly beyond our comprehension. It is a startling exhibition of the heart of God. In the Cross we have an eternal symbol of God's point of view. I have come to see that the only way I can hope to look like Jesus and bring life to others is by way of the Cross. If I do not follow the way of the Cross and put to death the things in me that are not of God, then they will put to death the things that are of God, in me and in those whose lives I touch.

SPIRITUAL DISCIPLINES

God uses five tools to create his life in me and in others. I will refer to them as disciplines. I choose that word because I am a disciple undergoing training. These are simply the methods of instruction that God is using.

The Discipline of Worship

God began to teach me about worship when I reached a critical juncture with a client and simply did not know what to do. At those times I tend to go to God and ask him, "What should I do?" I do not know about you, but when I go to God with a question, I am often surprised by his response.

At that time I was in great need of an answer and waited for one expectantly. I needed to know what to do and what to say. Even hearing God's answer at that time required a radical shift for me. I believed action was required immediately. The initial response from God was a very "loud" silence. Typically, my response to silence is to jump in and try to figure it out for myself. As a young therapist, I often responded to my clients' silences by filling them with words. It was always a mistake to do so. Being educable, though somewhat on the slow side spiritually, it dawned on me that if filling those silences between people with words or actions was a mistake, then perhaps the same thing might be true in my relationship to God.

As I waited, the answer came. It was not an answer that said, "Do this or that." It was an answer that surprised me. I had come to see that Christians live out their lives in the context of the most important battle of time and eternity. It is a battle against a relentless, deceptive, brilliant schemer with massive forces we cannot see. In such a context, every fiber of our being calls for action. And yet in that context, the answer I got back was, "Worship me. You want to outsmart this schemer? You want to win in this battle? You want what you do to be deathless and redemptive? You want to leave behind you the aroma of Jesus? Then worship me."

To truly follow the way of the Cross is to fall down and worship. What other possible response is there to the sight of the great God of the universe bending down to bear our sin? It is very easy when working with hurting people to think that speaking God's truth is of first importance or that loving God's people is foremost. But the great essential, the source from which all else springs, is the private relationship of worshiping God. Nothing—no crisis, no need, no work, no person would ever remove us from being what Amy Carmichael calls "a worshiper at the feet."

The discipline of worship reminds me that God is God. The discipline of worship is what keeps me from being shaped by the evil and suffering I confront on a daily basis. Who or what we worship shapes us in profound ways. None is worthy of our worship except the Lamb that was slain. The discipline of worship reminds me that although this world is teeming with evil and injustice, God is holy and just. Worship reminds me that he who is high and lifted up also dwells with the humble and broken and that because of the Cross, none of us, no matter how small or crushed, need be afraid.

The Discipline of Truth

Many years ago, when I first began hearing about sexual abuse from my clients, I was shocked and found it incomprehensible—not unbelievable, simply difficult to understand. When I was asked to speak on the topic of abuse, I did what I often do—I began my study by looking up the word *abuse.* Our word for abuse comes from the Latin *abutor,* which means "to use wrongly." Further definitions include, "to insult, to consume, to violate, to tread underfoot, to tarnish."

I realized that if abuse occurs when we treat another in injurious ways, then I must admit to being an abuser. I have used others wrongly. I have shown partiality or favoritism. I have tried to manipulate others to serve my own ends. I have trod others underfoot by ignoring them or by treating them as if they did not matter.

The discipline of truth as seen at the Cross says that I am guilty of abuse. I, who react with shock, surprise, and disdain for the perpetrator, also abuse or violate others. I, who find abuse of children with one's genitals incomprehensible, have abused others with my tongue. The ground at the foot of the Cross is indeed level. The discipline of truth helps me see who I am before God lest I become haughty and blinded to my own mistreatment of others. The discipline of truth prevents me from getting filled up with hate or condescension toward perpetrators, lest an arrogant rage cause me to mislead others in the way they confront evil. The discipline of truth keeps me ever before God, pleading with the psalmist, "Keep back Thy servant from presumptuous sins; let them not rule over me" (Ps. 19:13, NASB).

The Discipline of Study

God has said that his thoughts and mine are not the same (Isa. 55:8-9). I have found that my thoughts are easily influenced by the people and experiences I encounter. If I am to think God's thoughts, then I must engage in disciplined study. I will fail to bring light and life to others unless I live and think among the facts as God sees them.

Two kinds of study need to inform my life and my work. The first of these is the study of Scripture. Whatever I am dealing with in my own life or another's, it must be built on and permeated by the truths of Scripture. My life and my mind need to be saturated by the facts in God's Book, living among them and continually asking God how to apply them. When Jesus gave us the first and greatest commandment, he said that we were to love the Lord (worship) with all of our minds. There is much discussion today about the fact that Christian *thinking* is a rare and difficult thing. If part of what the Cross teaches is God's point of view, then part of its call to me is to acquire the mind of Christ, to learn to think God's thoughts. The discipline of study will train my mind to see things from God's perspective rather than from my own. As I bow to it, the discipline of study will work out the truths of God in my life so that I do not just *know* what he says, I *live* what he says. We fool ourselves if we think we have actually studied the Word when we have merely read it and failed to obey it. Any truth of Scripture that we have read and not obeyed, we have not truly studied.

The second kind of study that needs to inform my life and my work is the study of people. If I am not a student of people (not just theories), I will be of little use when it comes to skillfully applying God's truth to their lives. God brings me as a therapist into contact with all sorts of sordid human "stuff." If I arrogantly assume that I know what other people are like, I will very likely misunderstand them and ineptly apply God's Word to their lives as well. The study of human beings can be confusing and messy. Many of us prefer to study our theories, theological and/or psychological. I am not suggesting that theories are not helpful. I am saying that unless we discipline ourselves to live among the facts of God's Word as well as the human facts, we will miss the mark in our work.

The discipline of study keeps me ever a student, one who listens, examines, and pays attention. The study of God's Word in its proper sense keeps me from merely acquiring more and more knowledge and causes me to bow continually before what I learn so that my Teacher might work in me what his life and death have taught me. The ongoing study of human beings keeps me listening acutely so that my responses—verbal and nonverbal—might be wise, loving, and timely applications of the truth of God.

The Discipline of Prayer

Prayer does not seem to be anything we do naturally or easily. It is a discipline Jesus modeled for us and exhorted us to do. Jesus was continually in contact with God through prayer, and we are called to do the same. As the years pass, I am coming to view prayer quite differently from the way I did before. I used to think of prayer as a way of getting things from God. However, if I consider prayer by looking at the Cross, I realize that my former view is backward. The purpose of prayer is not for God to indulge my spiritual propensities, as if somehow I need things to go my way in order to serve him. Rather, the purpose of prayer is for me to know God and to allow him to develop his life in me.

Jesus' prayer just before his crucifixion was that "all of them may be one, Father, just as you are in me and I am in you. May they also be in us so that the world may believe that you have sent me" (John 17:21). Surely that prayer above all others is the one that God will honor. To be one with him means to think like him, to be like him, to look like him. If that is Jesus' prayer for me, then how can I pray for anything else?

I find that my prayers tend to run down two different channels. The first of these is that I am continually asking God to teach me how to think about something the way he does, to love someone the way he does. In essence, no matter what I encounter, in the office and out, the request is, "Show me how you would be, and then make me like you." Because of the work of Jesus on the cross, I can boldly enter the presence of God and ask him to make me like himself so that his name is glorified wherever he puts me.

Second, rather than simply praying for what I want, I am learning that therapy and the ministry of intercession go hand in hand. It is true that as counselors we have a profound impact on those we counsel. It is also true that we human beings are very limited in what we can do. So prayer not only enables me to apprehend the nature of God and begin to assimilate his thinking but also allows me the inestimable privilege of being part of God's unseen work in another's life. As we intercede, God works out things that he often chooses not to show us for a long, long time. Entering the school of intercession means learning to believe that God will do his work, even though we see no evidence of it in the broken life before us. It is a strenuous school. We would much rather push and pull on the lives in front of us in order to change them than live out Christ before them and wait for him to use our intercession as a means to touch them.

The Discipline of Obedience

Certainly the concept of obedience is woven throughout all of those mentioned above. I find within myself, however, a propensity simply to externalize the truths of God. By that I mean acquiring knowledge about God and his Word, and even exercising the disciplines I have mentioned, without being shaped and altered by them. Therefore, I find it helpful to remind myself of my need for obedience or for the outworking of what God has wrought at the Cross.

We cannot be conductors of the life of God unless his life permeates our being. Only by the work of the Spirit of God is death transformed into life. If the disciplines of worship, truth, study, and prayer do not result in obedience, then death will reign. We will not be redemptive in the lives of others unless we have learned to bow to God's work of redemption in us. Obedience results in lives that explain to others the grace and truth of the Father. Obedience results in lives that are used to buy back others from the realm of death in the name of Jesus.

As therapists who have seen the power and darkness around us and who have seen and felt the great suffering of others, we desire to bring life. As Christians who have seen glimmers of the greatness of our God, tasted of the love of the Father, and experienced the beauty of redemption in Christ, how can we not obey? The discipline of obedience means that our faithfulness to him is demonstrated by taking heed to both ourselves and our doctrine (1 Tim. 4:6) so that we bear an ever-growing likeness to the person of Jesus.

SUMMARY

Research and experience both attest to the fact that unless we are in a healthy and vigorous condition, we will catch the soul disease with which we are working instead of helping to cure it. As therapists to those devastated by the evil of others, we will not survive unless we know how to become like the cedars of Lebanon. Their most striking characteristic is that instead of feeding parasites, the strength of the life within those trees kills the parasites. May God teach us to be so filled with his life that, like the cedars of Lebanon, our very existence destroys those things that are of the nature of death. May our work in the dark and painful places of others' lives be a redemptive work because his life is being poured out through us at all times.

PART SEVEN

Profile of a Compassionate Church

26

The Church Community

❦

During the past decade the fact that sexual abuse occurs in Christian homes has surfaced in the church. It is a problem many have long denied and one that even now is hotly debated as to its occurrence, its frequency, and what is to be done about it when it does come to light. This is particularly true when a church member or leader is accused of sexually abusing someone in his own home or in the congregation, or when an adult begins the painful process of facing his or her own childhood abuse. Some churches have been known to blame victims, ostracize them, or simply ignore them until they are "all better." At the same time, some church communities or individuals have come alongside to walk with survivors as they attempt to find healing for the violence and injustice done to them.

During my years of working with survivors, I have seen all of these responses and more. I have seen many men and women deeply injured by the church community at a profoundly vulnerable time. Some have been silenced, neglected, criticized, and abandoned. Others have just been "sweetly" ignored. I have also had the great privilege of watching men and women who love God make a sacrifice of time and money to walk compassionately alongside survivors during the darkest days of their lives. They have given men and women who are suffering torment a safe haven and a beautiful example of family as God intended it to be. I have been blessed by their support. And in keeping with the wonder of his ways, God has blessed these compassionate people in indescribable ways as well.

While churches have begun struggling with the problem of sexual abuse and all its ramifications, Christian counseling has been a growing movement in this country, and a hotly debated topic as well. There are arguments about the sufficiency of Scripture, the evils of secular psychology, general revelation, and whether or not there is anything "Christian" about Christian counseling. Sadly, some of the criticism has been justified. Certainly some has not. However, the point that concerns us here is that often a great gulf has existed between the world of Christian counselors and the community of the church. I believe such a division has enabled many, many suffering people to fall through the cracks or be injured even further. Frankly, I deplore such a division. How much better for the body of Christ if both elements work together, bringing their different gifts and skills to the aid of those who suffer!

One reason we have been vulnerable to such a division is that human beings do fall into a rather unique category: They are both physical and spiritual beings. As a result, some people ignore the spiritual aspect and study humans only as physical beings reducible to scientific categories and explanations. Others ignore the physical aspect and treat humans only as spiritual beings, some even going so far as to ignore any need for medical treatment. I suspect the majority of us fall somewhere in between. The problem comes when we decide that our particular place on the continuum is the only biblical position. Instead of setting up such dichotomies, how much better to call the *whole* body to a radical obedience that will result in holy living and godly thinking and to a sacrificial love that will produce a healing community for all. Such a call would enable us to bring our theological understandings, our psychological understandings, and our scientific understandings together before God, asking him to help us think his thoughts about creatures who are so "fearfully and wonderfully made."

It is my hope that one result of this chapter will be a clear call to the whole body, both counselors and church community, to join hearts and hands to serve the people who have suffered beyond comprehension. What better proof of the redemptive power of Christ, and what better example of how the body of God's church should function!

Before offering the church community some concrete suggestions regarding an effective response to survivors of abuse, I think we need first to have an understanding of how the church was intended to function. If we do not have at least a basic grasp of God's call to the church, we will make many errors in how we respond to those who suffer. A solid foundation will help keep us from some common mistakes.

THE CHURCH AS A BODY

"The body is a unit, though it is made up of many parts; and though all its parts are many, they form one body.... Those parts of the body that seem to be weaker are indispensable, and the parts that we think are less honorable we treat with special honor.... There should be no division in the body, but...its parts should have equal concern for each other. If one part suffers, every part suffers with it; if one part is honored, every part rejoices with it" (1 Cor. 12:12, 22-23, 25-26).

According to this Scripture passage, all of us who know Christ are connected in a very vital way. Not only does each part affect the others, but we are to function by demonstrating a common concern for one another. No one is to be ignored or neglected, and in fact, those members who seem to be weaker are the very parts we are to invest with special honor. How unlike us, who would typically remove or hide the weaker among us. How like Christ, who again and again reversed the natural order of things and made that which was last to be first.

Paul also tells us here that when one member of the body suffers in some way, the other members suffer too. If this is so, then to be a part of the body is to enter into a costly relationship. It is a relationship that will bring on us the suffering of others. We usually work to avoid suffering, yet to enter into the community of the church is to bend down to bear the weight of the burdens of others. It is to invite suffering other than our own into our lives. Such a concept is contrary to human nature. Clearly such community is a supernatural work!

If we accept this Scripture passage as truth, then I believe we can conclude the following:

1. Whatever a member of the body suffers with—whether I understand it, fear it, or am made uncomfortable by it—God has called me to have the same concern for that person as I would for myself. Think about how we typically respond to pain in our own lives. When something hurts (even something as small as a paper cut), we focus our care and attention on it. That suggests that a great deal of time, effort, and interest would be given to members who are suffering.

2. Those members of the body we deem more feeble, less worthy of honor, or ignoble are the very ones we are called to surround with more honor, more attention. That means that the greater the pain, the greater the destruction, the more ravaged a life is by disease or trauma—the greater the care and nurture that should result.

3. *When any member of the body suffers, I suffer.* That potentially has tremendous impact for the church cross-denominationally and internationally, but for our purposes we will consider the implication for a local body. The passage in 1 Corinthians does not seem to say that I will suffer only when I am aware that you are suffering. It appears to suggest that I suffer as a result of the suffering in your life, whether or not I know about it. To suffer with another in God's way will be redemptive to both parties because it is the nature of God to bring light and life. I think we can also say that to ignore God's way is to erode or drag down the body, to bring death.

This vital connection in the body of the church is a mystery far beyond our understanding. However, we do not need to grasp all of how it works in order to be obedient to it. To pretend that we can ignore the suffering of others and fail to treat the weak with honor without tremendous cost is to deny the truth of God's Word.

THE CHURCH AS A SANCTUARY

In the Old Testament, the Israelites, God's chosen nation, were given regulations both for worship and for an earthly sanctuary. God told Moses to "have them make a sanctuary for me, and I will dwell among them" (Exod. 25:8). Since the coming of Christ, we now have a living tabernacle or sanctuary, for God dwells within his people both individually and corporately. In different ways, both the old and the new sanctuaries have been the dwelling place of God. Scripture is clear about the fact that the place where God dwells is to be a holy place as well as a place of refuge for the poor and oppressed of the earth. The psalmist says, "Lord, who may dwell in your sanctuary? Who may live on your holy hill? He whose walk is blameless and who does what is righteous, who speaks the truth from his heart...who does his neighbor no wrong...who despises a vile man" (Ps. 15:1-4). The sanctuary of God is to be a holy place that provides a refuge from evil. Surely what characterized the sanctuary made by hands is to be manifested in the tabernacle made by God, the body of his church.

Sadly, instead of manifesting holiness and safety, the dwelling place of God has sometimes mirrored the horror we find in the tribe of Benjamin. In Deuteronomy 33:12, Moses pronounces the following blessing on the tribe of Benjamin before his death: "Let the beloved of the Lord rest secure in him, for he shields him all day long, and the one the Lord loves rests between his shoulders." One would think that a group of people so secure and shielded by the Lord God himself would offer that same refuge and security to those who entered their borders. Instead we find in Judges 19 the horrific story of the rape and death of the Levite's concubine.

In Judges we are told that this particular concubine was unfaithful to the man to whom she was legally attached. In her anger she left him and returned to her father's house. He went after her four months later. After several days, the Levite finally extricated himself and his concubine and began his journey home. It was dangerous to sleep in the unprotected countryside, and the Levite chose to stay in Gibeah, where Benjamites lived.

Although the law of hospitality was strong in the Middle East, it was some time before they were offered shelter. Finally an old man took them in. Some of the wicked men of the city came pounding on the door later, demanding to have sex with the Levite. The owner of the house felt that would be disgraceful since the Levite was his guest, and instead the owner offered his own virgin daughter and the Levite's concubine. The men would not listen, so finally the concubine was handed out to them by the Levite himself, and they raped and abused her all night long. At dawn when they let her go, she worked her way back to the house where her master was and fell down at the door, her hands on the threshold. Her master's response upon finding her there was to tell her to get up so they could go home. There was no answer; she was dead. He put her across his donkey, took her body home, cut it in twelve pieces, and sent them into all the sections of Israel.

We could consider many aspects of this account: the fact that the Levite was just as guilty of the concubine's death as the men who killed her; the fact that when he told the story to the Israelites, he lied and said that the Benjamites wanted to kill him rather than rape him; the fact that our shock at histories of sexual abuse is surprising given the bluntness of Scripture regarding the horrors humans commit. However, I want us to note two points in reference to an understanding of the church as sanctuary.

First, within the borders of a tribe that was to understand and experience the rest and safety of God himself, a woman was brutally abused. She died outside the door with her hands across the threshold. What a picture! How often we believers, who know and experience the rest and safety of God in Christ, have allowed the vulnerable and abused among us to "die" outside the door! How many battered wives have been "sent out" and returned to their abusers? How many survivors of sexual abuse have been "left" outside the sanctuary, told to take their struggles elsewhere, to just put it behind them, and in effect, to "get up and go"? What must it have felt like to be handed out to a group of crazed, strange men and be gang raped all night long? Her wounds and bruises must have been clearly visible. How could someone look down on such injuries and simply say, "Get up; let's go"?

Had the Benjamites reflected the God who had blessed them with security, shielding, and safety between his shoulders, this woman would have found safety and comfort such as she had never known. She who was weaker and less honorable would have been protected from destruction and injury. The Benjamites missed a phenomenal opportunity to give to another a taste of the God who is our refuge! May we who name the name of Christ never be guilty of such missed opportunity!

Second, when the rest of Israel learned of the devastation that had occurred, they were shocked, and they all assembled before the Lord in Mizpah. We are told that "the leaders of all the people of the tribes of Israel took their places in the assembly of the people of God" (Judg. 20:2). After hearing the Levite's story, they united as one man against the Benjamites. First they asked the Benjamites to surrender the men who had committed the abuse. The Benjamites would not listen and chose instead to protect them, exhibiting a misplaced loyalty to the abusers in Gibeah. They chose to fight on behalf of the evil men against their own "brethren the children of Israel" (Judg. 20:13, KJV). As a result, Israel went to God at Bethel, the house of God, and asked him what they should do. God directed them to go against the Benjamites.

I think we would expect that if God told Israel to go against the Benjamites, he would then give them victory. Instead, the Israelites lost twenty-two thousand men on the battlefield that day. They went to God and wept before him, asking again what to do. God sent them again to fight the Benjamites. This time they lost eighteen thousand, all armed with swords. In other words, they sent in prepared men and lost them in the fray. A third time they went weeping before the Lord. They fasted and offered sacrifices. Again they asked whether or not they should go up against their brothers. This time God said yes and also promised them victory.

The horrific sin of the Benjamites resulted in brother having to go against brother at great cost to many. It was the only way to "purge the evil" in their midst. The holiness of God demands that the sin be dealt with. Doing so required perpetual seeking after him with tears, fasting, and sacrifices (which meant in part dealing with their own sin). Thousands of innocent men died as a result. The cost was great. God continued to send them into the fight, knowing about that cost. He did not make it easy. The effects of that hideous rape and murder and the Benjamites' attempted protection of the evildoers cost thousands of lives. Had they allowed the perpetrators to be brought to justice, it would have been far less costly to the nation of Israel. Whenever the body of Christ, through denial or actual choice, ignores such sins in its midst, the entire body suffers terribly as a result.

Obedience to God in circumstances such as these is very costly. We in the church of God are engaged in a battle. Scripture makes it abundantly clear that all of life is a battle for those who love God, yet few seem willing to bear it as an occupation. Yes, we will get hurt. We said in chapter 1 that suffering leaves its mark all over those who must endure it. Entering into the suffering of others will also leave a mark. God does not promise that such battles will be without cost. However, as we seek him and weep before him, he will enable us to fight. He will give wisdom so that we do not send people out to be abused. He will grant us open hearts so that no one dies on our thresholds but rather everyone is welcomed in and protected. He will grant us courage to enter the fray, knowing that whatever the cost, the ultimate price has been paid by his Son, enabling all of us to find God as our fortress, our deliverer, our refuge, and our shield. May we as the body of Christ provide sanctuary to others, never causing someone to cry out with David, "I have no refuge; no one cares for my life" (Ps. 142:4).

27

How Can the Church Help
Survivors of Sexual Abuse?

As we move on to consider how the church might effectively respond to the problem of abuse, we need first to look at three foundational tenets to helping of any kind. We noted earlier that the church is a body of vitally connected parts, each affecting the other. It is a vast, complex network of relationships, both heavenly and earthly. In chapter 3 we said that relationships are, in part, about knowing and loving one another in truth. These components of relationship are important to keep in mind as we proceed.

We have also stated that unless ministry is both incarnational and redemptive in purpose and in process, we will not bring true life as embodied in Christ to those we serve. We pointed out that because of the nature of human beings, God needed to come to us in the flesh in order for us to understand him and be restored. As believers, we too are called to live out the mystery of the Incarnation. In our relationships with one another we are to bring down into flesh-and-blood actualities the nature of God himself. As the church community bears others' burdens, we are to do so in a way that explains God to others.

Christ's purpose in entering this realm was redemption, the buying back of that which was lost. As we relate to one another in ways that bear the stamp of Jesus Christ, we also will see redemption unfold in the lives of others. We will see light replace darkness, life replace death, and healing replace brokenness. As workers in the church of God, what do we need to know in order for our lives to be incarnational and redemptive?

Let it first be said that if we are to minister effectively to others, we must at all costs not allow ourselves merely to become wedded to a series of principles. We cannot reduce dealing with the lives and souls of human beings to a set of rules. If we do, our ears will cease to listen intently to individuals, we will prescriptively apply Scripture, and we will blame the sufferer when results do not occur according to our plan.

There is no shortcut for dealing with human beings and their difficulties. God is a living Spirit; the Word is living and active; the Spirit indwells living souls, who in turn are ministering to other living souls. To attempt to reduce life to a series of rules causes us to end up like the religious leaders who thought that diligent study of the Scriptures would give them life. Jesus told them that it was not the Scriptures alone but the fact that they testify of him, who is life (John 5:39-40). We do not bring the life of God to exhausted human beings by way of principles. The life of God is brought another way entirely.

Three Facets of Incarnational Ministry

1. We must constantly rely on the Holy Spirit for guidance about what to do or say in every situation. If that vital connection is not there, we are reduced to formulas. That means we must not simply rely on memory, book knowledge, what worked with someone else, or something used by someone we deem effective. Systems, principles, and rules can be helpful. However, we must first and foremost learn to listen to the Spirit. It is he who understands the heart and mind of the one we are trying to help. Beware of any method or teaching that does not first throw you back onto complete reliance on the Spirit of God. It is in that place, and only in that place, that you will find truth, life, wisdom, and comfort for others.

2. We must constantly search the Scriptures. Any thinking we do about people must be done through God's Word as well as governed by his Spirit. Learn how to study the Scriptures deeply, all the while understanding that according to those Scriptures the true student is one who allows the words to permeate his or her own life first. Study of the Word as God intends it is study that transforms the life of the student. If that does not occur, we tend toward a wrong use of the Word of God. Someone comes to see us, we figure out what we think the problem is, and then we hurl a verse like a projectile. Such a thing bears no fruit. If we do not experientially know who God is and if we are not governed by God's Spirit, what we do will not be redemptive.

3. We must truly understand what it means to be flesh. We must learn how to communicate that understanding in a way that lets others know they are heard and known. We must go to school among people. We cannot skillfully apply God's Word to people unless we understand them. How do they think? How has their particular kind of suffering affected them? What do we need to learn about what it means to be them? What is it like to live with chronic pain? What is it like to be beaten daily by the man who promised to cherish you? What is it like to be used sexually by the man you called Daddy?

We are surrounded by people who are not like us at all. We will meet people whose lives are nothing like ours. Their difficulties are things we have never encountered. We need to lay aside our assumption that everyone else is like us, that they can do what we do. A woman who grew up with a father who loved and nurtured her is not like a woman whose father was her greatest fear, ripping apart her body and her soul on a daily basis. We need to get ourselves out among people. We need to listen, learn, and watch. We need to allow the "stuff" of others' lives to touch us. Beware of the tendency to assume that you know and the equally great tendency to live a life apart from the "stuff" of others.

May we be people who are governed by God's Spirit, continually reliant on his leading. May we live among the facts of God's

Word, transformed by and obedient to its truth. May we also learn to live among human facts, not hiding behind fortresses of theories and principles, but being willing like Jesus to get down into the midst of sickness, torment, and disease. It is only as the church of God manifests these characteristics that the life of God will be demonstrated in a redemptive way!

Given that all that we do must flow out of the foundation stated above, how then can a body of believers effectively and compassionately assist an adult survivor of sexual abuse? I recently had the great privilege of interacting with a group of women who were pooling their thoughts about how to help the church respond to those in crisis. The group consisted of women in leadership positions in the church, Christian counselors, a survivor, and a woman who had opened her life and home to a recovering survivor. Our goal was to discuss how we could come together in our diverse roles to provide refuge for those who suffer. It was a rich meeting, and I want to use the discussion it generated as a basis for providing some thoughts about survivors' needs and some hindrances to meeting those needs.

SURVIVORS' NEEDS

All survivors of sexual abuse need

1. A significant sense of belonging. Men and women who grew up sexually abused feel isolated and unwanted. Often they have no sense of what it means to belong to a family group. The church can provide a place of support, love, and significance for survivors. Not only can the church provide a place where the survivor experiences the love and affirmation of a family, it often is the only family some survivors have. Many survivors have either homes they cannot return to for safety reasons or families who do not acknowledge the truth of their lives. One survivor told me that interacting closely with a few families in her church community gave her the first experience she ever had of seeing firsthand a man loving his wife and children faithfully and safely. Many women have said they had no idea what a marriage should look like until observing some marriages in the church.

2. To be pursued. One of the characteristics of incarnational love is that it is a pursuing love. God came to be with us. When others suffer, we often expect them to come to us, pursue us for what they need, and attend our functions. How unlike Christ, who died for us while we were yet sinners! We need to take the initiative to keep suffering people connected with us. If we tell a survivor to call us when she needs something, we will probably not hear from her. We need to lovingly pursue with calls, encouraging notes, and invitations that are sensitive to her needs at the moment.

3. To have physical and/or financial needs met. Is the survivor safe from her abuser? Is she safe from her own destructive impulses? Is she suicidal? Does she abuse any substances? Does she need financial help? Is she physically able to care for herself? Is she able to care for her family? Does she need someone to call in the middle of the night? Does she live alone? Is she safe doing so? Where does she spend holidays?

4. Hope without condemnation. In the darkest of times we struggle to have hope and faith. Sometimes we are less than successful. Suffering people often need others to have faith and hope for them. Admonitions to hope or trust only result in despair; if the sufferers were able, they would do so. How much better to come alongside and tell survivors that where they are lacking and/or unable, we will stand in the gap and believe God for them.

5. A balance of ministry and fun. Often when we do reach out to those who are suffering, we reduce our relationship with them to one of pure ministry. Sadly, that has the effect of causing sufferers to feel like nothing more than a problem that needs to be fixed. That perspective also prevents us from bringing good and fun things into a dark life. When we bring fun into sufferers' lives, we provide an oasis that will help them feel loved simply for who they are. It is also important for survivors to feel needed by those who care for them. Although an "I can't do..." needs to be honored, very few people want simply to be takers. Give them dignity by allowing them to contribute to your life, even if it means just letting them do the dishes after a meal.

6. Others' willingness to witness great pain and believe the "unbelievable." Sitting with an incest survivor brings you face-to-face with the sickest, most twisted and evil things human beings do to each other. Adults rape and sadistically torture babies and children. Many men and women have lived in terrible isolation, thinking their secrets were too horrible to be told. Calling back memories that one has never been able to voice is a massive struggle. Hearing about such things can cause great denial in the listener. Yet we who believe that sin is so hideous as to require the death of God himself should of all people find evil believable.

7. A listener, not a fixer or a blamer. How little value we place on listening! To attend to the struggle of another by listening is to bestow honor on that person. You cannot "fix" a history of childhood abuse. You can stand with someone while she courageously faces the truth of her life and love her while she struggles to learn to live with it. Learn how to sit and be quiet. When we don't know what to say, it is usually best to say nothing rather than allow our discomfort with silence and pain to drive us to rattle off an answer. One of the ways we cope with horror is by attempting to explain it or find out what made it happen. Searching for such explanations can easily lead to blaming the survivor. *Never* imply that the survivor is to blame for the abuse. *Nothing* a child has ever done, no matter how provocative, is justification for abuse. Incest is a criminal act. The abuser *always* carries responsibility for the abuse.

8. Resources. If the survivor needs and wants professional help, assist her in finding competent counseling. She may need you to help her know what questions to ask of the counselor. Is the counselor a licensed professional? Does the counselor accept third-party payments? Does the counselor have training and experience in the treatment of sexual abuse? What kind of experience and from where? The survivor may need you to go with her to the first few appointments and simply wait in the waiting room. The idea of sitting down with a perfect stranger and telling the secret of incest for the first time is utterly terrifying to most.

9. Touch. Be very aware of your vocabulary, your timing, and your body language. A survivor has been repeatedly abused by another's body and words. She will be afraid of yours. At the same time she may be starved for touch and affection. Do not touch her without her permission. Never touch her in a sexual way. Learn to read and acknowledge her body cues. Often it is through her body language, rather than words, that she will communicate emotions like fear or anger.

10. Knowledgeable friends. If you are going to walk alongside someone who is dealing with the issue of sexual abuse, then you need to be knowledgeable about the subject. It would be wise to read several books on the topic. See the Suggested Reading list at the end of the book. If you do not understand the problem, you will more than likely make some hurtful mistakes.

11. To resolve spiritual issues. Understand that the spiritual ramifications of incest are complex and powerful. When a "Christian" father, uncle, grandfather, camp counselor, or pastor sexually abuses a child, beliefs and feelings about who God is, his love, and his protection are all shattered and are not easily reassembled. A few verses will not put it all back together.

12. Time. Healing from the devastating consequences of childhood sexual abuse takes a long time, usually years. Should you choose to walk alongside someone who is struggling in this area, it is important to recognize that you are facing a long process. The survivor will wrestle with powerful urges to resist facing the truth; she will fight hard and long to rid herself of lies. She may endure months or years of terrifying nightmares that rob her of much-needed sleep. A small network of trustworthy people will often work better than one person alone. If the survivor is married, her husband will also need a support network that will walk with him on the long road. Healing takes time. God created us to live in time, and so we heal over time. Sexual abuse shatters many fundamental aspects of personhood. Although our God is a God of redemption, he usually works that redemption out through people and over time.

13. Intercession. Jesus himself is at the right hand of the Father, interceding for us. The Spirit prays for us when words will not come. Should we not then pray for those who are suffering and are often unable to pray for themselves? Pain silences and isolates. We who would come alongside need to pray for and with those who are silenced and isolated.

It is crucial to keep in mind that at times a survivor will want you only to pray *for* her and not *with* her. However, there are also times when a survivor who is going through her darkest hours will want and need a small group (perhaps those in her network) to come together to pray for her in her presence. To deal with sexual abuse is to battle the prince of darkness. To hear others pray with faith and boldness to the God who can and will redeem is to bring a beam of light and a surge of hope where darkness reigns.

HINDRANCES TO EFFECTIVE HELPING

As you come alongside survivors of sexual abuse, be aware that several dynamics may prevent you from giving effective help.

1. Activities. Most of the women at this meeting discussed how activities can easily take precedence over people in church life. We get so busy with "doing" the next event that we do not take time to know people and love them. Suffering slows people down, and if we are going to walk with others in their suffering, then we must slow down too.

2. "If you would only…" We become a hindrance rather than a help when we greet those who suffer with statements such as: "If you would only…attend church, read Scripture more, believe more, stop thinking about yourself, put the past behind you." Rather than saying, "Here, let me help you carry that heavy load," we end up putting heavy burdens on already bowed backs. Remember that God our Savior did not greet us with, "If you would only…" Instead he said, "Here, let me show you how. Let me shoulder the burden. Let me be with you."

3. Lack of maturity. How often confidences are betrayed under the guise of sharing a prayer request! If we are to help those who struggle with things that frighten them, humiliate them, and shame them, then we must be trustworthy people. We must learn that there are things we can share with no one but the Father. To work with survivors is to minister to those who know betrayal well. We want them to learn to trust. The only way to help them do that is to be trustworthy ourselves. Unless a life is threatened, confidences should *never* be broken.

4. Resistance. We often fail to give victims of abuse credibility. We want to believe that incest cannot occur in "good Christian" homes. It can. It has occurred in pastors' homes, elders' homes, choir directors' homes, and in the homes of people about whom it has been said, "Oh, he was such a fine man." We fail to give credibility when someone says to us, "I can't." I am not sure why this is so. When a paraplegic says, "I can't walk," we have no difficulty believing him or her. Somehow we change the rules when the injuries are not visible. When a survivor says, "I can't...be in crowds right now, sleep, think straight, pray, etc.," we need to believe her. To say, "Of course you can," is to say, "You don't know what you are talking about." How much better to respond with, "How can I help? What do you need me to do?" If we were trying to help a paraplegic, we would find out how to best be his or her legs. We need to do the same for the survivor.

5. Short-term thinking. Like managed care, the church seems to think that short-term is right and should always work. The more spiritual among us get better quickly. Those who struggle long term clearly do not love God enough. And yet we say we believe this to be a dark world where sin is rampant and destructive. We believe that God is long-suffering and merciful. Where do we get our quick-fix model? How fortunate we are that God does not adhere to short-term sanctification!

6. Male leadership. At least within the evangelical world, most of those in church leadership continue to be male. Whatever we think or feel about that, we need to keep it in mind when dealing with women in crisis. A woman who spent her childhood being sexually abused by a man will have all kinds of reactions to male leadership. One of those responses will be fear. It is possible that this will prevent her from seeking the help she so desperately needs. Many churches are now training women to work alongside women in crisis so that when a woman is dealing with an issue like abuse, she has some recourse other than male leadership. We need to respond to the fear and damage resulting from abuse with tenderness and sensitivity.

7. Structure and expectations. In many ways, the church seems to be structured to accommodate the whole and the healthy. Often activities are designed for intact couples and families. Activities assume a certain level of ability for handling events and people.

We expect people to come, learn, listen, grow, and participate. On one hand there is nothing wrong with that. However, that perspective does not account for sickness, suffering, trauma, dying, terror, and torment. To experience these things is to fail to fit into the structure. When that results in responses of judgment, humiliation, impatience, and denial, we have failed to be the church God has called us to be. According to the apostle Paul, the church should bestow more abundant honor on those members who lack it rather than applaud those who have no need of it (1 Cor. 12:23-24).

8. *Disbelief.* All of the women at this meeting talked about how many in the church do not believe that abuse of any kind has touched so many lives. That means it is kept secret because many fear they will not be believed. Attention to the problem is not a priority because the problem is believed to be rare. Years ago I spoke to a woman in leadership and suggested to her that many of the women she ministered to had probably experienced some kind of abuse. She was incredulous. I asked her to consider simply adding the word *abuse* to any list of problems women struggled with whenever she spoke. Not long afterward I got a phone call from her. "They are coming out of the woodwork! What do I do now?" Again, knowing we live in a world ruled by the prince of the power of the air and knowing that human hearts are deceitful above all things, why are we surprised?

9. *Fear of expressions of pain.* One survivor said that it is a hindrance when others cannot distinguish between a "roar of pain" (venting rebellious-sounding verbiage about God)—like a lioness with a thorn in her paw—and genuine rebellion. The Psalms contain a lot of "roaring" (Where are you, Lord? Why have you abandoned me?). She said that when such a thought occurred repeatedly, she knew she was believing one of Satan's lies and needed to deal with it. She also learned how dangerous it could be to express such things in the presence of someone who could not distinguish heresy or rebellion from hard questions and a "roar of pain."

10. *Lack of understanding.* We often do not understand the nature of evil and suffering, the complexities of human development, the mysteries of how children think and respond, the fact that incest is a criminal act, and that redemption in a life never comes easily.

Yes, the God we worship is capable of redeeming the pain beyond words into something that gives life and brings glory to him. However, the transfiguring of agony into redemption cost Jesus inestimably. Death (and incest *is* of the nature of death) does not normally transform into life in this dark world. The beauty of redemption in a life *never* comes easily.

SUMMARY

God's Word says that the church is to consider those parts of the body that are weaker as indispensable. How contrary to the natural order of things such thinking is! If that is true, it means that you and I, as members of the body of Christ, *cannot* live without those we typically deem feeble or less honorable. We need them. We think those who are suffering need us and that we bestow honor on them by pausing from our busy schedules to give them a little time. Such thinking is not only insulting, it is wrong.

If I have learned anything from my work with those who have been sexually abused, it is that I have indeed needed them. They have taught me many wonderful things about God. Perhaps more important, as I have allowed those who came to me for help to teach me, the result has been a greater transformation into the likeness of Christ. I have gained a greater understanding of the depth of my own sinfulness, my frailty, my great need for God, his infinite grace and love, the wonder of the Cross, and a thousand other things. I can never repay the debt I owe.

If we as the body of Christ will heed his call and act as those who are so connected that we suffer whenever any one of us suffers, reaching out to love sacrificially and act redemptively, we will find ourselves blessed beyond measure. Yes, to walk the way of our Savior is costly. The forces of hell rose up to stop him, and we will find it no different. Our suffering left its mark on him, and the suffering of others will do the same to us. We are told that the servant is to expect the same as the master. A body that does not follow its head is a sick body. A healthy body lives conformed to the directions of the head. It is a great loss to us when we do not follow our Head in these ways.

We are a people who lay claim to God as our refuge and our help. We are a people called to be like the God we worship. We represent the person of Jesus Christ to a watching world. When we fail to be a sanctuary for the oppressed and suffering, we misrepresent him, for they will conclude that he is not safe. When we fail to give credibility to the suffering of others, we confirm for them that power is on the side of their oppressors and that there is no one to comfort them (Eccles. 4:1), even though our words say that God is a comforter. When suffering is greeted with impatience, judgment, distance, and verses thrown like missiles, we tell lies about God with our lives while attempting to speak truth with our mouths. God help us!

The pain of one wounded by a church that preferred she stay on the other side of the threshold is articulately expressed in the following poem:

On Leaving the Church I Loved

Your wounds cried out for vengeance,
Stunning me with the fierceness of their cry.
I had only brushed—unwittingly—against your injury,
And you visited all the fury of your pain upon my head
As if I was the culprit and wounder of your soul.
My baffled protestations only made you cry more fiercely—
"Crucify her! Crucify her!"
I flailed against Christ's mounting pin
Thrust through my heart,
Seeking to fly from such resolute pain.
But God's grace overwhelmed my human sense of justice
So that I could not help but see you through eyes of love.
I gave you what you wanted and quietly slipped away.
But, although my sense of justice has been
Tamed by Christ's Holy Love,
His Body is now double scarred.

—Lynn Brookside

May we who name the name of Jesus never send out another to be abused, never leave another to die on our thresholds, never cause further wounding to that sacred body by our fear, our judgment, and our lack of love. Rather, may we who now make up his body here on earth live out the truth that there is indeed a Redeemer and a Refuge for all who will come.

Endnotes

Chapter 1: Why I Write

1. Elie Wiesel, *In Confronting the Holocaust: The Impact of Elie Wiesel,* ed. Alvin H. Rosenfeld and Irving Greenberg (Bloomington, Ind.: University Press, 1978), 200.
2. Elie Wiesel, "A Personal Response," *Face to Face: An Interreligious Bulletin* 6 (1979): 36.

Chapter 2: Meeka's Story

1. Amy Carmichael, *Things As They Are* (London: Marshall, Morgan & Scott, 1903), 228.

Chapter 5: Understanding the Nature of Trauma

1. N. C. Andreasen, "Posttraumatic Stress Disorder," in *Comprehensive Textbook of Psychiatry,* ed. H. I. Kaplan and B. J. Sadock, 4th ed. (Baltimore: Williams and Wilkins, 1985), 918–24.
2. Judith Lewis Herman, *Trauma and Recovery* (New York: Basic Books, 1992), 33.

3. *Diagnostic and Statistical Manual of Mental Disorders IV* (Washington, D.C.: American Psychiatric Association, 1994), 424–9.
4. Ibid., 424.
5. Ibid., 477.
6. Herman, *Trauma and Recovery,* 108.

Chapter 6: Understanding the Nature of Child Development

1. Frank W. Putnam, *Diagnosis and Treatment of Multiple Personality Disorder* (New York: The Guilford Press, 1989), 122.
2. John Bowlby, *A Secure Base: Parent-Child Attachment and Healthy Human Development* (New York: Basic Books, 1990), 11.

Chapter 7: Definitions, Frequency, and Family Dynamics

1. Christine Courtois, *Healing the Incest Wound: Adult Survivors in Therapy* (New York: W. W. Norton, 1988), 16.
2. Ibid., 17–8.
3. Sam Kirschner, Diane A. Kirschner, and Richard L. Rappaport, *Working with Adult Incest Survivors: The Healing Journey* (New York: Brunner/Mazel, 1993), 34–8.
4. Ibid., 41.
5. Courtois, *Healing the Incest Wound,* 115.

Chapter 8: Symptoms and Aftereffects of Childhood Sexual Abuse

1. Robert McAfee Brown, *Elie Wiesel: Messenger to All Humanity* (Notre Dame: University of Notre Dame Press, 1983).
2. Bessel A. van der Kolk, *Psychological Trauma* (Washington, D.C.: American Psychiatric Association Press, Inc. 1987).

Chapter 12: Memory Retrieval

1. G. S. Klein, *Perceptions, Motives, and Personality* (New York: Jason Aronson, 1970), 112.
2. Bessel A. van der Kolk, "Trauma and Memory," in *Traumatic Stress: The 20Effects of Overwhelming Stress on Mind, Body and Society* (New York: The Guilford Press, 1996), 296–7.
3. S. D. Solomon, E. T. Gerrity, and A. M. Muff, "Efficacy of Treatments for Posttraumatic Stress Disorder: An Empirical Review," *Journal of American Medical Association* 268, no. 5 (5 August 1992): 633.
4. Bessel A. van der Kolk and Onno Vander Hart, "The Intrusive Past: The Flexibility of Memory and the Engraving of Trauma," *American Imago* 48, no. 4 (1991): 444.
5. Helga Newmark, "Stolen Childhood," *McCall's* (August 1994): 100.
6. Bessel A. van der Kolk, *Post-Traumatic Stress Disorders: Psychological and Bio- logical Sequelae* (Washington, D.C.: American Psychiatric Press, 1984), 63–6.
7. Judith Lewis Herman, *Trauma and Recovery* (New York: Basic Books, 1992), 176.
8. Elie Wiesel, *A Jew Today* (New York: Random House, 1978), 81.
9. Robert McAfee Brown, *Elie Wiesel: Messenger to All Humanity* (Notre Dame: Notre Dame University Press, 1983), 19.
10. Ibid., 20.
11. Amy Carmichael, *Things As They Are* (London: Marshall, Morgan & Scott, 1903), 65–6.
12. Ibid., 228–8.

Chapter 13: Facing Truths about the Past

1. John Bunyan, *The Pilgrim's Progress* (Garden City, N.Y.: International Collectors Library, n.d.), 38.

2. Elie Wiesel, "Art and Culture after the Holocaust," in *Auschwitz: Beginning of a New Era? Reflections on the Holocaust,* ed. Eva Fleischner (New York: KTAV Publishing House, 1977), 403.
3. Judith Lewis Herman, *Trauma and Recovery* (New York: Basic Books, 1992), 101–2.

Chapter 14: Facing Truths about the Present

1. Primo Levi, *Survival in Auschwitz: The Nazi Assault on Humanity,* [1958] trans. Stuart Woolf (New York: Collier, 1961), 106–7. As quoted in Judith Lewis Herman, *Trauma and Recovery* (New York: Basic Books, 1992), 85.

Chapter 16: Relationships

1. Elie Wiesel, *Night* (New York: Bantam Books, 1960), 30.

Chapter 17: Reclaiming the Body

1. Elie Wiesel, *Night* (New York: Bantam Books, 1960), 81.
2. Judith Lewis Herman, *Trauma and Recovery* (New York: Basic Books, 1992), 108.
3. Bessel A. van der Kolk and M. Greenberg, "The Psychobiology of the Trauma Response: Hyper Arousal, Constriction, and Addiction to Traumatic Reexposure," in *Psychological Trauma,* ed. Bessel A. van der Kolk (Washington, D.C.: American Psychiatric Press, 1987), 63–7.

Chapter 20: Dissociative Disorders

1. Richard P. Kluft, "Treatment of Multiple Personality Disorder," *Psychiatric Clinics of North America* 7 (1984): 9–29.
2. *Diagnostic and Statistical Manual of Mental Disorders IV* (Washington, D.C.: American Psychiatric Association, 1994), 487.

3. R. Horevitz and R. Loewenstein, "The Rational Treatment of Multiple Personality Disorder" in *Dissociation: Clinical and Theoretical Perspectives,* eds. S. J. Lynn and J. W. Rhue (New York: The Guilford Press, 1994), 290.

4. David Calof, *Multiple Personality and Dissociation* (Center City, Minn.: Hazeldon, 1993), 1–2.

5. Frank W. Putnam, *Diagnosis and Treatment of Multiple Personality Disorder* (New York: The Guilford Press, 1989), 131–66.

6. Frank W. Putnam, "Discussion: Are Alter Personalities Fragments or Figments?" *Psychoanalytic Inquiry* 12 (1992): 95–111.

7. Richard P. Kluft, "Varieties of Hypnotic Intervention in the Treatment of Multiple Personality," *American Journal of Clinical Hypnosis* 24 (1982): 230–40.

8. Richard P. Kluft, "An Introduction to Multiple Personality Disorder," *Psychiatric Annals* 14 (1984): 19–24.

Chapter 21: False Memory Syndrome

1. Bessel A. van der Kolk, R. Blitz, W. A. Burr, and E. Hartmann, "Nightmares and Trauma: Lifelong and Traumatic Nightmares in Veterans," *American Journal of Psychiatry* 141 (1984): 187–90.

2. Lenore Terr, "What Happens to Early Memories of Trauma?" *Journal of the American Academy of Child and Adolescent Psychiatry* 1 (1988): 96–104.

3. Bessel A. van der Kolk, "The Body Keeps Score: Memory and the Evolving Psychobiology of Posttraumatic Stress," *Harvard Review of Psychiatry* 1, no. 5 (1994): 253–65.

4. Jean Piaget, *Play, Dreams and Imitation in Childhood* (New York: Norton, 1962), 98.

5. Bessel A. van der Kolk, "Trauma and Memory," in *Traumatic Stress: The 20Effects of Overwhelming Stress on Mind, Body and Society* (New York: The 20Guilford Press, 1996), 296–7.

6. Samuel Knapp and A. Tepper, "Risk Management Issues in

the False Memory Debate," *The Pennsylvania Psychologist* 55, no. 3 (May 1995): 26–7.

Chapter 22: Male Survivors

1. David Finkelhor, *Sexually Victimized Children* (New York: Free Press, 1979), 79.
2. D. Liask, "Research on Male Victims of Childhood Sexual Abuse: What Do We Know and What Do We Need to Know?" (paper presented at the Fifth Annual National Conference on Male Survivors, Bethesda, Maryland, September 1993).
3. T. Nielsen, "Sexual Abuse of Boys: Current Perspectives," *Personnel and Guidance Journal* 62 (1983): 139–42.
4. John Briere, *Therapy for Adults Molested as Children: Beyond Survival* (New York: Springer Publishing, 1989), 152.
5. David Finkelhor, *Child Sexual Abuse: New Theory and Research* (New York: Free Press, 1984), 82.
6. John Briere and K. Smiljanich, "Childhood Sexual Abuse and Subsequent Sexual Aggression against Adult Women" (paper presented at the 101st Annual Convention of the American Psychological Association, Toronto, Ontario, Canada, August 1993).
7. Briere, *Therapy for Adults Molested as Children,* 159.

Chapter 23: The Impact of Trauma Work on the Therapist

1. *Diagnostic and Statistical Manual of Mental Disorders IV* (Washington, D.C.: American Psychiatric Association, 1994), 424.
2. Charles R. Figley, "Compassion Stress and the Family Therapist," *Family Therapy News* (February 1993): 1–8.
3. Laurie A. Pearlman and Karen W. Saakvitne, *Trauma and the Therapist: Countertransference and Vicarious Traumatization in Psychotherapy of Incest Survivors* (New York: Norton, 1995), 31.
4. Judith Lewis Herman, *Trauma and Recovery* (New York: Basic Books, 1992), 141.

5. Charles R. Figley, *Compassion Fatigue* (New York: Brunner/Mazel, 1995), 8.
6. Herman, *Trauma and Recovery,* 141.
7. Oswald Chambers, *Christian Disciplines* (Grand Rapids: Discovery House, 1995), 30.

Chapter 24: Strategies That Foster Endurance

1. Laurie A. Pearlman and Karen W. Saakvitne, *Trauma and the Therapist: Countertransference and Vicarious Traumatization in Psychotherapy of Incest Survivors* (New York: Norton, 1995), 393.

Suggested Reading

Dan Allender, *The Wounded Heart* (Colorado Springs, Colo.: NavPress, 1990).

John Briere, *Therapy for Adults Molested As Children* (New York: Springer, 1989).

Christine A. Courtois, *Healing the Incest Wound* (New York: W. W. Norton & Company, 1988).

John Courtright and Dr. Sid Rogers, *Your Wife Was Sexually Abused* (Grand Rapids: Zondervan, 1994).

Jennifer Freyd, *Betrayal Trauma* (Cambridge, Mass.: Harvard University Press, 1996).

Eliana Gil, *Treatment of Adult Survivors of Sexual Abuse* (Walnut Creek, Calif.: Launch Press, 1988).

Lynn Heitritter and Jeanette Vought, *Helping Victims of Sexual Abuse* (Minneapolis: Bethany, 1989).

Judith Lewis Herman, *Trauma and Recovery* (New York: Basic Books, 1992).

Cynthia A. Kubetin and James Mallory, M.D., *Beyond the Darkness* (Dallas: Word, 1992).

Steven Jay Lynn and Judith W. Rhue, *Dissociation* (New York: The Guilford Press, 1994).

Arlys Norcross McDonald, *Repressed Memories: Can You Trust Them?* (Grand Rapids: Fleming H. Revell, 1995).

Laurie Anne Pearlman and Karen W. Saakvitne, *Trauma and the Therapist* (New York: W. W. Norton & Company, 1995).

Frank W. Putnam, *Diagnosis and Treatment of Multiple Personality Disorder* (New York: The Guilford Press, 1989).

Bessel A. van der Kolk, Alexander C. McFarlane, and Lars Weisaeth, editors, *Traumatic Stress* (New York: The Guilford Press, 1996).

Charles L. Whitefield, M.D., *Memory and Abuse: Remembering and Healing the Effects of Trauma* (Deerfield Beach, Fla.: Health Communications, Inc., 1995).

About the Author

Diane Mandt Langberg, Ph.D., has been a licensed psychologist in private practice for nearly twenty-five years. She is a speaker at local and national conferences for clergy, women, couples, students, and professionals. Dr. Langberg writes the counselor column in *Today's Christian Woman* magazine and has also written for *Partnership Magazine, Urban Mission Journal,* and *Christian Counseling Today.* Her books include *Feeling Good, Feeling Bad* (Servant, 1991) and *Counsel for Pastors' Wives* (Zondervan, 1988). Diane lives in Jenkintown, Pennsylvania, with her husband and two teenage sons, Joshua and Daniel.

Printed in the USA
CPSIA information can be obtained
at www.ICGtesting.com
LVHW090421061123
762866LV00053B/1150